Unwanted Company

Unwanted Company
Foreign Investment in American Industries

JONATHAN CRYSTAL

CORNELL UNIVERSITY PRESS

Ithaca and London

First published 2003 by Cornell University Press

Printed in the United States of America

Library of Congress Cataloging-in-Publication Data

Crystal, Jonathan, 1965–
  Unwanted company : foreign investment in American industries / Jonathan Crystal.
    p. cm.
Includes bibliographical references and index.
  ISBN 0-8014-4123-4
  1. Investments, Foreign—United States. I. Title.
  HG4910.C79 2003
  332.67'3'0973—dc21
                          2003001243

Cornell University Press strives to use environmentally responsible suppliers and materials to the fullest extent possible in the publishing of its books. Such materials include vegetable-based, low-VOC inks and acid-free papers that are recycled, totally chlorine-free, or partly composed of nonwood fibers. For further information, visit our website at www.cornellpress.cornell.edu.

Cloth printing   10 9 8 7 6 5 4 3 2 1

To Caroline

Contents

Acknowledgments

In the course of doing research for this book, I received financial support from the National Science Foundation, the Mellon Foundation, the Center for International Affairs at Harvard University, and the Donald McGannon Communication Research Center at Fordham University. I gratefully acknowledge all these institutions.

I also received help and encouragement from a number of individuals. Yuen Foong Khong has been my mentor and friend since I was a sophomore in college. Robert Keohane, Andrew Moravcsik, and James Alt advised me in graduate school and helped me immeasurably. Many of my fellow graduate students also gave me useful advice, especially Brian Burgoon, Raj Desai, Stephanie Golob, Michael Hiscox, Henry Laurence, and Kip Wennerlund. Among the scholars who were generous enough to offer me suggestions and comments at various points, I would particularly like to thank Lawrence Broz, Robert Denemark, Jeffry Frieden, Vicki Golich, Christianne Hardy, Louis Pauly, and Kenneth Thomas. I am grateful to my colleagues in the Political Science Department at Fordham, especially Richard Fleisher and Jeff Cohen, for their encouragement and friendship. I also thank Roger Haydon from Cornell University Press for his enthusiasm, support, and excellent advice. All these people helped improve this book; as I did not always take their advice, none should be held responsible for the remaining flaws.

Some material in this book appeared in an earlier form as "A New Kind of Competition: How American Producers Respond to Incoming Foreign Direct Investment," *International Studies Quarterly* 42:3 (September 1998), 513–43, published here with permission from Blackwell Publishing Ltd.; and "Globalization, International Corporate Alliances, and Political Conflict: The Experience of the U.S. Airline and Telecommunication Industries," *Business and Politics* 1:3 (1999), 343–73, published here with permission from Taylor & Francis (http://www.tandf.co.uk).

My parents, Harvey and Irene Crystal, have been there, literally, from the beginning, and I am enormously grateful for everything they have done for me. My two boys, Nathan and Seth, did a great deal to delay the writing of this book, but I would not give back one minute of the time they took from this project. Finally, my wife, Caroline Ewing, offered to proofread the entire manuscript. I imagined that since she is a former English major, this task would entail correcting grammatical mistakes and fixing up the prose. To my chagrin, she discovered structural problems and logical flaws in virtually every chapter. As usual, her advice was right on target, and ultimately, her assistance improved the manuscript enormously. Without her love and support, I doubt this book would even exist.

Acronyms

AAMA	American Automobile Manufacturers Association
AEA	American Electronics Association
AFBMA	Antifriction Bearing Manufacturing Association
AIADA	American International Auto Dealers Association
AISI	American Iron and Steel Institute
AMT	Association for Manufacturing Technology
APAA	Auto Parts and Accessories Association
CAMI	Canadian-American Manufacturing, Inc.
CBEMA	Computer and Business Equipment Manufacturers Association
CIFIUS	Committee on Foreign Investment in the United States
COMPACT	Committee to Preserve American Color Television
CVD	countervailing duty
DOD	Department of Defense
DOJ	Department of Justice
DOT	Department of Transportation
DRAM	dynamic random access memory
EIA	Electronics Industries Association
FCC	Federal Communications Commission
FDI	foreign direct investment
FTZ	foreign trade zone
GAO	General Accounting Office
GATS	General Agreement on Trade in Services
GATT	General Agreement on Tariffs and Trade
ICA	international corporate alliance
IFDI	incoming foreign direct investment
ITC	International Trade Commission
MEMA	Motor and Equipment Manufacturers Association
MVMA	Motor Vehicle Manufacturing Association
NAFTA	North American Free Trade Agreement
NCMS	National Center for Manufacturing Science
NMTBA	National Machine Tool Builders Association
NUMMI	New United Motor Manufacturing Inc.

OMA	orderly market agreement
SEMI	Semiconductor Equipment and Manufacturing International
SIA	Semiconductor Industry Association
SM&E	semiconductor materials and equipment
STA	Semiconductor Trade Agreement
TPM	trigger price mechanism
UAW	United Auto Workers
VRA	voluntary restraint agreement
WTO	World Trade Organization

Unwanted Company

ONE

The Challenge of Incoming Foreign Direct Investment

In the late 1970s many U.S.-owned firms found themselves in an unfamiliar situation. For the first time since the nineteenth century, foreign-owned subsidiaries were becoming a significant presence on American soil.[1] The trend accelerated throughout the 1980s, and by the end of that decade the United States had emerged as the world's largest host of incoming foreign direct investment (IFDI).[2] For American firms, foreign competition no longer came only in the form of imports. Now it also consisted of local production by foreign-owned companies. Questions about regulating IFDI that had long been the subject of debate in other countries now turned up on the political agenda in Washington. American-owned multinational corporations, accustomed to facing criticism of their own outward FDI from labor unions at home and from nationalist governments abroad, began to perceive inward FDI as a potential threat to their own fortunes. For these U.S. firms, the globalization of production had finally hit home.

Faced with this challenge, how did U.S. producers respond to IFDI? How did they perceive and interpret the problem? What solutions did they consider? Did they look to the government for help? What kinds of policies did these producers favor regarding the regulation of IFDI and the treatment of foreign-owned firms? What explains their reactions? Are there any common threads that run through their responses? These are the questions that this book examines. The answers shed light on how firms within the United States adjusted to the transformation of America's international economic position: from being primarily a *source* of FDI to being like most other developed countries—both *source and host* of direct investment. This shift inspired an outpouring of literature on IFDI in the United States, overheated journalistic accounts and more careful analyses of the economic effects of IFDI alike.[3] But IFDI also provoked a *political* uproar. Scholars have devoted much less attention to this aspect of the issue, especially compared with the extensive political economy literature about international trade. Domestically owned firms often stood at the center of these political controversies. As a result, their reactions to the arrival of foreign-owned firms in the United States provide an excellent starting point for studying the politics of IFDI.

The reaction of American producers to IFDI also reveals deeper problems with the dominant explanations of the political behavior of societal actors. Specifically, most models of foreign economic policy making derive the interests of different societal actors by calculating their relative returns from various government policy options. Economic theories are used to determine which policies will provide the most benefits for a particular actor or group, which, it is assumed, will favor the policy that maximizes its returns. Scholars then go on to debate the role societal actors play (as compared with other potential forces such as international pressures, state officials, domestic institutions, and beliefs) in affecting policy outcomes.

The first step of this process—specifying the interests of societal groups—is crucial, since one cannot assess the importance of something until it is accurately identified. Most scholars, however, spend little time on this step and move quickly to investigating policy outcomes. The justification for this neglect is that a well-developed body of economic theory allows scholars to map the policy preferences of societal actors, thus freeing them to focus on the more controversial question of what explains governmental behavior. The discussion of IFDI in this book makes it clear that this neglect is problematic. Chapter 2 argues that the root of the problem is that producers, and especially multinational firms, are complex actors with multiple interests, and it is often unclear which of these interests a firm will (or should) act on. In order to explain their behavior, one needs to examine *how societal actors translate economic interests into policy preferences*. Firms prefer higher profits to lower profits. In deciding what positions to adopt on political issues, producers will choose the one that is most likely to provide them with the highest level of benefits. But this decision is seldom straightforward. Often a number of policies (not all of them mutually compatible) would serve producer interests. Firms must then decide how to turn their underlying preference for more profit into *policy preferences* for a particular governmental action. Formulating a political strategy precedes entering the policy-making arena. The argument of this book is that economic interests together with domestic political structures—institutions and prevailing norms—shape the behavior of producers.

INCOMING FOREIGN DIRECT INVESTMENT IN THE UNITED STATES

The complexity of the politics surrounding IFDI in the United States helps explain the relative neglect of the topic by political scientists and economists. At one level the political dynamics around the issue appear simple and straightforward. Labor, U.S. multinationals, state and local government officials, and much of the executive branch of the federal government all have had strong reasons to endorse a welcoming attitude toward IFDI. Though the public at times may have reacted uneasily to the influx of foreign (and especially Japanese) investment, eventually the concrete benefits that foreign producers brought with them (such as jobs and tax revenue) outweighed this discomfort. With few important groups in favor of restrictions, it is no wonder the often-predicted legislative backlash never materialized.[4]

In fact, U.S. policy has encompassed far more variation than the absence of formal barriers suggests. Those who favored a more restrictive approach toward foreign investors did not lobby for legislative restrictions, perhaps because they knew such goals were unrealistic. Instead, they sought other measures, such as local-content requirements, deviations from national treatment (that is, treating foreign-owned firms differently from domestically owned firms), rejections of (or the attachment of conditions to) particular foreign acquisitions, and classification of local production by subsidiaries as "foreign" for the purpose of implementing trade legislation. Many of these battles did not attract much public attention, nor were they aimed at explicitly altering the official U.S. position toward IFDI. But taken together, they constituted regulation of foreign investors in the United States, and hence it is appropriate to refer to these actions as de facto U.S. IFDI policy.

Furthermore, the reactions of American firms—even multinational firms—to IFDI have been anything but straightforward. As the case studies in this book detail, U.S. firms have neither uniformly opposed IFDI nor uniformly welcomed it. In fact, their response has varied greatly both across and within sectors. Even individual firms have shifted their positions, supporting a nationalist stance on some issues and a more liberal position on others. This book attempts to account systematically for that variation.

PUZZLING REACTIONS TO IFDI

Most of the existing literature that predicts societal policy preferences by determining how alternative policies affect relative returns has focused on trade and finance. Chapter 2 extends these models to FDI by using the existing political economy literature to generate predictions of the reactions to IFDI that one should expect from American-owned firms. However, as the experiences of the industries examined in chapters 3 through 6 illustrate, it is very difficult to make sense of the pattern of producer behavior using these predictions. The central problem is that although economic self-interest accounts for any particular episode, taken together the reactions to IFDI varied in ways that seem to defy explanation. The solution to this quandary lies not in rejecting the existing political economy models but in recognizing that this approach is incomplete and cannot by itself explain the observed behavior of U.S. producers.

In what ways have the reactions of U.S.-based firms deviated from theoretical expectations? The first puzzling outcome concerns firms that have spent significant time, resources, and political capital in successfully seeking trade protection. In a world where foreign competitors can relocate production instead of (or as well as) exporting, trade protection no longer delivers the benefits it promises to local producers who find themselves under siege from foreign competitors. In some circumstances import barriers may end up inducing foreign firms to set up local operations, intensifying competition within the host market and thus "exacerbat[ing] the economic decline of those [domestic] producers which the protectionist policy was initially introduced to assist."[5] Faced with a new and equally threatening form of competition, U.S. producers had to decide how they would respond.

One would expect that domestic firms would redirect their efforts toward fighting IFDI. It would be odd if firms that were in enough distress to seek trade protection did nothing when production by local subsidiaries eroded the value of this protection. As one economist wrote, when IFDI was just beginning to attract attention, "For industries in which ownership and internalization advantages are important, 'protection' is likely to have little protective effect unless inward DFI is also restricted. . . . This suggests that in some industries where IDFI has recently become important, a next step in the political pressure for protection from foreign competition will be demands from affected domestic firms and unions for restrictions on inward DFI."[6] This is precisely why so many observers expected IFDI in the United States to become a controversial issue in the 1980s and 1990s, as it had been in many other host countries during the 1960s and 1970s. Although the United States and Japan fought repeatedly and bitterly over trade issues, by the end of the 1980s sales in the United States by local Japanese-owned warehouses, assembly plants, and factories accounted for twice the total value of U.S. imports from Japan.[7] A large part of the so-called Japan problem, then, came in the form of local subsidiaries. Surely the focus of lobbying activities by besieged U.S. firms should have shifted to some extent from trade to the regulation of IFDI.

In fact, U.S.-owned firms have not lobbied for restrictions on IFDI to nearly the same degree they have for import barriers. Logically, it should not matter to domestic producers whether their profits are being reduced by competition from foreign rivals located abroad or from foreign rivals that have relocated to territory within the host state. In either case the affected firms would demand policies that would increase their own profits at the expense of competitors. Yet U.S. producers largely refrained from doing so in the case of IFDI. Why?

Many firms did not immediately appreciate the nature of the threat IFDI posed. Yet even when producers recognized that threat, their responses were relatively subdued. Being multinational themselves, American firms were unlikely to try to block (or even express opposition to) incoming FDI. Such a position would be perceived as inconsistent and hypocritical; more important, such measures could backfire and end up injuring U.S. firms.

Although U.S. firms did not seek investment protection to the same degree they sought import protection, neither did they ignore the threat IFDI posed to their market position in the United States. In fact, many domestic producers sought a range of indirect measures designed to discriminate against foreign-owned firms. Significantly, even internationally oriented firms adopted decidedly nonliberal policy preferences toward IFDI. This, then, presents a second puzzle: Why would globalized firms support measures that would discriminate against foreign investors when they themselves had fought long and hard against such measures in other countries? Why would they risk provoking retaliation against their own investments or, at the least, setting a risky precedent by supporting restrictive or discriminatory policies? One possible motive centers on the issue of reciprocity. As discussed in the next chapter, internationally oriented companies have sometimes favored restrictive commercial policies despite the risks to their own overseas interests. When firms find themselves at a competitive disadvantage with foreign competitors owing to some trade or industrial policy on the part of the foreign companies' home government, multinational firms have adopted "strategic trade demands" that make access to the home market contingent on liberalization abroad. The logic of strategic trade demands carries over to IFDI; that is, if firms put forth these kinds of trade policy preferences, they ought to adopt a similar position on the treatment of IFDI and foreign-owned firms. In practice, however, firms that put forth strategic trade demands sometimes refrained from doing so with respect to IFDI, even though logically they had every reason to extend these policy demands.

The case studies in this book examine the variation not only between trade policy preferences and IFDI policy preferences but also among different sectors' responses to IFDI. Within industries variation also existed among different firms. In fact, even for particular firms, political demands varied over time and across policy issues. Thus policy preferences varied on a number of dimensions, and the case studies assess the extent to which the commonly used models can account for this. In the end, approaches that emphasize how foreign competition affects the relative economic returns to societal actors, though useful, cannot fully explain the responses of U.S. firms to IFDI and how these responses vary.

EXPLAINING REACTIONS TO IFDI

Firms have a number of conflicting economic interests with regard to IFDI (just as they do, incidentally, with regard to many other issues, such as trade and exchange rate policy). With IFDI, firms want protection against foreign competitors and therefore will favor restrictive or discriminatory policies. They also want to promote liberal investment policies abroad and avoid any actions that may provoke foreign retaliation against their own investments and so therefore will favor liberal policies. Finally, they want to counter the existing restrictions—on both trade and FDI—that some foreign countries have imposed and so therefore will favor contingently restrictive policies.

To predict which of these conflicting policy preferences firms will act on, one needs to look not just at the relative benefits of various government policies but also at the relative costs of obtaining them. One component of these relative costs involves the difficulty of mobilizing group members and overcoming collective action obstacles. Another component that has received less attention is the domestic political environment's effect on the ability of even well-organized groups to pursue their goals. Specifically, societal actors are likely to seek policies for which domestic institutions exist to channel their policy demands and to supply the desired policy outputs. Also, societal actors will seek policies that can be easily reconciled with prevailing norms concerning the appropriate role of the state in the economy. Institutions and ideas, frequently used to account for government policies, in fact are crucial independent variables in explaining firm behavior.

Focusing on political structures sheds light on the contrasting outcomes of trade and IFDI policy preferences. Given the more developed institutional framework that exists for responding to imports, firms in the United States have more opportunities to obtain policies that will give them relief from trade competition. By contrast, producers that might want to limit

IFDI have fewer options. Although some institutional channels exist for restricting IFDI, they supply protection only under certain conditions. This explains seemingly contradictory demands from a single industry across different issue areas. For instance, when a foreign investment affects national security or industry concentration, policy tools exist that can be used to restrict or regulate IFDI. Because the tool exists, and because using it is widely perceived as a legitimate departure from liberal norms, the political cost of combating IFDI will be reduced. Creating new tools, though not impossible, is costly and difficult, and therefore firms are more likely to lobby for discriminatory IFDI policies when these institutions and norms can be readily employed.

A long-standing debate has pitted those trying to explain policies in terms of societal interests against those who emphasize domestic political institutions. Those who focus on domestic institutions argue that societal demands are filtered and refracted through—sometimes blocked by—the domestic political system. Both sides, however, assume it is appropriate to derive societal policy preferences directly from economic interests. The question they argue over is how important these policy preferences are compared with state actors or institutions (or ideology or international forces). In debating the role of societal actors in influencing policy, all sides have missed the crucial point that the policy preferences of societal actors are derived not solely from relative economic returns but also from political structures. In other words, these political structures affect not only how likely a group is to get the policy it wants but also what policy it wants in the first place. Ignoring this point prevents an accurate assessment of the impact of groups on policy making.

It merits emphasizing that the argument presented here does not supplant the standard explanations but rather *supplements* them, telling us how economic interests are translated into different types of policy preferences. Nor is this argument—that political variables influence societal policy preferences—entirely unfamiliar to social scientists. Expected utility theory says that in calculating the costs and benefits of various options, actors estimate the probabilities that various outcomes will occur (including the likelihood that they will be able to obtain the benefit they are seeking). Other scholars have also noticed that there is a feedback effect in which policy outcomes are not only influenced by but also influence the position that groups take.[8] However, students of international political economy have yet to incorporate these basic insights into models of how the global economy affects domestic politics. The most likely reason is that doing so would diminish the parsimony of the theoretical explanations. But not doing so imposes its own cost: ignoring this factor makes it difficult if not impossible to establish the policy preferences of societal actors and thereby accurately gauge their impact on political outcomes.

Chapter 2 provides a theoretical framework for examining the industry case studies. First, it defines the dependent variable *policy preferences*. Confusion between this concept and *preferences* more generally has been one of the major obstacles to greater understanding of this issue. Briefly, firms are assumed to "prefer" greater profits, but that tells us little about what policies they will seek. When examining "strategy" (what actors do to achieve their preferences), most authors emphasize the means by which actors seek their preferred policy outcome. But the preferred policy outcome itself is a strategy since many different policies can lead to greater profits. Subsequently, the chapter asks where policy preferences come from and examines existing models that are based on an actor's economic interests. The discussion derives IFDI policy preferences by extrapolating from the more voluminous literature on trade politics. In this way the chapter generates hypotheses for explaining IFDI policy preferences on the basis of (1) a firm's competitive position in the world economy, (2) the extent of its international interests, and (3) the costs of its being excluded from foreign markets. But when these hypotheses are taken together, based as they are on the multiple and conflicting economic interests of firms, it becomes unclear which motives or incentives will dominate a firm's calculation of its policy preferences. The chapter lays out an approach emphasizing the importance of political variables in the translation of economic interests into policy preferences. The domestic institutional context shapes the state's response to certain kinds of political demands, in turn influencing the kinds of demands societal actors are likely to put forth.

The political structures that shape societal policy preferences do not arise from thin air. They are a product of, among other things, pressures from domestic interest groups. But if these institutions are at the same time a cause *and* an effect of societal actors' political positions, one must guard against the danger of overestimating the extent to which these structures really shape policy preferences. This issue of endogeneity is discussed at more length in the next chapter, but in this case the problem is not as serious as one might fear. Producers prefer certain kinds of institutional structures to others, but they face formidable costs in attempting to alter existing institutions. Empirically, as the case studies show, producers did not expend much effort trying to create new institutions; most of the time, these structures were taken as fixed.

The case studies detail the reactions of producers in various industries as they experienced inflows of IFDI. Chapter 3, which looks at the consumer electronics and steel industries, serves as a useful starting point in two ways. Chronologically, these were the first industries in which foreign investors developed a significant local presence. And theoretically, the reactions of local firms in these sectors come closest to the predictions of the economic-interest theories. U.S. color television producers responded to IFDI in accordance with the extent of their internationalized interests: global producers favored liberal policies whereas domestically oriented producers favored more stringent regulations. Steel producers adopted a welcoming attitude toward foreign investors since many of the investments came in the form of joint ventures that promised infusions of capital without posing an independent competitive challenge. These industries were in the weakest economic position of any examined in this study; they therefore had less flexibility in determining what measures to take to deal with the challenges posed by IFDI. As the first industries that dealt with this challenge, they also had less experience figuring out what approaches would work best to safeguard their interests.

By contrast, the industries that faced the second wave of IFDI in the mid- to late 1980s (examined in chapters 4 and 5) responded to this new competitive threat in a more multifaceted and in some ways contradictory manner. At times producers favored liberal policies, but in other instances they lobbied for restrictive or discriminatory measures. Chapter 4 looks at the semiconductor and automobile industries, two of the most prominent advocates for protectionist trade policy during that decade. Each industry had ample motive to seek restrictions on IFDI since each saw the value of its trade protection undermined by foreign-owned production in the United States. Yet in both cases firms sought such restrictions only under certain conditions: for the semiconductor industry, when IFDI affected national security or antitrust concerns, and for the auto industry, when foreign-owned firms could be attacked for low levels of domestic content (meaning few American jobs) in their vehicles. These arguments were widely perceived as legitimate reasons to restrict investment or discriminate against foreign producers, and because they were accepted ends, in most cases institutional structures already existed that could further these goals. The cost of adopting restrictive policy preferences was therefore lower in these instances.

Chapter 5 looks at two industries that relied heavily on the national security argument for trade protection: machine tools and antifriction bearings. In both cases, playing the security card was much more difficult with respect to IFDI than it had been for arguing in favor of import restrictions.

In lobbying for trade protection, industry and government officials had emphasized production location over ownership; the prospect of losing access to advanced machines persuaded policy makers to grant the domestic industry the protection it sought. The problem with this strategy was that domestic producers found that few available remedies existed for addressing the new competitive threat of foreign production on U.S. soil.

Finally, chapter 6 centers on two service industries: airlines and telecommunications. In these cases there existed a much more developed institutional framework for regulating foreign firms. Indeed, for much of the period under examination, IFDI was expressly limited. As a result, foreign firms that wanted to establish a physical presence in the United States (and this was usually a prerequisite for serving the local market) were forced to enter via joint ventures and strategic alliances. Although U.S. firms in these sectors were very competitive and simultaneously engaged in expanding their own overseas operations, they took a surprisingly strong position in favor of further government restrictions on foreign competition. This behavior was motivated by the desire to use U.S. market access as a crowbar to open foreign markets, but such demands were possible only because of the existing structural context. Domestic producers found a favorable institutional environment that limited the options those foreign firms had and provided openings for discriminatory policy preferences.

The industries examined here were not the only sectors in which IFDI occurred. But because the central puzzle concerns the disjuncture between trade and IFDI policy preferences, the analysis focuses only on sectors that were already facing severe import competition from overseas and in which foreign penetration of the U.S. market had already become a political issue. The two service industries examined in chapter 6 did not experience import competition only because trade in these particular services was impossible without an accompanying local presence. Here it was the inability to gain access to foreign markets that led American firms to lobby for more stringent regulation of foreign-owned firms in the U.S. market. In effect, there needs to be some underlying motive—either to bolster trade protection or to pressure foreign governments to liberalize—that would lead a firm to make IFDI an issue in the first place. In competitive sectors in which IFDI occurred but in which domestic firms did not seek import barriers and were not shut out of foreign markets, there would be no reason to expect demands for changes in IFDI policy and so no reason to include them here.

Each case study explores the effect that the globalization of production had on industry actors and explains the policy demands with which they responded. The focus is less on the private beliefs of business executives than on the public positions taken by these actors—the societal policy preferences or demands that government officials could observe. These positions were made manifest by corporate behavior, including lobbying activities, testimony before legislative and administrative bodies, press releases and other statements to the media, and so forth. Once the policy preferences of the industry actors are established, the case studies examine the economic-interest hypotheses (introduced in chapter 2) to see how far they can take us in understanding the reactions to IFDI and to what extent emphasizing domestic political structures adds explanatory leverage. The chapters examine a variety of issues that arose concerning the regulation of IFDI and the treatment of foreign-owned firms. As we shall see, in many of these cases domestic industry actors played an active role in pressing the government to adopt a stricter position; in others, however, there was little if any political activity by local firms. In the analysis of this variation there are a number of instructive comparisons. In addition to the comparison between demands for trade policies and demands for IFDI policies, there is a cross-industry comparison among the sectors as well as a contrast between the reactions of manufacturing and service industry actors. Finally, there is significant variation within the industries over time and across specific issue areas related to IFDI and foreign ownership. To begin the task of explaining these different patterns, the next chapter derives hypotheses for what we should expect to influence the policy preferences of corporate actors.

TWO

Political Responses to Foreign Investment

How did industries within the United States respond to the globalization of production when it threatened their own economic fortunes? What kinds of policies did they support regarding the regulation of incoming foreign direct investment and the treatment of foreign-owned firms? This chapter begins to consider these questions by presenting a theoretical framework within which the empirical case studies can be examined. The chapter first discusses the ambiguous nature of policy preferences and then analyzes the prevailing explanations for these preferences. Although an enormous literature explores the origin of trade policy preferences, and a smaller (though rapidly growing) body of work focuses on monetary policy preferences, scholars of international political economy have virtually ignored policy preferences regarding FDI policies.

Nevertheless, borrowing from the existing literature on trade, one can apply the logic underlying these theories to construct explanations for how producers respond to incoming foreign direct investment. Trade and FDI are, of course, not equivalent, but the close links between these two methods of penetrating foreign markets suggest that the trade literature can at least serve as an analytic starting point. From this body of research the chapter derives three explanations for IFDI policy preferences that emphasize three different (though not wholly exclusive) criteria firms use for evaluating whether to seek restrictive or discriminatory policies: the severity of the competitive threat that IFDI poses, the extent to which domestic producers have international interests themselves, and the extent to which producers have an incentive to use domestic barriers as a bargaining tool to improve foreign market access. All three of these explanations derive policy preferences from economic interests. In other words, given its economic circumstances, a firm should respond to IFDI in a predictable way regardless of the political environment. Although environmental characteristics may affect whether or how societal policy preferences translate into policy outcomes, the policy preferences themselves are seen as primarily economic in origin.

This approach provides a good starting point for analyzing policy preferences, but it also raises a problem: taken together, these criteria generate contradictory predictions. Producers have a multiplicity of often-conflicting economic interests, and it is not always evident which will prevail in determining policy preferences. After the fact, one can always explain a particular action by pointing to some motivating economic interest, but this does not allow for predicting the policy preferences actors will adopt. The industry case studies examined in this book provide empirical support for *all* the hypotheses, thus further compounding the analytical problem. This is not to say that firms are acting irrationally; seemingly inconsistent and contradictory behavior simply reflects the producers' complex bundle of underlying economic interests.

To understand why producers choose to pursue different elements of their economic interests at different times, one must look beyond the returns that actors receive from various policies. When choosing strategies to obtain their basic goals, actors calculate not only the potential benefits they would receive from a given policy but also the costs of seeking it. One crucial but often overlooked component of this calculation is the estimated probability that the government will react favorably to a particular demand. This probability will depend on the political environment—the alignment of domestic interest groups as well as structural elements of the political system such as institutions and prevailing normative beliefs. With sector-specific demands there were few opposing coalitions, and political structures mattered most in affecting how producers translated their economic interests into policy demands.

WHAT DO PRODUCERS WANT?
PREFERENCES AND POLICY PREFERENCES

Although the concept *preferences* seems simple enough, the term has been plagued by confusion. Most analysts argue that *preferences* refers to ends or goals, the substantive outcome or state of the world one ultimately wants. These "preferences over outcomes" are considered exogenous to the situation one is analyzing, and they do not change as long as actors behave rationally and consistently. Preferences in this sense are mental constructs and thus not directly observable.[1] What we can observe are the varying strategies by which an actor tries to achieve these goals. These "preferences over actions," or "policy preferences," vary with the environment or the actor's information. A firm facing import competition *prefers* more profits, but its *strategy* or policy preference to achieve this goal—adjust economically, exit the industry, seek tariffs or nontariff barriers, seek subsidies or regulatory relief, and so on—will depend on a host of external factors. Political scientists most often take actor preferences as given and unproblematic; they then investigate how the preferences interact with these other environmental variables to affect behavior.[2] Many scholars have emphasized the need to keep preferences and strategies distinct when analyzing the behavior of individuals, groups, or states.[3]

Any given policy can simultaneously be regarded either as a strategy (to achieve some underlying goal) or as a preference (for which one engages in some strategic action). In most studies of foreign economic policy the analyst treats the policy that a group wants—say, trade protection—as a preference. The strategy is then conceptualized more narrowly, for instance as the type of protection the group seeks (tariffs, quotas, antidumping duties) or the kinds of tactics it engages in (advertising, campaign contributions, lobbying) to obtain the policy outcomes.[4] But what a group demands— protection, free trade, or something in between—is really a strategic policy preference. After all, other governmental outputs exist (direct government subsidies, regulatory relief, an undervalued exchange rate, and the like) that can satisfy the producer's preference for profit maximization. In analyzing trade politics, therefore, one cannot simply assume that a particular firm will favor trade protection because of its economic situation. The producer's strategy (policy preference) will depend on a number of environmental factors. This is not a particularly controversial claim; nevertheless, most existing models of policy making simply do not treat policy preferences as strategic choices. It is also easy to see why there has been so much confusion on this issue. One analyst might take a preference as fixed within a given situation whereas another might probe into the origins of these preferences. But in the latter case the preferences are now a strategy chosen to achieve some other deeper set of preferences.[5]

DETERMINING POLICY PREFERENCES

Scholars have used three methods for determining preferences: assumption, theoretical derivation, and empirical observation.[6] The first two are essentially equivalent since as soon as one moves beyond the most basic and general goals (e.g., survival or wealth-maximization), any useful assumptions will be derived from some underlying theory. The real question, then, is whether to deduce or induce preferences. The underlying issues in this debate relate directly to differences in how analysts determine policy preferences as well.

If preferences are unobservable mental constructs, inferring preferences from behavior is notoriously unreliable (not to mention tautological if those preferences are then used to explain outcomes). Other factors besides preferences (such as the strategic environment) may be prompting observable behavior. Conversely, actors may have preferences that they do not act on, again because of environmental considerations.[7] Jeffry Frieden has argued that "an actor's behavior incorporates *both* its underlying preferences *and* its strategic response to the setting it faces. There is no way to separate the two by observation alone." This is why, he claims, deducing preferences from theory is better than trying to observe them.[8]

Other scholars, by contrast, believe there is no substitute for empirical observation. These analysts argue that one can avoid the danger of tautological reasoning by inferring preferences from observing choices in other, similar situations. However, even if we assume preferences will remain constant in a different situation, there is still the problem of how to distinguish them from context-specific strategies.[9] One could interview actors and ask them directly what they *really* want. Such an approach is probably more useful for discerning the views of the public than that of lobbying groups since the latter have myriad incentives to misrepresent their true preferences.[10]

International relations scholars who believe that nation-states are too complex to yield clear theoretical predictions about what they want favor observing preferences.[11] But the goals of societal groups—at least with respect to economic issues—ought to be more amenable to theoretical generalizations. Indeed, for many students of international political economy, these group policy preferences present no real puzzle. Producers, for instance, are assumed to want to maximize their profits; those that do not follow this approach will not survive long. These actors will thus formulate policy preferences based on how various governmental actions will affect their bottom line. For the analyst, determining the returns from various policies becomes a simple matter of using the appropriate economic theories.

This is by far the dominant approach in IPE, and it has proved to be valuable in furthering our understanding of how societal interests are affected by the international economy and what kinds of policies they are likely to support. Scholars have used this approach to study trade, exchange rates, and international finance. The next section of this chapter uses the trade literature to derive economic microfoundations for an explanation of FDI politics.[12] The economic links between trade and IFDI involve substitution (local production by foreign subsidiaries taking the place of imports) and complementarity (local production facilitating and promoting imports). In the first case local producers should shift their attention from trade competition to FDI competition; in the second case local producers should be concerned about both forms of competition. In either case domestic producers' demands on regulating imports and IFDI should be related; the variables that affect the former should have an analogous effect on the latter. Any inconsistency in producers' reactions to different forms of competition requires an explanation.

EXPLANATIONS OF IFDI POLICY PREFERENCES

There are three ways to explain demands for trade protection, each with its own implications for incoming foreign direct investment, leading to three hypotheses for what kinds of policy preferences we would expect to see regarding the regulation of IFDI and the treatment of foreign-owned firms. In the end, each of these approaches provides plausible explanations for the observed policy preferences. All are consistent with maximizing profits, and in the abstract, there appears to be little justification for favoring one over the other. Furthermore, the cases examined in chapters 3 through 6 provide empirical evidence that both supports and weakens each of the three hypotheses. In responding to IFDI, domestically owned producers have a multiplicity of economic interests and consequently put forth conflicting and even contradictory demands reflecting the importance of the variables highlighted by all three explanations. The task for the analyst is to explain when and under what conditions each of the hypotheses will hold true.

This chapter provides an explanation of how the domestic political context shapes policy preferences. Firms with a number of contradictory interests will put forth only those demands that they perceive as conforming to the requirements of existing domestic political structures and as being in accordance with widely held beliefs concerning the proper role of the state. Domestic institutions channel group demands, and norms provide ideological legitimacy for certain policy preferences. Actors determine, through feedback from the domestic political system, which potential demands are most likely to be satisfied and make their decisions accordingly.

(1) The Production Profile Hypothesis

The first approach, common in much of the political economy literature, derives policy preferences from the position of an industry or firm in the international economy. Analysts use a number of specific indicators in this assessment.

First, capital specific to import-competing sectors will be hurt by free trade whereas an export orientation should lead industries to support liberalism.[13] The higher the foreign share of the domestic market, the more likely the affected domestic industry will feel threatened by overseas competitors and will demand protection.[14] To the extent that incoming foreign direct investment substitutes for or augments import flows—that is, to the extent foreign companies are able to exploit their firm-specific advantages within the host country—domestic capital specific to these affected sectors should react in a similar (negative) way toward IFDI and favor more restrictive or discriminatory policies.[15] It should not matter to these firms where their foreign rivals are located, at home or abroad: if these threatened producers succeed in obtaining protection from imports, then they should seek policies to restrict IFDI in order to preserve the value of the rents they have obtained.[16]

Second, domestic firms in a relatively less competitive position (e.g., firms with little physical or human capital per worker, low value added per worker, low R&D spending, etc.) will be less likely to succeed in fighting off the challenges of foreign competition and therefore are more prone to seek trade protection.[17] Again, extending the logic to IFDI, firms that have trouble competing against imports will also be hurt by the output of foreign subsidiaries; if these domestic firms demand trade barriers, they should similarly be worried about IFDI.

Finally, policy preferences will vary with business conditions. When demand is relatively flat, producers are more likely to seek protection.[18] Although overcapacity and slack demand should lead labor (concerned with employment and wages) to oppose imports but welcome IFDI, for business (concerned with profits), depressed economic conditions will prompt opposition to both imports and IFDI.

In sum, the Production Profile explanation sees variations in demands for tighter IFDI regulation and/or departures from national treatment as resulting from variations in a firm's economic situation: the extent of foreign competition, the firm's competitive position, and prevailing business conditions. To the extent the value of any of these three variables shifts against domestic producers, these actors will become more likely to demand restrictions on IFDI for the same reasons they demand import barriers: to protect profits that are threatened by foreign rivals. Lorraine Eden and Maureen Appel Molot, in a discussion of FDI in the North American automobile industry, claim that in response to foreign competition, locally based firms attempt, first, to sharpen their government's perception of the distinction between "insiders" and "outsiders" and, second, to lobby for policies that provide them with benefits at the expense of the latter. According to the authors, the underlying motive is to "reap economic rents from getting a larger market share and squeezing out the competition," and the shift in the form of this competition from import penetration to IFDI only "raises the stakes."[19]

In most cases, after describing a country's production profile, scholars go on to debate the influence of these societal demands as compared with state actors, institutions, international forces, ideology, and other variables that might affect government policy.[20] Societal policy preferences, then, function in much of the literature as independent variables. Few studies spend much time questioning these assumptions about what groups seek.

(2) The Global Industry Hypothesis

The second approach emphasizes how even in the face of severe international competition, many producers refrain from seeking trade protection. A number of studies have shown that demands for import barriers vary inversely with the extent of a firm's international interests. The liberal trade preferences of multinational corporations result from the potential costs of disrupting intrafirm trade, the danger of provoking retaliation, the disproportionate benefit to domestically based rivals, and the possibility that protection might spur foreign multinational corporations (MNCs) to evade trade protection by creating new and potentially more threatening competition in the domestic market.[21] Another study found that industries dependent on exports and/or imported inputs were (along with retailers, foreign companies, and foreign governments) most likely to take an active role in fighting product-specific trade protection.[22]

Extending the argument to IFDI policy would suggest that international firms ought to be even more likely to favor policies of openness and national treatment. The danger of foreign retaliation in response to IFDI restrictions could inflict greater injury on U.S. multinational companies than trade retaliation could. MNCs can adjust to trade sanctions by relocating production, but if foreign governments were to strike at U.S. outward investment, firms would have fewer options with which to respond. Similarly, producers with little intrafirm trade can weather trade wars but would suffer from investment-related retaliation. Restrictive IFDI policies in the United States would also hinder attempts to move toward a stronger and more liberal multilateral regime governing FDI—a long-standing goal of U.S. MNCs. It thus seems very unlikely that internationally oriented firms would support restrictive or discriminatory IFDI policies even when competition from foreign-owned firms hurts them in the short term.

The Global Industry hypothesis suggests not only that domestically based MNCs will oppose IFDI restrictions against their foreign competitors but also that these firms will have a similar open attitude toward IFDI in vertically related sectors (upstream industries that supply them with inputs, and downstream industries that buy their products). Import-consuming industries oppose trade protection because it increases the prices of their inputs.[23] Following a similar logic, firms will welcome IFDI in upstream sectors insofar as the entrance of more firms—domestic or foreign—into the supplier industry will increase competition and drive down input costs.[24] Firms should also favor a liberal policy toward IFDI in downstream industries, as this would increase the local demand for their own products. In sum, this hypothesis predicts that policy preferences concerning IFDI will vary with the international orientation of producers. For the same reasons that global producers favor liberal trade policy, they will also support a liberal IFDI policy.

(3) The Strategic Investment Demand Hypothesis

A third hypothesis suggests that firms will make "strategic" demands, aimed at putting political pressure on the country where the foreign investor is headquartered. Specifically, domestic firms are concerned with whether or not the foreign government provides reciprocal treatment of the firm's own exports and investments. According to strategic trade theory, in certain oligopolistic sectors (those characterized by large economies of scale, steep learning curves, and substantial R&D requirements) protectionist or discriminatory policies on the part of foreign governments give their companies first-mover advantages as they are able to reap scale economies and reduce their marginal costs, damaging the overall competitive position of the shut-out firms.[25] Consequently, MNCs that would otherwise favor free trade (because of their international orientation) instead put forth "strategic trade demands" consisting of support for conditional import barriers designed to pressure foreign countries to open their markets.[26] The damage these companies sustain from being discriminated against outweighs the risk of foreign retaliation. Many economists have expressed skepticism about the wisdom or practicality of strategic trade policies, but what matters here is whether and under what conditions producers believe these measures will benefit their competitive position.[27]

The theory of strategic trade demands relates to the issue of IFDI in two ways. First, when firms successfully put forth strategic demands, the issue of regulating FDI will almost inevitably arise.[28] Foreign firms (assuming they possess the requisite firm-specific advantages) can jump over trade barriers, set up local subsidiaries, and thus frustrate any hope of bringing pressure to bear on the foreign government. If foreign producers ultimately find operating local subsidiaries to be equal or preferable to exporting, then domestic trade barriers become all but worthless as a bargaining tool. The domestic firms will have to (1) drop their strategic trade demands, (2) proceed with their efforts but accept that the effects will be diminished (if not eliminated) by IFDI, or (3) demand tougher IFDI policies toward MNCs from foreign source nations that they perceive as not providing reciprocal treatment for the host country's exports.

Second, global firms are concerned about access to international markets via both exports and FDI. Hence, a restrictive FDI policy in a foreign country can provoke demands on the part of the excluded domestic firms to their own government for policies of contingent IFDI closure. As suggested earlier, foreign restrictions on FDI may be more harmful than restrictions on exports since firms can evade trade barriers by shifting production.[29] Some argue that in "strategic" industries, gaining access via outward FDI will not be a satisfactory substitute for exporting because the inability of the subsidiary to take advantage of economies of scale and learning effects would damage its efficiency.[30] Often, however, the production process can be broken into stages and dispersed geographically. Firms can evade foreign trade restrictions by relocating manufacturing while retaining production of certain high-tech components (which are subject to these scale and learning effects) at home. Even if economies of scale dictate centralizing production, the domestic MNC could relocate abroad and export back to the home country. Therefore, global firms are unlikely to adopt contingently restrictive policy preferences if foreign countries, although protectionist, at least allow IFDI.

By contrast, a foreign country that denies access to FDI, even if it were to grant trade access, would cause significant harm to MNCs that were shut out.[31] First, to the extent that trade is carried out *within* a multinational corporation, anything that restricts investment will also restrain trade. Majority-owned subsidiaries create final markets and intermediate channels for their parents' exports. When import and export flows are driven not by relative prices but by discretionary managerial edicts, equity ownership and control (and, by extension, IFDI policies) will matter greatly in determining trade patterns. Firms prevented from investing will simply be unable to sell their products in that market.[32] Second, it is becoming increasingly critical that producers of noncommodity goods establish a physical presence close to their customers in overseas markets. Not only does this reduce transportation costs and turnover time for orders, but even more important, a local presence allows firms to understand and respond to ever-changing local needs and tastes. Though sales and distribution subsidiaries can often perform this task, as production becomes more complex and specialized and customers more demanding, this limited presence no longer suffices. The production process itself must become flexible and able to respond quickly to an unpredictable demand.[33]

Reducing foreign investment barriers abroad, then, has become a prerequisite for the ultimate end of expanding sales in foreign markets. Firms that are unable to establish a local presence in an important overseas market will find their overall competitive position damaged. They will therefore suffer losses not only in the country from which they have been excluded but in other markets as well.[34] Where these conditions hold, firms in strategic industries will put forth contingently restrictive trade and investment demands to press foreign countries to liberalize.

Concerns about reciprocity have emerged as a salient issue in a wide range of sectors, not just those considered strategic. Although the original theory of strategic trade demands limited its domain to industries with scale economies, steep learning curves, and heavy R&D requirements, the theory's premise can be fruitfully applied to technologically mature industries such as automobiles or steel.[35] Nor have reciprocity concerns been confined to formal market barriers to access. Many of the structural barriers in Japan that have frustrated potential foreign investors (for example, the restrictive marketing and distribution system) constitute barriers to entry for any new firm, foreign or domestic. Acquiring a Japanese firm would allow foreign investors to avoid many of these high entry costs, but this step has also proved to be extremely difficult in Japan because of cross-shareholding among kereitsu members.[36] These issues have been the subject of controversy and negotiation between the U.S. and Japanese governments. In formulating their policy preferences, U.S. firms certainly take these matters into consideration.

Finally, the Strategic Investment hypothesis also has implications for how producers will view IFDI in vertically related sectors. As mentioned earlier, firms that use imported inputs should normally favor an open IFDI policy insofar as it will lead to a more competitive supplier-industry structure at home and thereby reduce costs. However, domestic producers may perceive upstream foreign firms to be engaging in predatory behavior through their investment activities.[37] If domestic firms believe that foreign targeting is attempting to lay the groundwork for future cartelization of an upstream industry and that oligopolistic cooperation will then be likelier among firms of the same national origin, they may fear becoming dangerously dependent on foreign producers. This will lead firms to oppose IFDI to the extent that it replaces domestically owned suppliers with foreign-owned suppliers. And if the potential upstream cartel would be controlled by the very same vertically integrated foreign enterprises that compete against the user firm, there will be an extra incentive to fear the foreign control of suppliers.[38] Though the issue is really the structure and behavior (rather than nationality) of the supplier industry, nationality becomes politically relevant to the extent foreign companies are the ones that pose the danger. The dangers in becoming dependent on foreign upstream producers include the possibility of price increases, unreliable supplies in times of shortages, and restrictions (or delays) in access to state-of-the-art technological innovation.[39] The more rapid the pace of innovation, the more worrisome it is for downstream firms to see their suppliers favor other customers, whether via price, speed, or reliability of supply, or simply through customizing output. This argument does not require any conspiracy or conscious decision on the part of foreign suppliers to injure domestic firms. Where close and regular collaboration with suppliers is necessary to remain competitive, industrial culture may inhibit cooperation among firms of different national origins, and this can constrain domestic firms from capturing the benefits from technological innovations by foreign-owned suppliers.[40] In short, ownership nationality can matter.

The situation is somewhat analogous for IFDI in downstream industries. If foreign companies disproportionally buy inputs from suppliers of their own nationality, domestic suppliers will have reason to oppose FDI into their customers' industry. Again, this was a common accusation against Japanese manufacturing firms, which, it was alleged, induced their own suppliers to follow them overseas and replicate the keiretsu relationships in the host country.[41] Domestically based suppliers complain they are being shut out of a foreign market (though in this case, the "foreign market" is physically located on domestic territory).

In sum, the Strategic Investment hypothesis predicts that policy preferences regarding IFDI in the host state will vary with the prevailing government policies and informal practices in the nation where the foreign investor is headquartered. Internationally oriented firms will seek more confrontational policies—tightening regulation on IFDI or departing from national treatment—in order to pressure foreign countries either to liberalize their commercial policies or (if the practices in question are matters of private-sector practices or industrial structure) to agree to quantitative market-share guarantees.

Deducing Policy Preferences from Economic Interests

The three approaches just presented provide alternative accounts of the origin of corporate policy demands, pointing to different independent variables as having the most important causal effect (see table 1). These hypotheses are not mutually exclusive; policy preferences are surely af-

Table 1. Summary of Hypotheses

	These conditions . . .	. . . should result in these policy preferences toward IFDI . . .	. . . and these policy preferences toward IFDI in upstream and downstream sectors
Production Profile	High foreign market share, weak competitive position, adverse business conditions	Favor restrictions on IFDI and deviations from national treatment	N/A
Global Industry	International ties (e.g., outward FDI, out-sourcing, international corporate alliances)	Favor liberal IFDI policy and national treatment	Favor liberal IFDI policy and national treatment
Strategic Investment	Market access barriers (formal and informal) of foreign investor's home country	Favor contingently restrictive IFDI policies	Favor contingently restrictive IFDI policies

fected by more than one variable. Producers have a multiplicity of economic interests. They care about their competitive position in the world economy (so they might favor stricter regulation of foreign-owned firms), but they also care about furthering their own interests as global investors (so they might support liberal policies), and finally, they also care about the consequences of asymmetric market access (so they might demand contingent restrictions). Depending on the extent to which the various preconditions for these hypotheses are met, firms will adopt incompatible policy preferences at different times.

Although each of these approaches generates clear predictions concerning policy preferences, when more than one motive exists at once there is no way to deduce which one the decision maker will privilege. Economic interests by themselves do not spawn determinate predictions. As a result, the analyst finds it difficult to deduce what policies groups will advocate. One study of U.S. IFDI policy minimizes the role societal groups played simply because ascertaining their power "can become problematic when a group's interests are multiple or uncertain; the analyst searching only for group interests may not be able to discover an adequate explanation for policy formation."[42] But an inability to explain policy preferences is not a legitimate reason to downplay the importance of societal actors. Uncertainty concerning interests may dampen the involvement of societal groups if it leads them to become confused as to the best course of action and therefore to sit on the sidelines of policy debates. However, this seems unlikely for groups that have a large stake in an issue.[43]

When faced with uncertainty and multiple interests, how do producers decide what approach to adopt? More detailed information could lead to a more precise delineation of the actor's policy preference. For instance, one could quantify the costs of foreign market exclusion and compare them with the costs of foreign retaliation (multiplied by the probability of its occurrence). But the result of incorporating the likely reactions of other actors into the utility function is that the informational requirements become formidable, not just for the analyst but also for the actor formulating its policy preference. And even if producers could cope with the uncertainty, it would still be difficult to predict which approach they would choose. There is, in short, an inescapable element of ambiguity in predicting the policy preferences of societal actors.[44] The economically derived hypotheses provide only a partial explanation of policy preferences. They uncover the incentives that firms confront, but because several of these incentives coexist, the question becomes how and why these economic interests have varied effects on political demands.

COSTS, EXPECTED BENEFITS, AND DOMESTIC POLITICAL STRUCTURES

Analysts have long recognized that actors make cost-benefit calculations in deciding what course of action to take to obtain their underlying goal (in this case, maximizing wealth). Thus the costs of alternative policies are as important as the benefits (that is, the returns derived from the economic models discussed earlier) in predicting policy preferences. In describing the cost side of the ledger, most scholars have focused on collective action costs.[45] Collective action costs can explain why firms have trouble organizing to pressure government officials in order to obtain favored policies, but they say less about why firms have decided to favor one policy over another in the first place. Producers in sectors with high organization costs may anticipate the difficulties of mobilizing and thus choose an alternative course of action (such as economic adjustment).[46] On the other hand, the opposite argument also has merit: large oligopolists able to overcome collective action costs will also have the necessary resources (financial, managerial, technological, etc.) to regain their competitiveness without government assistance or will be sufficiently diversified to shift resources to alternative uses. It is the firms in fragmented industries that will be more likely to pursue political strategies.[47] Clearly, collective action costs on their own cannot explain why firms adopt certain policy preferences.[48]

In sum, economic models detail the benefits of various policies, and those scholars who have looked at the cost side focus primarily on organizational costs, especially collective action issues. However, actions depend not only on the net benefits from a given policy but also on the probabilities that various outcomes will occur.[49] Policy preferences are political strategies, and to understand where they come from, one needs to look at what might make them more or less likely to succeed in influencing government policy. As Daniel Verdier has pointed out, "Producers try to maximize the product of two variables (return discounted by political risk [the chance of winning the return through lobbying]). High risk might make an expected high return look less attractive, whereas low risk might make an expected low return appear more attractive. . . . To a great extent, producers choose sides on the basis of political feasibility."[50] Political feasibility, in turn, is a function of the domestic political system. Political variables that reduce the chances of obtaining one's demands will increase the relative costs of pursuing that option and will lead the actor to consider pursuing an alternative course toward the same underlying goal.

What, then, determines chance of success? What makes some demands more likely to be acted on than others? A huge literature has explored how domestic political structures affect policy outcomes, privileging the demands of some groups while disadvantaging those of others.[51] But because the institutional structure affects a group's chances for political success (in other words, which demands will be listened to), it also affects whether and what demands are put forth in first place. Actors will anticipate that they are either likely or unlikely to succeed, given the existing institutional structure, and (assuming it is costly to create new institutions, as discussed later) decide accordingly to pursue or not to pursue a particular strategy.

This argument echoes recent statements by "historical institutionalists" who maintain that "not just the *strategies* but also the *goals* actors pursue are shaped by the institutional context."[52] As mentioned earlier, some rational choice critics of historical institutionalism argue that many of the examples cited to support this claim "are more usefully interpreted as examples of institutions influencing the strategies actors choose."[53] But strategies involve more than just tactical decisions about what actions one should take to increase the chances of having a favored policy adopted; strategies also involve what kinds of policies one should favor in the first place. Rationalist models that assume profit-maximization as the underlying goal are perfectly compatible with institutionalist analyses of how actors determine what policies they should advocate. Some rationalist models also assume one can determine policy preferences by deducing them from economic theory, and that is the assumption this book challenges.

When producers have multiple economic interests, their policy preferences will be affected by domestic political structures. They will be more likely to seek a given policy when (1) domestic institutions exist to organize and channel their demands and supply the desired output, and (2) the demands are in accordance with widely held norms concerning the appropriate exceptions to liberalism.

Domestic Institutions

Political scientists have long employed variations in domestic institutional structure to explain the *supply* of foreign economic policies across nations, across policy areas, and over time.[54] Fewer have discussed the effects of institutions on policy *demands*, though there have been some efforts along these lines. Geoffrey Garrett and Peter Lange emphasize the role socioeconomic institutions (such as the form of labor organization) may play in affecting societal demands.[55] James Alt and Michael Gilligan discuss how political institutions affect trade policy coalitions, that is, whether firms and workers will organize along class or industry lines.[56] Finally, Ronald Rogowski has explored how political institutions (the franchise, mechanisms of representation, and decision rules) can affect the "strategies of influence" that domestic groups adopt, though he focuses on explaining lobbying tactics rather than the substance of the policies that groups favor.[57]

On the most basic level, domestic institutions reduce the costs of making demands by providing information to private actors about what remedies are available for redressing their complaints and what actions they should take to achieve their goals. More important, social groups are more likely to receive the policies they desire if institutions exist that have been authorized to supply that policy output. With the probability of success higher, actors will then be more likely to pursue the political strategy that involves making demands through that institution. By contrast, groups will be less likely to mobilize in order to champion a policy in the absence of any institutional channels to address their complaints. Industry actors will not expend resources (including political capital) on a battle with little chance of victory or victory only at an extremely high cost.[58]

Norms and Legitimacy

Norms about what policies are considered legitimate also affect the formulation of policy preferences. The idea that preferences may reflect more than material interests—that they may incorporate ideas and norms as well—is now a familiar theme in social science. But although the importance of ideas in preference formation has been applied at the individual level and at the state level, it has rarely been applied at the intermediate level of societal groups.[59] When dealing with group policy preferences over foreign economic policy, most scholars have seen little reason to abandon a materialist approach. Nonetheless, Judith Goldstein and Robert Keohane suggest that when actors experience uncertainty as to how various policies will affect them, causal ideas function as a "road map" helping these actors determine how best to obtain their preferred outcomes.[60] As a result of this uncertainty, societal groups often express policy preferences that appear "irrational." That is, these preferences do not seem to maximize economic returns. One reason is that actors view their environment through the lens of particular ideas or ideologies. Actors can "rationally" translate their goals into a variety of policy preferences, depending on the ideas they hold.[61]

Although personal beliefs are important, actors will also respond to widely shared norms that underlie the policy-making process. In seeking government regulation, firms want to emphasize normative arguments they know will resonate with the public and politicians. This emphasis, in turn, will affect which of many potential interest-promoting policies producers will actually lobby for. In fact, it matters little whether actors sincerely believe these ideas or not. The ideas form part of the political landscape that producers must take into account when formulating their policy preferences. Often these ideas are embodied in institutional structures. Goldstein's study of U.S. trade policy illustrates how institutions channel demands by determining "what constitutes a legitimate claim against the state for aid."[62]

The Domestic Political Context of IFDI in the United States

The policy preferences of U.S. producers regarding IFDI were shaped by both underlying economic interests and the domestic political context. The case studies in this book provide details of the institutions and prevailing ideas that constituted the environmental context within which groups decided which of their economic interests to pursue. This section provides a rough sketch of this institutional structure. For the most part, U.S. policy toward IFDI has been characterized by neutrality, which in turn consists of two principles: the right of foreign firms to establish subsidiaries and the principle that once established, foreign-owned firms will be treated no differently than domestically owned firms (national treatment). The institutional apparatus governing IFDI is relatively rudimentary.[63] Unlike many other countries, the United States has not had an agency to screen IFDI or negotiate with foreign investors. Indeed, there are few existing tools that Washington could use to hinder IFDI even if it wished to.[64] There are some important exceptions, including a handful of long-standing sector-specific limitations on foreign ownership[65] and the 1988 Exon-Florio amendment.[66] A few regulations govern foreign participation in government activities such as defense contracting and federally funded R&D programs. Various agencies in the government have also set forth criteria (albeit not always consistently) for what constitutes a domestic or foreign company for the purposes of implementing other trade and regulatory legislation. According to the argument here, producers will tailor demands to match the specific rules and stipulations embodied in these institutions. They will be less likely to seek policies, however potentially advantageous, in cases in which the existing rules do not cover their situation or do not promise a favorable outcome.

The second component of domestic political context—prevailing beliefs about what policies are legitimate—is more difficult to observe independently of the outcomes one is trying to explain. One way to avoid this problem is to examine the types of norms that are salient in political activity surrounding other issue areas, such as outward FDI or trade. If, for example, firms successfully lobby for trade protection by stressing national security concerns, the absence of reciprocity, or employment preservation, then one might expect that these same firms will put forth demands for IFDI restrictions when the positions can credibly be phrased in these terms.[67] Firms that are seeking more restrictive policies must have a strong argument to counter the prevailing ideological consensus (at least among policy makers and influential elites) in favor of openness and national treatment.[68]

The Origins of Political Structures

Producers formulate their demands not just on the basis of what will increase their returns (since a number of policies will accomplish this goal) but also on the basis of what political strategies appear most promising. This, in turn, is a function of domestic political structures: the presence of institutions to channel demands and provide policies and the existence of widely shared beliefs that legitimize the demands. The question naturally arises, Where do these institutions and beliefs come from? If institutions and ideas reflect rather than (or as well as) shape the political demands of producers, the argument here will overestimate the effect these variables have on political demands; economic interests would dictate demands for policies *and* for changing political structures. Of course, it makes perfect sense that powerful groups will try to alter institutions and to affect public ideas about what policies are legitimate. As Frieden and Rogowski write, "Given that socio-economic and political agents have preferences about policies, and political institutions affect the adoption and implementation of policies, it follows that private agents must have preferences about institutions themselves."[69]

But although it is surely true that producers have preferences over institutions, there is little evidence for the claim that industry actors had, or even tried to have, significant influence over the nature of the state structures concerning the issue of IFDI. Perhaps surprisingly, the level of corporate lobbying over sector-specific IFDI policies far exceeded the negligible effort expended to shape overall U.S. IFDI policy, even though these general policies set the parameters as to what outputs are available at the sector level. Although there were vigorous debates over legislation that would impose greater regulation on foreign-owned firms (for instance, the Bryant amendment, mandating stricter reporting requirements on FDI; the Exon-Florio amendment, giving the president increased powers to block acquisitions on national security grounds; and the Manton amendment, imposing reciprocity standards for participation in consortia funded or organized by the government), in these debates and others like them, U.S. firms did not actively put forth demands for changes in U.S. policy. If anything, large business organizations consistently opposed the measures (though these were not major priorities for the groups). Nor were there demands from U.S. producers to create screening bodies, to create a United States Investment Representative (as a counterpart to the United States Trade Representative) or an Economic Security Council (as a counterpart to the National Security Council), to impose federal regulations on state offerings of investment incentives, or to instigate general negotiations to alter Japanese IFDI policies (along the lines of the Structural Impediments Initiative in trade policy). These were not outlandish ideas; all of them (and others) had been put forth by a number of scholars or policy makers as institutional changes worthy of consideration. Most of these changes would have favored domestic producers. Therefore, the utter lack of political support for these structural innovations among U.S. producers who opposed IFDI is something of a puzzle, for as Frieden and Rogowski suggest, producers ought to have had a preference on these questions. At the least, changes in these wider institutional constraints would have made it easier to obtain the desired outcomes in the industry-specific contests.

One reason for this anomaly is that the collective action costs were much higher for general IFDI policies that would create or modify domestic institutions. Producers did not want to bear the costs of demanding policies for which the benefits could not be appropriated. In their work on trade politics I. M. Destler and John Odell found that recent antiprotection political activity was confined to product-specific trade protection and that there was no comparable increase (if anything, a decline) in opposition to generic trade-restrictive proposals. These issues, because of collective action costs, do not generate political participation by narrow industry-specific interest groups. Instead, these questions interest the larger business coalitions, which do not face the collective action problems but which find themselves immobilized on product-specific issues because of the heterogeneity of their members' interests.[70] It was far more common for industry actors to be affected by rather than to affect domestic structures. This is not to say that institutions never change; rather, they do not change often and especially not in the short run. Producers deciding on policies for which to lobby treat these institutions as if they were exogenous. The same argument holds for the ideological variable. Again, industry actors participated in public debates and tried to affect the public's view of what would be seen as legitimate. But these efforts were constrained by a preexisting consensus which firms did not create and to which they could only react.

INDUSTRY CASE STUDIES

The experiences of various American-owned industries that confronted the challenge of IFDI are considered in chapters 3 through 5. The manufacturing industries discussed here all suffered from foreign trade competition, sought and obtained import barriers, and subsequently saw the value of their trade protection undermined as foreign MNCs relocated production through various forms of IFDI. In these chapters the contrast between protectionist trade policy demands and more ambiguous IFDI demands requires an explanation. In the case of the service industries examined in chapter 6, FDI itself was already strictly regulated and hence foreign firms gained entry through international corporate alliances. Here the focus is on the political demands that domestically owned firms put forth for government regulation of these alliances.

Each of the case-study chapters examines every political issue in which the question of IFDI or foreign ownership was relevant in determining the nature of producer policy preferences. Under the first hypothesis (emphasizing the position of the industry within the world economy), one would expect to see demands for tighter IFDI regulation, especially when domestic firms are particularly threatened by foreign subsidiaries.[71] Under the Global Industry hypothesis, one expects that these demands will not materialize, owing to the international interests of U.S. firms; if the demands do exist, their intensity will vary inversely with the extent to which the domestic industry is globalized. Under the Strategic Investment hypothesis, one should expect demands to vary with the policies and industrial structure of the source country.

After describing the industry's behavior, the chapters assess the extent to which its policy demands are explicable in terms of these three approaches. If these hypotheses are able to account for the observed pattern of demands (either by themselves or interactively), then no additional variables are necessary and examining political structures would be superfluous. If, however, these hypotheses cannot explain variation in the observed outcomes (within and among industries), then the case for bringing in other factors is strengthened. Because of the indeterminacy of economic interests, policy preferences will not vary directly with these economic variables but rather will vary with the presence or absence of domestic political structures—rules governing IFDI regulation and ideas about what policy options are legitimate. To be more precise, these political structures will affect which of the economic interests are translated into policy demands.

In most (though not all) of the cases examined, economic explanations are not in fact sufficient to explain the policy preferences of societal actors. These explanations are most useful in analyzing the reactions of the sectors involved in the first wave of IFDI, steel and consumer electronics. By contrast, the semiconductor and auto industries both put forth ambivalent demands regarding IFDI. Neither industry showed the same level of concern toward IFDI as it did toward import competition, even though FDI was undermining hard-won gains in trade protection. At the same time, many firms in both sectors were far more willing to advocate IFDI restrictions than one would expect given their international interests. The machine tool and antifriction bearing industries took a more liberal approach toward dealing with IFDI, which was surprising in that these industries were less globalized. Conversely, the more competitive and globalized service sectors—airlines and to a lesser degree telecommunications—were surprisingly vehement in their opposition to foreign entry, even via international alliances.

The case-study chapters explain these outcomes by examining the way political factors affected the relative costs of presenting various policy demands. To the extent that different state actors make IFDI policy in different arenas with different instruments, firms face a choice as to which policies they should seek to further their underlying goals. All else being equal, they opt for the policy they feel they have the greatest chance of obtaining. Specifically, firms will demand policies that are seen as feasible (which depends on domestic rules and regulations) and legitimate (which depends on how the policy accords with widely held beliefs regarding appropriate exceptions to liberalism). If these factors vary, the demands of different industries on IFDI issues (or of the same industry over time or across issue areas) will vary in a way that cannot be explained by economic considerations alone. Policies that are feasible and legitimate will be demanded; policies that are neither will not be. The intermediate cases are more ambiguous. Policies that are feasible but not legitimate may be advocated in a low-key or behind-the-scenes way, but they will not become the object of major public political activity. Policies that are legitimate but not feasible may be given extensive lip service by industry representatives in public statements but will also not become the object of a major expenditure of political resources.

The important role played by these two political variables suggests that one cannot just apply the economic logic behind trade demands and come up with accurate predictions of policy demands on IFDI, despite the fact that domestic producers may be affected similarly by the two forms of competition. In U.S. trade politics, institutions and legitimating ideas built up over two centuries have been used by policy makers to regulate import competition.[72] But with IFDI the country has had a very different historical experience, and as a result, a very different political context exists. Ultimately, the differences between how beleaguered industries respond to foreign competition in the form of imports versus local production via IFDI have more to do with this political context than with underlying economic interests.

THREE

An Economic Response
Consumer Electronics and Steel

By the time incoming foreign direct investment attracted the attention of the public in the 1980s, the consumer electronics and steel industries had already faced substantial competition from local production by foreign-owned subsidiaries. In both cases domestic producers had expended considerable effort and political capital in obtaining import protection, only to see their overseas competitors skirt these barriers by investing directly in the United States. These sectors were the first to confront what would later become a common problem: how to respond to production by foreign-owned firms in the United States. This chapter examines the political reactions of domestic producers in these industries as they confronted this new form of competition.

On the face of it, the two sectors exhibited quite different reactions to IFDI. In stark contrast to its position on trade, steel producers presented the least hostile reaction to IFDI of any industry in this study. There were some initial attempts to use antitrust measures against foreign firms, but these were soon abandoned and substantial opposition to IFDI never materialized. Later some companies raised objections to the import of semi-finished steel slabs by foreign transplants, but enough domestically owned firms had also outsourced this part of the process to prevent the issue from catching on. The consumer electronics industry's reaction was more ambiguous; some firms called for stricter regulation both on antitrust grounds and on the basis of insufficient domestic content (particularly the foreign subsidiaries' reliance on imported picture tubes). There were complaints that Asian companies were circumventing negotiated trade agreements by assembling imported parts in their U.S. plants without adding much local value; this practice, critics argued, did not constitute "real" investment. However, it proved very difficult to persuade policy makers to regulate transplant production, especially when foreign investors could point to the jobs they were creating while domestically owned firms were outsourcing their own production. Ultimately, U.S. producers dropped their objections to IFDI.

Economic motives can largely explain the actions of the steel and consumer electronics industries, in contrast with the industries examined in subsequent chapters. Keeping in mind that the political-structures explanation of policy preferences is meant to supplement, not displace, economic explanations, by investigating cases in which political factors did not play a large role, we begin to understand when and under what conditions political structures will matter more.

The weight of economic interests in these cases reflects the extent to which these two industries had been devastated by import competition and lacked the capability to recover their competitive position, even with considerable help from Washington. With economic constraints weighing more heavily on these producers, they had very limited flexibility. As argued in chapter 2, political variables become especially important when economic interests are contradictory, and thus a multitude of strategies serve to further the actor's underlying goals; in these cases firms faced much more compelling economic pressures as to what actions they needed to take. In addition, IFDI was still a novel phenomenon during this period. The nature of the competitive threat these firms faced was not clear; there were questions about whether foreign firms would be able to maintain their competitive advantage on U.S. soil. There was also considerable uncertainty about the potential mechanisms by which the problem could be addressed via the policy process. By the time some domestic firms had begun to consider political action aimed at changing the government's IFDI policy, other developments made it unlikely this approach would provide any benefits for the domestically owned industry.

THE CONSUMER ELECTRONICS INDUSTRY

The American consumer electronics industry was not the first to experience the challenge of import competition during the post–World War II period.[1] However, foreign producers' evasion of trade barriers via the relocation of production was a new phenomenon. When foreign direct investment came to this sector, it transformed the ownership structure of the entire industry. By the early 1980s, before IFDI had even emerged as a salient political issue in Washington, production of color televisions in the United States had become thoroughly dominated by foreign-owned firms. After the purchase of majority ownership in Zenith by LG Electronics (a Korean company) in 1995, no U.S.-owned color television manufacturing remained.[2] Significant production still exists in the United States (nearly two-thirds of the 25 million color TV sets sold to Americans are manufactured locally), but foreign companies control this production.[3] There has been considerable debate over whether this matters. Most economists believe it does not, but a few dissenters blame the problems of the U.S. semiconductor industry in the 1980s on the absence of a domestic consumer electronics industry. Asian consumer electronics producers, they argue, sourced chips from their own suppliers while U.S. chipmakers, unable to form close links with potential customers, gradually lost the ability to manufacture these kinds of chips.[4] Regardless of the effects on other sectors or on the national economy as a whole, for U.S. consumer electronics producers, the foreign takeover of the industry was a harrowing experience.

The domestic industry's troubles began in the late 1960s and early 1970s. U.S. profits, market share, and employment all took a nosedive, reaching a low point by the mid-1970s. Japanese market share in the United States increased from 15 percent in 1975 to 30 percent the next year. Domestic production in 1975—5.4 million units—was down from 7.03 million three years earlier.[5] Some of the problems were self-inflicted (for instance, U.S. producers lagged behind their Japanese competitors in adopting solid-state technology), but American industry officials mostly blamed Japan's unfair trading practices: predatory dumping made possible by collusion, government assistance, and covert rebates to U.S. merchandisers.[6]

The American companies' reaction to the rise of import competition was twofold. First, many producers either abandoned the market or shifted production overseas in order to reduce labor costs. Second, and concurrently, the industry launched a massive lobbying campaign for government support. They used such a wide variety of political and legal channels—petitions for antidumping and countervailing duties, lawsuits in Customs Court challenging the commodity tax rebates that Japanese companies received on their exports, escape clause petitions seeking temporary protection in response to severe injury caused by increased imports, and the Section 337 petition claiming unfair trading practices—that opponents accused the domestic firms of "multiple harassment" designed to impose heavy legal costs on the competition.[7] Washington was reluctant to supply the protection that some firms were demanding, and consequently, throughout the course of the decade the domestic industry, distributors, Japanese producers, various government agencies, and courts (up to and including the Supreme Court) were embroiled in a complex and bitter series of disputes.[8] Despite the attitude of the executive branch, continuing demands for protection and the resulting trade friction made it appear increasingly likely that the government would eventually implement some form of import restrictions. Finally, after a March 1977 ruling by the International Trade Commission on the escape clause petition recommending substantial increases in tariffs for five years, President Carter negotiated a three-year orderly market agreement (OMA) with Japan, limiting the number of television sets it could export to 1.75 million per year, a figure that represented 60 percent of their highest level of shipments in 1976.[9] The agreement did not satisfy many of the escape clause petitioners.[10] Still, it was better than nothing, and the domestic industry gave the agreement its support.[11]

The OMA covered both complete sets (limited to 1.56 million units) and incomplete sets (190,000 units). Incomplete sets were defined as those assembled to the point that the picture tube is in place or those "at least assembled to the point where no more remains to be done, prior to installation in its cabinet, than the incorporation of the picture tube, tuner and incidental components."[12] This definition purposely excluded subassemblies and components. Also, TV sets that contained at least 40 percent U.S. labor costs were wholly exempted. Thus the agreement all but invited the foreign companies to evade export restrictions via IFDI, as long as there was a minimum amount of local manufacturing. Indeed, encouraging such IFDI was a deliberate goal of the OMA, and this was made clear to the Japanese government.[13] Before the negotiations were completed, every Japanese company explicitly proclaimed that trade restrictions would induce them to set up local subsidiaries or, if they already were operating such plants, to boost production levels so as not to lose market share.[14] From Washington's perspective, explicitly laying out what kind of investment would be considered domestic production for purposes of the quota would prevent "screwdriver" assembly designed purely to evade the OMA and would promote more substantial, and therefore more desirable, IFDI.[15] From the standpoint of the domestic producers, however, even "real" investment would diminish the protective impact of the OMA.

The OMA worked insofar as it reduced the number of imported televisions from Japan. In fact, although the OMA officially limited exports to 60 percent of the 1976 level, by 1979 they had fallen to 19 percent of that high-water mark.[16] But not surprisingly, locally produced Japanese TVs replaced these imports. In 1976 22 percent of Japanese sets sold in the United States were produced locally (up from zero four years earlier). In 1978, after the OMA was in place, local production caught up with imports. By the end of the decade four out of every five Japanese TV sets sold in the United States were produced in local subsidiaries.[17] The trade restrictions led to a renaissance of (foreign) manufacturing in the United States. U.S. television production capacity increased by 1.88 million units between 1977 and 1980, but 83 percent of that consisted of Japanese-owned companies.[18]

Initially, most of these investments were in the form of acquisitions (although the very first foreign investor, Sony, built a new plant in 1972).[19] For instance, Matsushita bought Motorola's Quasar division in 1974 and, adding that to its own Panasonic line, became the largest television manufacturer in the world.[20] In 1974 Magnavox was acquired by the American affiliate of the Dutch firm Philips, the largest European producer (and only non-Asian firm with direct investment in the U.S. TV industry).[21] In 1976 Whirlpool sold its controlling interest in Warwick (which produced television sets for Sears under the retailer's private label) to Sanyo.[22] Finally, in 1977 Hitachi announced a joint venture with General Electric under which the two companies would set up a new 50–50 company called General Television of America and produce sets at GE's existing plants.[23] However, the Justice Department rejected this venture on antitrust grounds. The OMA provoked Hitachi to try again, and in 1979 the company decided to build a greenfield plant in Compton, California.

Beginning in the mid-1970s and accelerating after the implementation of the OMA, a wave of greenfield investments supplemented these acquired subsidiaries. Mitsubishi, which had almost disappeared from the American consumer electronics market, reentered via a subsidiary in Santa Ana, California (augmented by a second, adjoining plant established in 1981). Toshiba built a plant in Nashville, Tennessee, that began assembling televisions in 1978. That same year, Sharp followed suit with a plant, also in Tennessee, and as already mentioned, Hitachi established local production in 1979. In 1982 JVC announced it would build a color TV factory in Elmwood Park, New Jersey. By the beginning of the 1980s, then, all the major Japanese companies had set up production in the United States.

Through IFDI Japanese producers minimized the effect of the OMA on their earnings and essentially prevented any loss in market share.[24] Because of this upsurge of IFDI, one analyst argued that "the 'protection' afforded by bilateral quotas on complete sets has been virtually eliminated." Domestic profits remained dismal and, in fact, continued to decline.[25] How, then, did the U.S. industry, or at least that part of the industry that had worked so hard to gain trade protection, respond to this situation?

The Production Profile explanation suggests that to the extent IFDI reduced the benefits the industry received from trade protection, domestic producers should have extended their protectionist trade demands to cover IFDI. That is, they should have supported stricter regulation of IFDI and policies that deviated from the norm of national treatment. Other methods of foreign OMA evasion were addressed in this way. For instance, because the trade agreement covered only Japanese imports, there was concern that imports from other countries would fill the gap. And in the years following the OMA's initiation, Korean and Taiwanese imports skyrocketed. In 1976 Taiwan exported 235,000 sets to the United States while South Korea exported 47,000. Within two years those figures had risen to 434,000 and 624,000, respectively.[26] Domestic producers complained that Japanese subsidiaries had shifted production to these countries in order to evade trade restrictions. In response, some producers called for global quotas with worldwide limits. Eventually, the U.S. government extended the OMA to cover Taiwan and Korea. Some U.S. producers were reluctant to support the extension since they had established operations in these countries.[27] But most domestic firms supported bolstering the trade agreement by eliminating these avenues for evasion. By analogy, when IFDI into the United States undermined the OMA, one would expect domestic producers to undertake similar political efforts to protect their profits.

The Global Industry hypothesis predicts that any hostile reaction to IFDI would be tempered, if not completely precluded, by the international ties of the domestically based U.S. producers themselves. American-owned firms varied in their global orientation, leading to a diversity of positions toward trade and IFDI.[28] RCA, the most global of the American television producers, remained aloof from the earlier trade battles, as (for the most part) did GE. By contrast, Zenith, the most domestically oriented, took the most actively protectionist role, and Magnavox and GTE-Sylvania frequently joined it in battle. Motorola took an intermediate position. Even the more nationalist companies altered their positions over time as their own orientations shifted (or, as with Magnavox and Sylvania, as they themselves were acquired by foreign firms). As noted earlier, import competition had led much of the domestic industry to accelerate moves toward increased multinational production to reduce labor costs. These new foreign plants were in addition to existing European subsidiaries that had been established to evade tariffs there. Some of the more diversified companies moved away from color television production altogether.[29] As a result, the industry was internally divided about what trade policy it preferred. The main lobbying group of the industry, the Electronics Industries Association (EIA), was split between the liberal International Business Council and the protectionist Consumer Electronics Products division.[30] The most active proponent of a protectionist policy was another group, formed in 1976, called the Committee to Preserve American Color Television (COMPACT), which included two U.S. TV makers (GTE-Sylvania and Wells-Gardener) but really reflected the efforts of labor unions and parts suppliers (especially companies that produced the glass for picture tubes). Domestic TV companies such as Zenith and Magnavox often participated in COMPACT-led campaigns, but they did not join the organization itself. After the OMA went into effect, the protectionist coalition began to crumble, especially after Zenith decided to lay off a fourth of its American workforce and shift production to Taiwan and Mexico.[31] Overall, these intra-industry divisions reduced the protectionist pressure on the government and help explain why the assistance the industry did receive was not larger or more permanent.[32]

Internationalized U.S. firms should have had even more reason to adopt liberal investment demands since their foreign activities consisted of multinational production rather than exports. They also engaged in only limited intrafirm trade.[33] Therefore, these firms would be unlikely to support any policy that set a precedent of restricting foreign direct investment. Furthermore, it would be odd indeed to observe U.S. firms supporting restrictions on foreign acquisitions when many of these firms themselves exited the industry by selling their operations to foreign producers. As mentioned, Motorola sold its Quasar division to Matsushita in 1974, and GTE sold Sylvania to N.A. Phillips in 1981. In 1986 RCA was purchased by GE, which subsequently sold the GE-RCA television division to Thompson CSF. Finally, LG Electronics purchased the last remaining U.S.-owned TV maker, Zenith, in 1995. It is possible that U.S. firms might oppose IFDI up to the point when they decided to put their own operations up for sale. In general, however, the extensive multinational investment among U.S.-owned producers suggests that they should at least be as hesitant, if not more so, in demanding restrictive IFDI policies as they were to adopt protectionist demands. Similarly, variation in policy preferences among firms or over time should also reflect variations in the extent of the U.S. industry's outward orientation.

Finally, the Strategic Investment hypothesis would suggest that U.S. firms would oppose IFDI by Japanese producers (though not by French or Dutch companies) because of the closed nature of Japan's market. As Zenith CEO John Nevin complained, "The exclusion of foreigners from the Japanese color television market has, so far, been close to absolute."[34] U.S. producers claimed that this policy allowed Japanese firms to use monopoly profits gained in the sheltered market to finance predatory dumping in the United States. Also, because of their exclusion from foreign markets, U.S. companies were unable to benefit from economies of scale and so had to suffer higher overall production costs. But as a motive for policy preferences, this explanation falters, for there is little evidence that domestic producers made any significant effort to export televisions to Japan, much less to establish subsidiaries there. Partly, this resulted from a vicious circle: it made no sense to devote resources to penetrating a market that was perceived as closed, but without devoting these resources, penetration was impossible. Even so, U.S. FDI in Japan was unlikely because American producers did not possess firm-specific advantages that would justify locating production there. Japanese labor was not cheap, and the local competition would have been fierce. U.S. producers were more concerned about protecting themselves in their own domestic market. The Strategic Investment hypothesis, then, is less relevant for explaining the consumer electronic industry's reactions.

The Reaction of Domestic Producers to IFDI

How, then, did the U.S. industry respond? Some U.S. companies expressed opposition to IFDI from the outset. For instance, in 1974, even before the OMA, Zenith and Magnavox publicly opposed Matsushita's bid to acquire Motorola's Quasar division. In a letter sent to the Justice Department, the two companies complained that Matsushita already had a large share of the U.S. TV market and was the world's largest television component manufacturer. Zenith's Nevin later explained, "The protest was based on the belief that Matsushita and other Japanese television companies had, through predatory pricing associated with dumping, so weakened the U.S. television companies that they were easy prey for acquisition or merger proposals. Zenith and Magnavox maintained that permitting the acquisition to proceed would allow Matsushita to benefit from the fruits of that behavior."[35] The Justice Department had already begun its own antitrust investigation. Ultimately, the department agreed not to interfere with the sale if it was delayed for thirty days, during which time Motorola would look for another buyer. But at the end of that period the deal went through, over the protests of the two domestic firms.[36] Justice did block a different foreign acquisition—the GE-Hitachi plan already discussed—on antitrust grounds, though there is no evidence that other domestic firms objected to this deal.[37] In any event, U.S. producers were no better off as a result of this second Justice Department decision since Hitachi reacted by setting up a greenfield plant in California.

In September 1974 Zenith filed suit in a Philadelphia federal court alleging that Japanese television producers had violated U.S. antitrust and antidumping laws.[38] The plaintiffs argued that twenty-one Japanese companies, including subsidiaries located in the United States, had engaged in a conspiracy to fix prices and grant rebates, discounts, and allowances and had attempted to "destroy, cripple, or injure U.S. competition in this market."[39] In its suit Zenith also requested that the court reverse the acquisitions of Motorola by Matsushita, of Magnavox by N.A. Phillips, and of Warwick by Sanyo.[40] Though ultimately unsuccessful, this case is noteworthy in that Zenith lumped local subsidiaries with their foreign parents as constituting a single competitive threat.

During the trade policy debates leading up to the OMA, those domestic firms that had supported import protection expressed concern that foreign companies might try to evade the trade restrictions through setting up screwdriver assembly plants. To prevent this practice, U.S. companies asked for additional quotas on components and subassemblies. A Zenith executive, in testimony over the escape clause petition, had argued that such quotas "would prevent television companies from circumventing the quota system by adding only modest increments of value to receivers that are essentially imported."[41] According to U.S. firms, then, it was not IFDI per se that concerned them but rather the *nature* of this investment—whether it was "real" investment or just the assembly of imported components. Just as the U.S. automobile industry would later do, many domestic color television producers assumed that "real" foreign direct investment in the United States would blunt the competitive advantage held by Asian producers. At the time the OMA was being negotiated, a GE executive, voicing widespread perceptions, indicated that the company was unconcerned about reports that Japanese firms would move their operations to the United States because if that were to occur, Japanese TV sets would no longer have a lower price than U.S. sets. Facing the same wage and production costs as their American competitors did, the new subsidiaries would no longer be able to beat U.S. companies on price.[42] This assumption later proved to be erroneous. Foreign producers were in fact able to transfer their firm-specific advantages to the United States, and the OMA had little effect in restoring the profitability of U.S.-owned firms.[43]

As the OMA neared its expiration date and the domestic industry's situation worsened, some executives began to complain about IFDI. COMPACT officials argued that the continued importation of incomplete models kept domestic firms from regaining their lost market position. According to the group, "The overriding purpose of these facilities [the subsidiaries] was obvious: they allowed the Japanese manufacturers to assemble color televisions in the United States from imported parts and to sell those televisions outside the discipline of the antidumping order."[44] However, most of the television manufacturers did not add their voices to these criticisms. Ironically, the one television producer that joined COMPACT in testifying at congressional hearings was the Dutch-owned Magnavox, which called for tightening the quota's coverage of incomplete sets so that it would apply whether individual parts were mounted on circuit boards or imported separately.[45] But this argument, later echoed by Zenith, suggested that trade protection was valuable precisely because it forced Asian companies to invest in local production. Unless the OMA was extended and tightened, these groups claimed, Japanese firms would revert to dumping or assembling imported components.[46] This was a strange argument for the domestic industry to put forth since increased IFDI would do nothing to help its own profits.

Ultimately, the Carter administration allowed the OMA with Japan to lapse but extended the agreement with Taiwan and Korea. In the opinion of the International Trade Commission (ITC) the successful international-ization of the Japanese industry meant that those companies now had no need or reason to boost exports.[47] The OMA was designed to restrict im-ports, not foreign competition as such, and so it did not matter to the ITC that the market share and profits of the domestic firms had continued to deteriorate. Meanwhile, the new agreements were even more permissive with respect to IFDI. Taiwanese firms (including Japanese and American firms with operations in Taiwan) were now allowed to export incomplete receivers without picture tubes to the United States in whatever quantity they wished.[48] Subsequently, Korean and Taiwanese firms followed the earlier example of the Japanese and began assembling color TVs in the United States.[49]

It is interesting to consider the response of the European TV industry to a similar situation. There, as in the United States, trade friction with Japa-nese companies led to extensive FDI, especially in the United Kingdom, with its large market, low labor costs, and weak currency. But the British government, concerned about overcapacity, imposed restrictions on the output of the transplants and high local content ratios (around 70%). In 1977, when Hitachi announced plans to build a color TV factory in north-eastern England, domestic producers, along with trade unions, asked the British industry secretary to reject Hitachi's application on the grounds that the Japanese company would be able to increase its market share. Hi-tachi promised it would source at least half its components locally, but the opposition persisted, and eventually the company withdrew its applica-tion. Subsequently, the British government suggested that Japanese com-panies invest via joint production with local firms rather than by setting up greenfield plants.[50] Other European governments pressured investors to respect minimum prices and to set up joint ventures with struggling local producers rather than invest in greenfield plants, a position strongly supported by European producers.[51]

Domestic Content and Picture Tube Imports

U.S.-based producers were nowhere near as active in opposing IFDI as were their European counterparts. Industry officials that did criticize foreign subsidiaries emphasized that they opposed only screwdriver assembly, not "real" foreign direct investment. It was a plausible argument because the percentage of domestic content in the televisions built by foreign-owned plants was low.[52] But the criticism was muted, and domestic producers never pressed the issue or supported any policies that would have addressed it. The reason was obvious: U.S. firms themselves had low levels of domestic content.[53] Domestic companies intensified their reliance on chassis subassemblies and printed circuit board assemblies imported from Taiwan and Mexico.[54] Zenith held out for a while, sourcing only about 10 percent of its parts from overseas up to the mid-1970s, but that changed in 1977, when the company shifted production abroad and increased foreign content of its sets to around 30 percent.[55] It was unlikely that the domestic industry would pursue a strategy of demanding stricter content rules.

There was one local content issue, however, that provoked conflict between domestic and foreign-owned firms. It involved picture tubes, the single most expensive component in a television set.[56] RCA, GE, Zenith, and (Dutch-owned) Sylvania produced their own tubes, and some Japanese companies had been induced by an existing 15 percent tariff to shift tube production to the United States.[57] But other foreign subsidiaries that did not produce tubes locally sought "foreign trade subzone status" for their factories. Under this program the federal government allowed manufacturers to import components duty-free in order to encourage local production for export. If the finished goods were sold domestically, the assembler had to pay the duty on the final product. In this case the duty on assembled sets (5%) was lower than that on picture tubes (15%), and designating a plant a "subzone" could therefore lead to considerable savings for an assembly plant. However, the granting of subzone status to foreign-owned plants stirred up controversy among domestically owned component producers. In fall 1981 Sanyo applied for subzone status at its Forest City, Arkansas, plant. Parts producers called the request a blatant attempt to evade tube duties.[58] COMPACT and the Tube Division of the EIA notified the Department of Commerce that they planned to oppose the Sanyo bid.

A few domestically owned TV manufacturers expressed support for the domestic tube makers. RCA (which did not play much of a role in the earlier trade battles) announced its opposition to Sanyo's request for subzone status, arguing that the financial advantages reaped from paying lower duties would give the Japanese company a leg up in competing for other export markets.[59] Other firms occasionally expressed concern about imported tubes. For instance, Zenith chairman Jerry Pearlman complained that the domestic industry had not benefited from import restrictions because Asian transplants imported kits "for snap-together assembly here . . . and those are [tube sales] that should be split up [among U.S. firms]. . . . We're not going to roll over and play dead. We feel we're getting beat up unfairly and we are going to keep fighting it."[60] Zenith continued to criticize the transplants on this issue, and eventually some foreign producers (such as Samsung) asked the U.S. government to clarify once and for all how tubes should be treated.[61]

TV makers offered some assistance during COMPACT's fight against imported picture tubes. When COMPACT filed an antidumping petition against Korea and Taiwan in 1983, it also lobbied the government to close a loophole that allowed companies to reduce the duties they paid on imported tubes by bringing them in as part of an unassembled kit that could be quickly put together by a local subsidiary.[62] A couple of domestic TV manufacturers expressed their support for the tube makers. At hearings over a bill to close the tariff loophole, Zenith complained about Matsushita's practice of shipping color tubes from Japan to a plant in Tijuana where they would be combined with a locally made chassis. From there the company imported the tubes as kits into the United States (without paying the 15% duty on tubes), assembled them into finished sets in Illinois, and sold them through its Panasonic and Quasar subsidiaries. Zenith, RCA, and COMPACT all pressed the government to tighten up on this kind of practice before other companies followed suit.[63]

Japanese producers saw the bill as penalizing them for having established plants in the United States. Since the OMA no longer applied to them, they could simply export complete television sets to the United States and pay only the 5 percent duty. Toshiba executives said, "The bill would penalize us for making TVs in America and reward the other U.S. companies who are moving jobs offshore."[64] Matsushita added that if the tariff were changed, the company "would be forced to examine very seriously the option of expanding our Mexican operation" to take over set assembly, which would mean laying off fourteen hundred workers at the Illinois plant.[65] These were persuasive arguments for policy makers, and the domestic TV industry backed off the issue. Nor did Congress take action to close the loophole.

Finally, in 1986 COMPACT filed antidumping charges against Japan, Korea, Singapore, and Canada for supplying the local "screwdriver" assembly plants with imported picture tubes at unfairly low prices. The petition received an affirmative ruling in 1987, but before duties could be imposed, foreign tube imports plummeted, falling from 2.3 million units in 1986 to 750,000 units in 1987 and to 274,000 units in 1988. COMPACT complained, however, that foreign suppliers were sending their tubes to Mexican plants instead. "All of the picture tubes that were being dumped into this country are now being dumped into Mexico, causing the same injury to U.S. [color picture tube] producers as when they were shipped directly."[66] COMPACT, joined by Zenith, petitioned the Commerce Department for relief under the anticircumvention provision of the antidumping law, under which televisions imported from Mexico were assessed duties on the tubes inside them.[67] But according to the terms of the law, two conditions are necessary for the government to find that foreign companies have circumvented antidumping duties. First, the merchandise imported into the United States must be of the same class or kind as the merchandise already subject to the existing duty. Second, the difference in value between the product imported into the third country and the completed product imported into the United States must be small. Finding that these criteria were not met, Commerce ultimately rejected the anticircumvention petition.[68]

Consumer Electronics: Conclusion

Given the intense effort the industry put into seeking trade protection, its reaction to IFDI was surprisingly muted. A few producers expressed concern about screwdriver assembly, but it never became a significant issue for the domestic manufacturers. The Global Industry explanation seems to account best for the outcomes in this case. Demands for more restrictive IFDI policies varied across firms and over time in a way that mirrored the growing extent of overseas outsourcing and, ultimately, exit from television production. Aside from component manufacturers, the only domestic TV maker who consistently supported restrictive policies against the transplants was the domestically oriented Zenith. Other, less globalized producers (for example, Magnavox and GTE-Sylvania) joined in these campaigns until they themselves were acquired or exited the industry. Global firms such as RCA and GE played no part in these debates (with the exception of RCA's opposition to Sanyo's free trade subzone, stemming from concern over competition in third markets). Thus the same divisions that characterized the industry in battles over trade policy, reflecting variation in global ties, account for divisions toward incoming foreign direct investment. Globally oriented firms could hardly oppose IFDI when they themselves were shifting production abroad at record levels. Meanwhile, the remaining domestically oriented firms, engaged in a fight for survival, extended their anti-import demands to IFDI.

At the same time, political structures still played a role in shaping how the domestic industry responded to IFDI. For instance, the comparison with European producers suggests that the absence of an investment screening mechanism in the United States inhibited complaints about IFDI, as there was no channel for demands to address overcapacity. Focusing on domestic content and preventing screwdriver assembly was the only way U.S. firms could address the IFDI issue. This theme came up as well at the hearing on the picture tube issue.[69] Ultimately, however, this argument could not make much headway. It was difficult to attack job-creating foreign subsidiaries while many U.S.-owned producers were reducing their domestic production. Thus even those firms that opposed IFDI had little to work with in attempting to build political support for a more restrictive policy. In sum, the Global Industry hypothesis explains the general pattern of behavior, and political factors add to our understanding of the specific actions that were or were not taken.

THE STEEL INDUSTRY

When incoming foreign direct investment in the American steel industry took off in the early 1980s, domestic producers were already in serious trouble. Steel imports had captured a quarter of the American market, domestic mills were operating at less than a third of their capacity, and unemployment in the industry had topped 60 percent.[70] The causes of these difficulties were the subject of some debate. Analysts commonly cited decreasing domestic steel consumption, increasing competition from domestic mini-mills (which used electrical furnaces to melt scrap metal), an overvalued dollar, the postwar reconstruction of western European and Japanese steelmaking facilities (incorporating the most up-to-date steelmaking technology), the rise of newly industrialized countries as low-cost steel producers, antagonistic labor relations, and a technological conservatism resulting from years of domestic market dominance.[71]

Domestic industry officials, however, put most of the blame on unfair trading practices—dumping, subsidized production, and market restrictions—by foreign competitors.[72] As early as the 1960s the domestic industry had been putting extraordinary effort into seeking protection from imports. The sheer scale of the industry's distress, the huge number of unemployed workers along with the visible devastation this joblessness produced in the affected communities, and the vigorous efforts of a congressional steel caucus (with more than two hundred members at its peak) led to the attainment and implementation of a variety of protectionist measures up through the early 1980s.[73] Although many observers com-

An Economic Response 47

plained that domestic producers failed to use the resulting breathing space to modernize as they had promised, the industry was still able to persuade the government to negotiate voluntary restraint agreements (VRAs) with the EC, Japan, Taiwan, and Korea in 1984 in order to reduce imports' share of U.S. sales.[74]

Unsurprisingly, the imposition of trade barriers prompted the relocation of foreign (and particularly Japanese) production to the United States. Tokyo actively encouraged investment as a way to ease trade friction with the United States.[75] By the early 1990s a quarter of all those employed in the steel industry in the United States were working at plants owned or co-owned by Japanese steelmakers.[76] Thus the VRAs may have boosted the profits of the steel industry, but a large portion of these increased profits went to foreign-owned companies, which, as one observer noted, "strengthen[ed] them in their international struggle with Bethlehem, USX, and other U.S.-owned steelmakers."[77] This could hardly be what U.S. firms intended when they originally sought trade protection.

The Production Profile approach suggests that steel producers should have resisted IFDI if it undermined import barriers. As was the case with consumer electronics, the domestic industry did not hesitate to pressure the government to prevent other types of VRA evasion. For example, when imports surged from the noncovered countries, the industry launched new antidumping and countervailing duty actions and called for the extension of the quota to these countries. The industry trade association, the American Iron and Steel Institute (AISI), asserted, "These uncovered countries have, to a significant extent, supplanted imports from covered countries. . . . Correcting this situation should be the first order of business in improving the program's effectiveness."[78] Transshipment through third countries was also perceived as a significant problem; in some cases countries without any steelmaking capacity were exporting to the United States, and in other cases mills were being constructed expressly to evade the VRA.[79] Moreover, domestic steel producers complained to Congress about the shift in the composition of exports to new higher value-added products and to downstream manufactured goods containing foreign steel.[80] U.S. firms lobbied for strengthening and extending the quotas. Sometimes they were successful, other times they were not. But correcting these problems—plugging the holes in the VRA—became a major focus of the domestic industry's political campaign for VRA renewal in 1989.

For critics of VRAs, this comes as no surprise. Kent Albert Jones, for instance, has argued that VRAs, rather than preempt more serious protectionist measures, inevitably lead the domestic industry to seek further protection in order to block foreign competitors from circumventing the agreement. Thus he predicts that domestic firms will "demand higher and higher domestic content rules, increased restrictions on foreign investment, or further restrictions on output or components imports based on the location of corporate headquarters. New crises in commercial diplomacy loom on the horizon as this cycle of trade restrictions and circumvention continues."[81] In other words, domestic steelmakers will support a more restrictive IFDI policy.

During this initial wave of IFDI, U.S. steel firms were not particularly global in their orientation. Until the early 1980s they had focused their attention on the lucrative domestic market, and exports were insignificant. Similarly, U.S. firms did not engage in much overseas manufacturing. Because steel production was widely perceived as a bedrock industrial activity, most governments around the world historically had encouraged the development of an indigenous steel sector.[82] Given their difficulties trying to stem loss of market share at home—indeed, merely trying to stay solvent—overseas expansion was not the most pressing priority for domestic firms. Even if they were in a position to afford to expand their operations, prevailing conditions of global overcapacity would have made such actions unprofitable.[83] As described later, however, U.S. firms came to develop extensive relationships with foreign companies in the form of joint ventures and strategic alliances. The logic of the Global Industry explanation suggests that these joint ventures should promote a more accommodating attitude, as they would buy off the potential opposition of domestic producers and give them a material stake in the success of foreign-owned operations.

Although U.S. steelmakers complained about restrictions in other countries, they were not in a position to make a sustained effort to penetrate these foreign markets. Therefore, demands for reciprocity never loomed very large. U.S. firms had their hands full coping with challenges in the domestic market, and to the extent they complained about foreign restrictions, their concern centered on how these barriers led producers from other countries to divert their exports toward the more open U.S. market.[84] Thus the Strategic Investment hypothesis has little to say about the industry's policy preferences.

The IFDI Strategy of Foreign Steel Producers and the Initial Reaction of U.S. Producers

In the spring of 1984 Nippon Kokan K.K. (NKK), Japan's second largest steelmaker, announced it would purchase 50 percent of National Steel Corporation, the seventh largest American steel producer, from National Intergroup, Inc., for $292 million. National hoped the deal would help it adopt Japanese technology to modernize its steelmaking facilities; its parent was more interested in reducing its steel business in an overall diversification strategy.[85] Only months before, National had tried to merge with U.S. Steel (USS, the steel division of USX), but the Justice Department made approval of the deal contingent on the two companies divesting themselves of two plants comprising six million tons of steel capacity (which was about what USS would have gained from the merger in the first place). When this deal collapsed, National was anxious to find a partner and welcomed the bid by NKK.[86]

NKK, for its part, had been attempting unsuccessfully to establish a presence in the American market, trying (and failing) to acquire Kaiser Steel and Ford Motor's steel division. The company's motives were twofold: to serve the Japanese auto transplants and to avoid potential U.S. trade restrictions. After announcing the bid, NKK actively tried to avert negative reactions with reassuring statements like that of the company's executive vice president, who emphasized, "National Steel Corp. is, and will continue to be, [an] American company and Nippon Kokan fully intends to respect it as such."[87] In a press conference NKK executives promised not to use NKK's U.S. presence as a circumvention mechanism to maintain its import level or to process semifinished steel products from its Japanese parent.[88]

Despite these pledges, other domestic firms expressed opposition to the deal on antitrust grounds. They especially objected to the contrast between the Justice Department's quick approval of this investment and its harsher treatment of the USS merger. Domestic executives saw a double standard at work, and they pointed to another recent Justice decision preventing Jones & Laughlin (LTV) and Republic Steel from combining.[89] USS, National's rejected suitor, was particularly annoyed now that its one profitable flat-roll plant in Indiana would bear the brunt of competition from the NKK-National combination. As USS chairman David Roderick testified before a congressional committee, "It's unfortunate that where an American producer is not permitted to tread, the only solution is one of foreign investment." But in the same statement he conceded that his company had "no plans to take a position pro or con on [the investment] as long as it's consistent with our laws."[90] A couple of months later Roderick reiterated that although he would have preferred "an all-American solution" to the industry's problems, he did not favor a stricter IFDI policy: "If anyone wants to invest, we wouldn't discourage them. It's really up to the foreign producers. . . . If they wish to come into a joint venture of a manufacturing operation in the U.S., they are perfectly free to do it."[91] Similarly, although the chairman of Wheeling-Pittsburgh objected to the merger, he declined to push the issue by, for example, filing an antitrust suit to force a court hearing.[92] Scattered and halfhearted protests thus comprised the extent of the industry's reaction to the takeover.

In 1990 NKK purchased an additional 20 percent of National and became the first Japanese steel company to own a majority stake in a major U.S. steel producer.[93] NKK executives noted that they had been very reluctant to take this step out of concern for the political repercussions.[94] But the Japanese company need not have worried. In fact, management and labor within National preferred the NKK takeover to the U.S. Steel merger, because they feared U.S. Steel would use National as a "cash cow" for its diversification efforts.[95] By contrast, they believed NKK would invest in rebuilding National's steel unit. It would have been difficult, therefore, for U.S. Steel to gain much political support in opposing the NKK takeover. The only issue that even arose regarding the investment was the effect on industry concentration; wider questions of VRA evasion or foreign ownership were not brought up.

Meanwhile, other foreign companies were also beginning to invest in American steel production operations. None of these investments provoked the slightest bit of opposition from the domestic industry. In fact, the domestic firms—even those that had been most critical of Japanese trade practices—were falling over each other to attract foreign buyers. Concurrent with the initial NKK investment in 1984, Wheeling-Pittsburgh Steel Corporation (then the eighth largest U.S. producer) entered into a joint venture with Nisshim Steel (the sixth largest Japanese producer).[96] That same year, Kawasaki Steel Corporation, together with a Brazilian iron ore producer, Companhia Vale de Rio Doce, bought a 50 percent share in a newly formed company, California Steel Industries (which basically consisted of operations at a mill in Fontana, California, owned by Kaiser Steel Corporation).[97] The next year, U.S. Steel and a Korean company, Pohang Iron and Steel Co. (Posco), formed a 50–50 joint venture to make sheet steel on the West Coast.[98] USS also teamed up with Kobe Steel to make bar and tubular steel in Lorain, Ohio, on a 50–50 basis. Originally, Kobe had considered its own greenfield plant but decided to pursue a joint venture, given the surplus capacity in the U.S. market.[99] Nippon Steel, the world's largest steelmaker, joined with Inland Steel in 1987 to announce a joint venture plant (dubbed I/N Tek) producing cold-rolled steel sheets in Indiana.[100] The two companies also arranged to construct two galvanizing lines, and in December 1989 Nippon announced that it would buy a 13 percent stake in Inland for $185 million.[101] In 1988 Kawasaki bought 40 percent of Armco for $350 million and quickly introduced the world's most advanced technology at the joint mills in Ohio and Kentucky.[102] Finally, LTV and Sumitomo agreed to produce electro-galvanized steel in a Cleveland plant whose ownership would be 60–40, respectively. This worked out well enough that the two companies agreed to a second, 50–50 joint venture in Columbus, Ohio, reportedly at the urging of the nearby Japanese auto transplants.[103]

Thus by the mid-1990s the Japanese had invested around $8 billion in the U.S. steel industry.[104] Some companies were, to varying degrees, already Japanese-owned—specifically, National Steel (70%), Armco (50%), and Inland (13%)—and nearly every major integrated steel producer was involved in an international joint venture (with the exception of Bethlehem).[105] Not even counting the joint ventures, foreign investors controlled around 20 percent of all steelmaking capacity in the United States and employed about 16.6 percent of production workers.[106] Aside from labor's objection to the USS-Posco venture and the brief flap over the antitrust implications of the NKK-National deal, there was no opposition from the domestic industry to this inflow of IFDI. Although the investments allowed Japanese companies to avoid trade restrictions, the American industry greeted them with open arms. The chairman of the American Iron and Steel Institute, in his 1986 "State of the Industry" address, observed, "Present managements seem to be viewing this prospect as an opportunity rather than as a problem. Companies who wish to sell in our market should be willing to invest and produce in our market."[107] In the automobile and machine tool industries, discussed later in the book, initial welcoming attitudes chilled considerably as the extent of IFDI continued to grow and especially as it became clear that Japanese-owned firms could perform as efficiently abroad as they did at home. In the case of steel, by contrast, the industry maintained its liberal position on IFDI.

There were powerful economic incentives for U.S. firms to adopt liberal policy preferences. First, U.S. firms were starved for funds to modernize and, in some cases, to survive. Estimates of the capital requirements required to bring U.S. facilities up to world-class levels varied from $4 billion to $8.5 billion per year; as one analyst noted, "The value of the industry's entire outstanding common equity is less than $8 billion."[108] In congressional hearings and in public statements the industry identified this capital shortage as the primary reason for its inability to modernize and recapture markets.[109] Steel companies (at least the big integrated mills) were in a vicious circle: unless they modernized, they would not regain their competitiveness, but because they were not competitive, they had no profits to invest in modernization, nor were capital markets eager to sink cash into the ailing industry. This was why, the steel producers argued, they needed tax breaks, relaxation of environmental regulation, and import protection.[110] But even with all this assistance, the gap between what they needed and what they could afford was too large.

Since the AISI claimed this capital shortfall was the result of predatory and unfair foreign trade practices and industrial policies, one might think the industry would look askance at Japanese investors using their ill-gotten gains to acquire American companies weakened by these same unfair acts.[111] But with low to nonexistent cash flow and huge restructuring costs, the domestic steel industry simply had no alternative but to search for funds wherever it could find them. As the chairman of Inland put it, "The alternative might be total surrender." An AISI official concurred: "I don't think we'd have much of a U.S. steel industry without joint ventures."[112] In addition to funds, the U.S. companies required up-to-date technology in order to modernize, and Japanese firms were strong in this department, especially in continuous-casting technology and in electronic control of steelmaking operations.[113] In 1988 Inland's president acknowledged that its joint venture partner, Nippon Steel, had the technological capability of the entire U.S. steel industry put together.[114]

The foreign investments just described also brought new capital and new technology in a way that directly benefited domestic firms. The first two Japanese companies to invest in the United States, NKK and Nisshim, entered into joint ventures, the first including all of National's operations and the second in a specific mill. Both pumped badly needed cash into the coffers of strapped domestic companies. Kawasaki kept open a moribund plant (and did so again with its investment in the two Armco plants). Nippon Steel, Sumitomo, and Kobe also entered the United States via partnerships rather than opening independent greenfield operations.

Why did Japanese firms choose this mode of investment, even at the risk of losing some control over firm-specific advantages?[115] If it was a result of pressure from the domestic industry, then it becomes circular to explain the position of the domestic industry by pointing to the nature of IFDI. No doubt foreign investors anticipated that joint ventures would face less political opposition than outright acquisitions or even new greenfield construction.[116] More important, however, were the economic forces at work. Overcapacity in the U.S. market combined with tremendous fixed capital requirements deterred greenfield investment. No matter how technologically advanced a foreign firm was, it simply would not have been profitable to build a new integrated steel plant in the United States. As for acquisitions, some takeovers occurred (e.g., NKK-National), but they started as joint ventures and only gradually became wholly owned. Again, this trend was less a deliberate political strategy than a reflection of the fact that acquiring American companies was not a particularly smart investment. Even with their joint ventures it was not until the mid-1990s that many of these Japanese subsidiaries climbed out of the red.[117] A Nippon Steel vice president spoke for the Japanese producers when he explained that because of a "confused" U.S. market, Japanese steelmakers would not expand their FDI as rapidly as Japanese auto or electronic manufacturers.[118]

For the U.S. owners of domestic steel operations, the dominant business strategy was one of diversification. In the 1980s top U.S. steel executives began making frequent trips to Japan to find Japanese buyers for their companies' steel units. These CEOs welcomed IFDI because they wanted to focus their attention on more lucrative activities. At the same time, lower-level managers in the steel divisions favored joint venture participation, as it promised freedom from "the constraints imposed by finance-oriented top executives and their constant quest for greater cash flow."[119] The fact that some of these joint ventures, once established, became increasingly Japanese-owned simply reflected the weakness of the U.S. partners. Japanese companies found they had to become more involved and integrate backward by acquiring their suppliers in order to ensure high-quality products while U.S. executives were looking to exit the industry.

The industry's liberal attitude toward IFDI contrasts markedly with its approach toward import competition. U.S. firms put enormous energies into seeking a renewal of the VRA in the early 1990s. David Goodman, Debra Spar, and David Yoffie argue that IFDI did not dampen protectionist demands by steel producers because much of the investment was import complementing (rather than substituting) and therefore import competition did not decline dramatically.[120] Also, U.S. producers continued to lose money, partly a result of greater domestic competition from the minimills. It is true that when the VRAs expired in 1992 and U.S. producers subsequently unleashed their barrage of countervailing duty (CVD) and antidumping duty (AD) suits against twenty-one countries, those companies with close ties to Japanese producers (LTV, Inland Steel, Armco, and National Steel) did not join the complaints against Japan. On the other hand, they also agreed not to oppose the complaints outright, which would have considerably weakened the American steelmakers' position.[121] So although import competition still provoked industry opposition, IFDI (coming as it did in the form of joint ventures) did not.

Regulating Semifinished Imports and Local Content
The one issue that caused a modicum of controversy involved the importation of slab (semifinished) steel. The 1984 VRA had, at the request of

the domestic steelmakers, limited imports of semifinished steel, but it was not long before many integrated steel mills—both foreign-owned and domestically owned—began considering importing slabs in an attempt to slash costs. In 1983 the steelworkers' union launched a full-scale campaign against USS's efforts to import raw steel from British Steel Company and Wheeling-Pittsburgh's attempt to import Brazilian slab.[122] The issue came to a boil in late 1986 when a labor dispute at USX created an anticipated shortage of semifinished steel for the following year. Under Commerce Department regulations companies could apply to import steel slabs over the VRA limits when domestic supplies were inadequate. NKK-owned National made just such an appeal to import twenty thousand tons of steel monthly from Japan, the largest appeal ever. But those companies that had invested in front-end production lobbied to prevent their rivals from importing slabs. Bethlehem and Inland filed objections to National's request, arguing that approval "will provide them [National] with a quick fix while we are making long range commitments in facilities for these same products and markets."[123] A couple of weeks later a much larger request to import semifinished steel (totaling over a million tons) in excess of the VRA quota was filed by two more foreign-owned firms—California Steel Industries (the Kawasaki Steel–CVRD operation in Fontana), USS-Posco—and one small domestic company, Lone Star Steel from Dallas.[124] The intra-industry dissension over this issue deepened. The AISI supported restricting semifinished imports, a position that was favored by companies such as Bethlehem, Inland, and LTV which had invested in front-end production. CSI became the main focus of the dispute after USS-Posco withdrew its petition following the end of the USX work stoppage. The California company claimed that it still needed to import the slab because domestic steelmakers had, in effect, abandoned the West Coast market.[125]

Although this was a dispute over local content in which the practices of foreign firms came under attack, domestic firms failed to link the issue to the wider question of foreign ownership (as the automobile and machine tool industries later did). The reason was that domestic firms were also adopting outsourcing strategies, especially on the West Coast, where domestic capacity was shrinking.[126] Tom Graham, president of the U.S. Steel division of USX (the most vigorous advocate of blocking the imports), admitted that outsourcing was inevitable: "The economies are so powerful that if we can overcome national chauvinism, it's about as sure as death and taxes."[127] The growing reliance on foreign inputs grew alongside the deepening of joint venture ties. When demand for steel increased, U.S. producers turned to their affiliated partners to find a sufficient supply of semifinished slabs.[128]

The Steel Industry: Conclusion

The observed outcome in the steel industry—strong opposition to imports combined with openness to IFDI—is not difficult to explain. The underlying economic incentives led to the welcoming attitude on the part of domestic producers. The industry's need for capital combined with the joint venture approach that foreign producers took toward investing in the United States inhibited domestic actors from complaining about IFDI even as the industry increasingly fell under foreign control. Political incentives also contributed to this situation: existing policies regarding foreign competition—the antidumping and countervailing duty administrative procedures, the trigger price mechanism, the VRAs, and so forth—were geared toward regulating imports. Had the domestic industry wanted to apply the same kind of restriction to IFDI, it is unclear what tools they would have been able to use. Not only were instruments to restrict IFDI unavailable, but also there was little potential of gaining political support for creating new instruments. The reason was that foreign investment was seen as creating jobs. Much of the political influence the industry had gained and the resulting success it had achieved on trade policy was a result of massive layoffs, visibly concentrated in specific regions with consequent spillover effects.[129] Slogans such as Foreign Steel Steals Jobs, which had been so effective in trade battles, would simply not work for regulating IFDI.[130] With little chance of success, firms would be less likely to make restrictive IFDI demands.

CONCLUSION

The consumer electronics and steel industries, the first to experience foreign competition via IFDI, were uncertain as to the ultimate effects foreign subsidiaries would have on the domestic industry's welfare. As it turned out, transplant production eroded the value of import protection and prevented domestically owned firms from recovering market share. However, the position of both industries (especially steel) was so dire that there was little room for choice in deciding how to respond to IFDI. Global TV manufacturers abandoned local production, though the remaining domestic producers battled against IFDI as best they could. This response resulted in an intra-industry division similar to that witnessed in trade. Domestic steelmakers welcomed the opportunity to form joint ventures and so had no reason to oppose IFDI as it manifested itself in this case. Political structures also shaped domestic producers' approach, though they were not decisive. These cases reinforce the point that the political explanation of policy preferences supplements rather than replaces the economic-interest explanation.

If these industries were the only cases in which IFDI diminished the value of trade protection, it would be questionable whether we need to develop a new theory to account for policy preferences, since the existing hypotheses explain a good portion of the observed outcome. But as we shall see in the next three chapters, the consumer electronics and steel industries were special cases. Their severe economic distress and the difficulty of finding an appropriate response to the transplant threat left them with little discretion. By contrast, in other sectors the economic incentives were much more ambiguous. In those cases political factors took on a more significant role.

FOUR

An Ambivalent Response
Semiconductors and Automobiles

During the 1980s, incoming foreign direct investment in the United States emerged as a salient political issue, especially investment from Japan. Although the media often focused on real estate landmarks or movie studios, Japanese manufacturing investment had a much more profound effect on restructuring the American economy. And of all the manufacturing sectors in which IFDI occurred, none generated more controversy than the semiconductor and automobile industries. In both these cases American producers responded to IFDI in a much more ambivalent way than the consumer electronics or steel industries had. As in these earlier cases, both semiconductor and automobile companies had sought and received trade protection in response to an inflow of Japanese imports. In both cases trade protection had contributed to the relocation of Japanese production into the United States. The nature of foreign competition changed, but not its intensity or its damaging effect on industry profits. However, many firms in these industries had international interests of their own—foreign investments, outsourcing arrangements, and joint ventures—and were therefore reluctant to support policies that could set a precedent ultimately resulting in restrictions on their own global operations. Finally, in both cases producers were concerned not just with IFDI in their own sector but also with developments in vertically related industries: semiconductor materials and equipment (SM&E) in the case of the chipmakers, and auto parts in the case of the car companies. The resulting ambiguity of economic interests in these industries meant that compared with the sectors examined in the previous chapter, there was more scope for choice in the formulation of IFDI policy preferences.

The semiconductor industry was initially wary of IFDI, seeking to count the output of local subsidiaries as imports for the purposes of antidumping legislation. Yet domestic producers could do little to stop Japanese companies from evading trade sanctions through relocating production. When IFDI came in the form of acquisitions rather than greenfield investments, however, the domestic industry had two arguments to use against it: antitrust and, especially, national security. Security concerns also justified the exclusion of foreign subsidiaries from government-funded R&D projects. Finally, during a wave of foreign takeovers in the upstream materials and equipment industry, semiconductor firms sought to block certain acquisitions that were politically vulnerable on either antitrust or security grounds. In sum, although the domestic industry did not simply transfer its protectionist or strategic trade demands to IFDI, it sought to use existing tools and legitimate arguments against IFDI to blunt the competitive threat of foreign subsidiaries.

Auto companies, by contrast, were slow to recognize the extent of the threat posed by so-called transplant production. They were also hemmed in by their own international activities; domestic producers could not support local content legislation favored by labor unions because it would hinder their own outsourcing strategies. It was the auto parts manufacturers who first took up the antitransplant cause by focusing attention on the low domestic content of the foreign assembly plants in the United States. Eventually, the automakers joined the campaign against the transplants and took a more restrictive position on IFDI-related issues such as the granting of foreign trade subzone status, rules of origin in the NAFTA agreement, labeling new cars with the amount of domestic content, and most dramatically, legislation that would have imposed quantitative limits on both Japanese imports and transplant vehicles. Though it was risky for domestic automakers to emphasize domestic content (given both their own vulnerability on this issue and the questionable assumption that addressing this problem would reduce competition from foreign subsidiaries), it was the only politically viable strategy. IFDI was widely perceived as creating jobs, but by attacking the transplants for their excessive reliance on imported components, domestic producers could neutralize this issue. They could also use existing institutional channels that were not available for a more direct attack on IFDI.

In sum, the experience of these sectors shows that economic interests motivate policy preferences but that the multiplicity of these interests makes it difficult to explain why actors ultimately choose the positions they do. Looking at the political context—the existing institutional apparatus that could be used to address the challenges of IFDI and the ideological arguments that were perceived as likely to win support—can help make sense of what seems like contradictory behavior. The political environment greatly affected the way producers in these two industries translated economic interests into policy preferences.

THE SEMICONDUCTOR INDUSTRY

IFDI in the U.S. semiconductor industry provoked political controversy disproportionate to the actual volume of investment.[1] The reason for this was the industry's perceived importance. Analysts frequently argued that semiconductors—the "crude oil of the twentieth century"—were an essential element of a giant "electronic food chain" extending from upstream materials and production equipment manufacturers to downstream systems producers such as computer and office equipment manufacturers.[2] According to this argument, the competitiveness of these end-product sectors—their rate of innovation, their export performance, and their productivity growth—depended on their ability to incorporate the best, most advanced, and least expensive chips. Most economists insisted that as long as semiconductors were obtainable on the open market, it made little difference who owned the companies that provided them. But proponents of a more activist policy (including many domestic producers themselves) claimed that the tight linkages between different stages in the electronics production process meant that ceding one sector to the control of a foreign rival could impose significant costs on other sectors along the "food chain."[3]

Industry representatives also emphasized the importance of having competitive domestic producers that could serve as dependable long-term suppliers for defense projects. Whether this required domestic ownership, however, was the subject of much disagreement among experts and government officials.[4] Throughout the 1980s and early 1990s the security question remained at the center of the debate over what policy to adopt toward the industry. By contrast, the jobs issue did not play as significant a role in IFDI politics as it had with steel and consumer electronics. By the early 1980s most American firms had already moved the labor-intensive portion of their production to low-cost sites in Southeast Asia to cut costs and battle foreign competition. When much of this production subsequently returned to the United States, its technological requirements (the need to squeeze numerous and ever-shrinking circuits onto a single chip and to eliminate any potential contamination during the process) led to widespread automation. Furthermore, most workers in this industry were either white-collar executives or skilled technicians, eminently reemployable in other high-tech sectors and seldom unionized.[5] Although foreign subsidiaries created American jobs, the numbers were insufficient to hold much weight as a persuasive argument for an open access regime. The cries of distress in response to Japanese competition during the mid-1980s came from capital owners rather than from workers.

As the American semiconductor industry watched its worldwide market share of DRAM (dynamic random access memory) chips fall from 70 percent in 1978 to 20 percent five years later, it gradually shifted its position on trade policy from one of supporting openness to championing policies of contingent protectionism and managed trade.[6] Japanese companies, which rose to dominate the industry during the same period, initially responded to trade friction with the United States by asserting their intention to expand chip fabrication in the United States. As the CEO of Oki Electric's American subsidiary warned, "The temporary relief provided to the American semiconductor industry by U.S. government action will be offset by fiercely competitive Japanese-owned manufacturing facilities located in the U.S." Hitachi, Mitsubishi, Toshiba, and Fujitsu all made explicit public statements linking the possibility of trade sanctions to increased FDI in the United States.[7]

The Production Profile hypothesis would lead us to expect that chip firms, especially those most adversely affected by Japanese competition, would favor regulating IFDI to the extent that foreign firms were able to avoid U.S. trade barriers and continue capturing market share.[8] By contrast, the Global Industry hypothesis would predict that those U.S. firms with extensive outward FDI would exhibit a liberal attitude toward IFDI and the treatment of foreign-owned firms.[9] Finally, the Strategic Investment hypothesis predicts demands similar to those of the Production Profile hypothesis: an extension of restrictive demands to IFDI, even from globalized companies, with the removal of the restrictions contingent on changes in Japanese trade and investment practices.[10] The Strategic Investment hypothesis also suggests that semiconductor producers would worry about Japanese firms gaining control over the upstream semiconductor materials and equipment sector because of the danger that foreign-owned suppliers might favor customers with which they had keiretsu ties.[11]

The Semiconductor Trade Agreement and IFDI

During the trade battles of the mid-1980s, domestic producers initially extended the principles underlying their strategic trade demands to the issue of IFDI. American firms expressed concern, detailed in briefs submitted to the International Trade Commission, that Japanese firms could circumvent antidumping regulations via the export of goods from third-country production facilities and IFDI. U.S. producers argued that any foreign-owned plants located in the United States that imported already-fabricated wafers to be locally assembled into DRAMs ought to fall under the antidumping ruling and their costs calculated the same way as for their parent company.[12] American firms distinguished between foreign-owned assembly plants and U.S. plants that fabricated the chips ("real" manufacturing). When NEC, a Japanese company, pointed out that its California plant fabricated (rather than merely assembled) 256K DRAMs, the American firms countered that because the designs were created in Japan and the process technology and equipment were developed in Japan, the NEC factory was still foreign and should be subject to the antidumping regulations. Under these criteria it is difficult to imagine that *any* foreign subsidiary could qualify as "domestic."[13]

Despite the domestic industry's testimony, the 1986 Semiconductor Trade Agreement (STA) between Japan and the United States did not subject chips that were fabricated in the United States by Japanese affiliates to the "fair market value" criteria designed to prohibit dumping. Even chips fabricated in Japan and assembled in the United States would be subject to a lower fair market value and thus less easily classified as dumped output.[14] The agreement did not completely treat transplant production as domestic; for example, any exports back to Japan by Japanese subsidiaries were not to be included in the 20 percent share of the Japanese market that U.S. companies were expected to obtain.[15] Overall, however, by favoring local output over exports, the STA created a large incentive for Japanese firms to avoid price regulation by relocating production to the United States.

After the STA entered into effect, however, U.S. firms dropped their hostile position toward IFDI. Producers everywhere were suffering from overcapacity, and it seemed very unlikely that Japanese firms would build new plants.[16] However, the issue of foreign ownership was to arise again shortly.

The Effects of Trade Sanctions

In April 1987 the Reagan administration, under pressure from Congress, determined that the Japanese had not lived up to the STA and imposed sanctions consisting of tariffs on a variety of electronic products. The immediate reaction of Japanese companies was to accelerate the relocation of end product manufacturing to the United States.[17] In September 1987 Toshiba began manufacturing laptop personal computers in Irvine, California. An NEC spokesman announced that the firm had suffered minimal damage from the sanctions, owing to its startup of U.S. PC manufacturing in early May. These were the two companies most severely affected by the sanctions, and yet one year later both confirmed that they had escaped penalty duties entirely by producing locally all the computer models that were covered by the sanctions.[18] They were not the only ones; a September 1987 article in the industry trade press reported that because of large inventories and stepped-up U.S. production, no Japanese company had actually exported any products that were subject to the 100 percent tariffs.[19] To the extent the sanctions were imposed to pressure Japan to open its market to U.S. producers, the ability of Japanese electronics firms to relocate production significantly diminished this pressure. The Semiconductor Industry Association (SIA) complained about this circumvention but suggested only that the administration adjust the trade sanctions upward in order to "restore the balance"—a suggestion that was rebuffed. Industry executives maintained that they had at least succeeded in getting Tokyo's attention, but there is little doubt that *effective* sanctions would have sent a more powerful message.[20] Still, U.S. producers did not extend their strategic trade demands into the realm of IFDI, even though it was arguably in their interest to do so.

Eventually, the Commerce Department took action to prevent tariff-jumping investment. Commerce determined that if Japanese firms were allowed to bring in chip-covered circuit boards (called "motherboards") duty-free to the United States, they could evade sanctions without really relocating any high value-added production.[21] This concern (along with an earlier ruling by the U.S. Customs Service reclassifying certain "computer parts" as "data processing equipment") led the department to rule that imported circuit boards with 16-bit and 32-bit processing capability would be subject to a 100 percent tariff. The decision also affected several American computer manufacturers that imported boards from Japan. The domestic Computer and Business Equipment Manufacturers Association (CBEMA), joined by the American Electronics Association (AEA), launched a vocal campaign to reverse the Customs ruling.[22] More surprisingly, the main association of chipmakers, the SIA, also opposed the ruling, even though it was intended to boost sales of domestic semiconductors. Partly, this opposition reflected the fact that the SIA included systems producers such as IBM, Hewlett Packard, AT&T, and Digital Equipment Corporation, which imported the motherboards. But even the other members worried about alienating the downstream electronics industry and losing its support for the broader trade battles with Japan.[23] Because both American computer firms and Japanese transplants in the United States imported Japanese components, it was difficult to prevent the rise of foreign screwdriver plants without simultaneously harming globalized American producers.[24]

The Fairchild-Fujitsu Affair

The attitude of benign neglect toward IFDI changed when investment came in the form of foreign acquisitions rather than greenfield investment.

The debate erupted in 1987, after Fujitsu had offered to buy 80 percent of Fairchild Semiconductor Corporation. Before he had even announced the deal, Fairchild president and CEO Donald Brooks personally questioned the president of the Semiconductor Industry Association, Andrew Procassini, about whether the SIA would oppose the deal. Procassini reportedly acknowledged that it was a private matter between two companies and pledged that the SIA would not interfere.[25] But when the deal was announced, the trade press was full of "reports of executive anger" and concerns voiced by other domestic companies.[26] The concerns centered on two major points. First, the low offering price was seen as reflecting the domestic industry's struggle against Japan's unfair trading practices. Not only was Fujitsu using the capital it had amassed as a result of these practices in order to avoid the STA's antidumping provision, but adding insult to injury, it was able to do so at a "fire sale" price because of its earlier transgressions.[27] Second, American producers believed that although this particular acquisition was friendly, future takeovers might not be, and given the recent large industry losses, the majority of domestic chipmakers would soon be vulnerable. The Fujitsu bid could signal the start of a trend, and it could also create the trend itself; if the deal went through, Hitachi, Toshiba, and NEC would have to react in order to remain competitive.[28] LSI Logic chairman Wilf Corrigan warned that if Fujitsu's "probe" succeeded, it would lead to "wholesale attacks on U.S. companies by cash-rich Japanese zaibatsu." He continued, "The handwriting is on the wall for other U.S. semiconductor companies. The question is, 'who's next?'"[29] Both objections explain the apparent paradox of American opposition to a foreign takeover of a subsidiary that was already owned by a French company, Schlumberger. It was Japanese, not French, companies which the American industry had accused of unfair trading practices and whose deep pockets and strong currency led the U.S. makers to fear further and more hostile takeover activity.

Despite this sentiment, however, the domestic industry did not lobby the government to prohibit the acquisition. At a meeting in October 1987 the SIA affirmed its official neutrality but, according to one participant, unofficially decided to make some phone calls in order to express its concerns about the deal to administration officials.[30] Industry actors also offered advice and support to public officials who were opposed to the deal.[31] These actions, though not insignificant, did not begin to approach the level of participation on trade issues. Some executives worried that restricting IFDI would set an unwelcome precedent (although it was already virtually impossible to acquire a Japanese company). Also, the SIA, which operated by consensus, had to take into account the more liberal views of its systems members (though this factor did not prevent the SIA from taking a hard line on trade policy).[32] The most important reason, however, was that there were no laws or regulations that could be used to block the takeover unless the deal was shown to have adverse national security or antitrust effects. Unfortunately for the chipmakers, those two arguments did not apply to this particular investment. Fairchild was not a sole supplier of components to any defense contractors, nor had it been involved in any classified projects since 1979.[33] Only about 30–40 percent of its production ended up as part of defense components. Had the security issue been the only stumbling block, the Pentagon could have directed that defense-related products remain a separate division (in effect a blind trust) managed solely by Americans, thereby denying Fujitsu access to this technology.[34] The antitrust angle was muddled by the fact that, technically, the product lines of the two companies did not overlap: Fairchild, like many other U.S. companies, produced logic chips, not memory chips.[35] One executive summed up the industry's dilemma: "I don't see the Fujitsu-Fairchild deal as being positive for the U.S. semiconductor industry . . . but I don't see anything that can be done about it."[36] Some opponents of the deal in Congress, the Pentagon, and Commerce argued that the deal threatened to harm downstream firms, particularly the U.S.-owned supercomputer manufacturer Cray Research, as Fujitsu would control nearly half the market for emitter-coupled logic chips, an essential supercomputer component. However, Fujitsu altered the terms of the deal in order to address these concerns.[37] Though many domestic chip companies still opposed the acquisition, they essentially sat on the sidelines as the battle played out in Washington.

As it turned out, the deal fell through after resistance within the executive branch (specifically, at Commerce, the Pentagon, and the USTR's office) created enough of a political stir to frighten Fujitsu into backing off. The Japanese company, which was simultaneously fighting charges that it was dumping chips, chose to withdraw its bid on the grounds of "rising political controversy in the U.S." The domestic industry responded with relief; an SIA lobbyist remarked, "We dodged a bullet."[38]

A de facto American policy emerged from the Fujitsu-Fairchild affair. One industry analyst noted, "In the absence of political intervention, more such acquisitions might have been predicted. However, Japanese firms seemed to have viewed the Fairchild incident . . . as a signal that the American government would prevent or forestall wholesale acquisitions of leading American semiconductor companies."[39] The effect was to discourage large-scale takeovers but not greenfield investment or joint ventures. Even Fujitsu did not completely abandon its attempt to enter the American market. Rather, it decided, first, to pursue smaller and less controversial takeovers that would not receive as much attention from the public and policy makers and, second, to follow a greenfield plant strategy, which also offered a more trouble-free (if expensive) way of establishing an American presence.[40] Fujitsu also maintained its relationship with Fairchild via second-sourcing, foundry relationships, joint product development, and a joint cell library. Here, too, security concerns did not arise over these cooperative agreements, despite the fact that Fairchild technology would be made available to Fujitsu.[41] Other Japanese firms also increased their American presence during this period, though not through acquisitions.[42] Although a few critics voiced concern about the long-term impact of this trend, virtually nobody argued in favor of raising barriers to investment.[43]

Partly in response to the Fujitsu controversy, however, Congress began debating the regulation of incoming foreign direct investment in more general terms. The business community largely backed the Reagan administration's opposition to any restrictions on IFDI. Eventually, the administration accepted a watered-down version of the Exon-Florio amendment (allowing the president to block acquisitions that threatened national security), partly in order to ensure defeating another amendment that would have tightened reporting requirements for foreign-owned firms.[44] The chip industry took a more favorable view of the Exon-Florio amendment; unlike other businesses, chip producers could use the national security argument to advocate blocking an unwelcome acquisition. But although the SIA expressed support for the law, the industry did not consider the issue a priority and did nothing to push for the bill's passage.[45]

Foreign Participation in Sematech

After the passage of the Exon-Florio amendment, chip industry executives turned their attention to the launching of a new government-funded research consortium called Sematech.[46] Initially, Sematech restricted membership to firms that were primarily owned and controlled by U.S. citizens with a domestic headquarters and that had a domestic manufacturing base (including fabrication and a substantial proportion of R&D). The first criterion would prohibit foreign-owned transplants, and the second would bar "fab-less" companies, which, although U.S.-owned, relied on offshore fabrication plants to supply them with chips. Furthermore, the consortium would work only with U.S.-owned semiconductor manufacturing equipment producers in its efforts to produce circuits of smaller and smaller line widths.[47] These criteria were not government policies; rather, they were the decisions of the consortium participants.[48] One Japanese transplant,

Hitachi America, approached Sematech in May 1988 about the possibility of membership but was rejected. In August NEC expressed interest as well. NEC operated a large fab near Sacramento and was in the planning process for a new production plant. Nonetheless, it too was turned down.[49] By contrast, U.S. producers with overseas chip production (such as Texas Instruments and IBM) or with extensive ties to foreign companies (such as Motorola) were allowed to participate.

Many critics viewed Sematech's membership criteria as "technological mercantilism" and argued that given the international ties of its members, the consortium "could not realistically hope to keep the results of its research within territorial borders."[50] Prohibiting foreign participation meant that Sematech would not be able to import technology—especially in the area of manufacturing process technology, which the consortium was specifically designed to promote—from the most efficient Japanese-owned chip producers.[51] Robert Noyce, the cofounder of Intel and Sematech's first CEO, agreed that U.S. firms might gain some technological knowledge from a more open policy, but he argued that overall, allowing foreign participation would backfire against the U.S. industry: "If the trade problem were resolved and our technology was not used by foreign countries in a predatory fashion as with TVs or semiconductors, I'd have no fear of diffusing our knowledge around the world. But American knowledge is being used to hurt Americans."[52] Industry officials saw no inconsistency in restricting membership at the same time as they formed alliances and joint ventures with their Japanese competitors. Anything that contributed to the underlying goal of strengthening the relative position of U.S. producers—whether through foreign partnerships or a national consortium—was desirable. Some pointed out that Sematech might enhance the position of U.S. firms in negotiating the terms of alliances. Others maintained that even if technology eventually diffused across national borders, the time lag involved would still create a crucial advantage for U.S.-owned firms.[53]

The industry's decision to adopt discriminatory measures against foreign-owned firms was facilitated by the political origins of the Sematech program. Initially, a report by the Defense Science Board Task Force on Semiconductor Dependency led Congress to put aside public funds to support domestic manufacturers at the same time that the industry was initiating the Sematech effort. The Pentagon, concerned about dependence on foreign suppliers, provided legitimacy for a project that controverted the dominant ideological tenets of a Republican administration.[54] Only the Defense Department had the existing capability, either in logistical or political terms, to channel funds to Sematech.[55] Some firms worried that

Sematech would become too oriented to the needs of Defense. But at the same time, this aspect of the program made it easier for the industry to adopt a more discriminatory position. In fact, some industry officials claimed it would be politically difficult to open the program up to foreign participants, given sentiment in the Pentagon and on Capitol Hill.[56]

All the while, domestic firms stepped up their participation in international alliances and joint ventures. Toshiba decided it had no need to participate in Sematech because of its joint venture with Motorola. Texas Instruments initially criticized Motorola when the deal was announced but the same year formed an alliance with Hitachi in which the two companies agreed to share technology in order to jointly develop a 16-mb DRAM.[57] These and dozens of other international alliances did little to alter the policy preferences of U.S. firms.[58] A vice president of Toshiba, responding to active lobbying by its partner Motorola for stricter commercial policies, admitted, "I am thoroughly confused."[59] But the inconsistency simply highlighted the multifaceted nature of U.S. producers' economic interests.

Foreign Acquisitions of Material and Equipment Suppliers

While the semiconductor industry was fighting to regain competitiveness, the U.S. semiconductor materials and equipment (SM&E) industry was also experiencing severe difficulty. Domestic firms saw their market share fall at an even sharper rate (from 85% in 1978 to 65% in 1985 and to under 47% in 1989) than that of their chip-producing customers.[60] Given the small size of most American companies (more than 80% had sales under $25 million), it is no surprise that a number of them, unable to weather the onslaught, put themselves up for sale. The prospect that foreign-owned firms would control SM&E production in the United States led many chip firms to fear that cooperation between customers and suppliers (vital for ensuring that production technology performs at its maximum potential) would erode. Historically, the relationship between the U.S. chipmakers and their suppliers had been relatively cool, but nonetheless, semiconductor firms saw significant risks in the prospect that the SM&E industry could fall under Japanese control.[61]

In late 1989 a takeover battle erupted over the sale of Perkin-Elmer's (P-E) Semiconductor Equipment group. P-E, which produced photolithography equipment (machines used to etch silicon chips), had seen its semiconductor tool sales fall from $305 million in 1985 to $40 million in 1989, and despite retaining a strong technological position, the company could not amass the funds necessary to remain competitive.[62] P-E originally had sought out American buyers for its money-losing division at the request of its largest customer, IBM. This appeal was seconded by Army officials, who did not want P-E's electron-beam technology to be sold to foreign investors.[63] After failing to find an American buyer willing to pay the $200 million asking price, however, P-E entered into talks with Nikon, a camera and semiconductor equipment firm that had keiretsu ties with Mitsubishi. Even before a bid was made official, however, the prospect of political controversy scared Nikon off. As the head of Nikon's semiconductor-equipment division explained, "Generally speaking, under the present political situation it will be very difficult for any company outside the United States to acquire Perkin-Elmer. . . . Even if we obtained the government's permission, there is the issue of public sentiment."[64] The Japanese company decided to wait and see how the issue played out; it could always resubmit a bid later if no other buyer stepped forward.

Opponents of a foreign takeover warned of the potential harm to U.S. chipmakers. A representative from the SM&E industry association, SEMI (Semiconductor Equipment and Manufacturing International), testified, "Photolithography equipment . . . is one very prominent example where the latest generation Nikon steppers have not been available in large quantities to American suppliers, while they have been available to Japanese users. This, in turn, puts American semiconductor makers in a non-competitive position because they do not have the most effective tools."[65] But the SIA did not take a position on the sale, nor did any individual chipmaker come to the aid of Perkin-Elmer. In fact, P-E's CEO complained, "The semiconductor industry wants protection, but they refuse to protect their suppliers. They want cheap machines and a laying off of the risks."[66]

While the chip industry outwardly maintained its neutral position, producers were in fact working through Sematech to oppose the takeover. Noyce, Sematech's director, told a Senate committee that allowing the deal would put the chip industry in a vulnerable position and recommended that the government charge foreign investors a premium in order to reimburse taxpayers for contributions Sematech made toward advancing P-E's technological position; after all, this technology was "paid for by the American people for the benefit of Americans."[67] Sematech also directly lobbied the administration, emphasizing (in Noyce's words), the "severe consequences to the electronics industry if Perkin-Elmer's equipment division fell into unfriendly [i.e., foreign] hands." The consortium announced that it would no longer use P-E equipment if the division was sold to a foreign buyer. Despite the fact that a Sematech spokesperson had initially said it would be "inappropriate" for Sematech to involve itself in talks concerning P-E's future, officials quickly overcame their qualms and played an active role in determining the supplier's fate.[68]

In February 1990 Sematech officials met to discuss the sale with IBM. The company did not want to buy P-E itself, claiming it had neither the expertise nor the desire to enter the manufacturing equipment business, but it wanted to keep P-E under American ownership. For a number of years, IBM had provided financing and technical assistance to P-E for the development of specialized equipment, and it was averse to seeing that technology come under the control of a firm with keiretsu ties to IBM's competitors. In the end, IBM organized domestic users and suppliers into a consortium, which averted the Nikon takeover by purchasing P-E's operations itself. IBM agreed to provide financing and to share its own R&D in order to bolster the new venture.[69] Sematech's charter prohibited investments in other companies, but nonetheless, it played the role of silent partner in the electron-beam lithography division that was spun off from P-E. Immediately after its formation Sematech awarded a joint development contract to the new company in order to support its development of an advanced photolithography stepper.[70] In the absence of government action to stop the takeover, the chip industry appeared to take a passive position, but in fact the Sematech consortium decided to "take the law into [its] own hands" and address the threat directly.[71]

Although Japanese firms dominated the silicon wafer manufacturing industry on which semiconductor production depended, it was a German company that set off the second major IFDI controversy by attempting to purchase an American SM&E firm. In December 1988 Monsanto agreed to sell its electronics material division—the last major U.S.-owned silicon wafer producer (which provided nearly 30% of the silicon used by U.S. chipmakers)—to the German chemical company Huels AG, a subsidiary of VEBA AG.[72] A few large firms (IBM, AT&T, and TI) produced their own silicon wafers, but this supply did not reach the open market (and often did not even meet the companies' internal needs). The initial response from the chipmakers was indifference, both because a German buyer seemed to pose less of a threat and because many felt the Monsanto division had declined in its technological capabilities.[73]

Opposition emerged among government actors, however. Those in Congress who had supported Exon-Florio expressed concern at the lenient administration of the law and made this acquisition a crucial test case. Congressional hearings were held, partly because some hoped that delaying the acquisition would allow more time for public concern to build or for a domestic buyer to step forward. Gradually, industry officials began a late lobbying blitz.[74] One SM&E executive involved in Sematech decision making explained, "Initially, we didn't think it was appropriate for Sematech to speak up in a sale involving private companies. Sematech went through some agonizing soul searching and decided we had no choice but to speak out on the question of silicon's strategic importance to the entire U.S. electronics industry."[75]

The semiconductor industry's opposition to the takeover was, however, too little and too late. In fact, critics of IFDI in the government and in the SM&E industry blasted the chip producers for their apathy and short-sightedness.[76] The Pentagon, which had initially requested a formal investigation, tried to broker a deal with an American company to keep the unit out of foreign hands (replicating the outcome of the Perkin-Elmer case), but no U.S. firm was willing to play the role IBM had in the previous episode. Those Defense Department officials who had expressed concerns about the takeover made DOD interference in the sale contingent on the presence of an alternative U.S. purchaser. None volunteered, even after the DOD offered to put up half the capital.[77] Eventually, DOD (as well as Commerce) withdrew its opposition and the deal was approved, contingent on written agreements by Huels to maintain production, R&D, and all technology in the United States for five years and make wafers available to Sematech and the U.S. semiconductor industry.[78] Monsanto's customers, though concerned, were not concerned enough to rescue the subsidiary themselves. The nationality of the buyer made the difference: Noyce, the head of Sematech, conceded, "With critical equipment and materials suppliers disappearing in the U.S., it is better to encourage the development of suppliers in Europe than have Japan become the sole-source supplier for these systems."[79]

Meanwhile, amid a flurry of SM&E acquisitions by Japanese companies, one in particular generated another major political battle.[80] In 1990 Nippon Sanso K.K. (a subsidiary of Nikon) offered $23 million to purchase Semi-Gas Systems, a subsidiary of Hercules, Inc. Both companies produced high-purity gas distribution and control systems for manufacturing, and the acquisition would give the Japanese firm nearly a third of the world market (and half the U.S. market) for gas distribution equipment.[81] Although a few individual semiconductor company executives immediately wrote to President Bush urging that he block the acquisition, for the most part the industry reacted passively. The American Electronics Association testified at Senate hearings that it was "deeply concerned" about the U.S. industrial base, but it emphasized that it favored "free and open markets" and did not voice support for blocking the sale.[82]

Although the industry associations and individual firms did little to protest the acquisition, Sematech once again leaped into action. Although a spokesperson claimed the consortium did not intend to take direct action to block the sale, he also indicated that Sematech would be "extremely and bitterly disappointed" if the sale occurred. Furthermore, Sematech warned that the sale would result in the cancellation of a contract Semi-Gas had involving the management of gas cabinets and cylinder gases at the Austin wafer fabrication facility. Two weeks later Sematech dropped any pretenses of noninterference and explicitly asked the federal government to block the sale.[83]

As they did in the Perkin-Elmer case, Sematech officials stressed the benefits the American company had received from American taxpayers. The consortium had invested heavily in Semi-Gas and claimed it would have to spend up to $100 million in order to develop an alternative domestic source of pure gas technology.[84] Nippon Sanso pledged that no technical data involved in the Sematech work would be transferred, but deal opponents claimed the technology involved could not be compartmentalized. Because the company had worked so closely with Sematech in the development of the gas delivery system, Semi-Gas had gained an "intimate knowledge" of the consortium's strategies and technologies, which would be transferred to foreign competitors.[85] Sematech argued that its own fate was tied up with that of Semi-Gas. It also complained that if the bidder had been American, the combined market share of the two companies would have violated antitrust rules. Finally, it pointed out that Semi-Gas was earning healthy profits, competing well in Japan, and had been put up for sale only because of problems in other parts of Hercules' operations.[86]

The Bush administration maintained its position of noninterference despite intense political pressure. Congress, responding to separate reports criticizing the administration's attitude toward IFDI from the Defense Science Board and the General Accounting Office, announced it would hold hearings to review the performance of the Committee on Foreign Investment in the United States. Nonetheless, CFIUS approved the sale, and the president announced he would allow the acquisition to go through. Sematech then proposed that Nippon Sanso be forced to give the consortium an exclusive license on any Semi-Gas technology developed as a result of its work at Sematech's Austin plant. The government rejected this plan and instead went along with Nippon Sanso's offer to create a separate arm's-length subsidiary to work on any Sematech-related technology development, an arrangement similar to other Pentagon agreements with foreign contractors.[87] By the fall of 1990 the only remaining obstacle was a long-running Justice Department probe into the deal's antitrust implications. At this point various members of Congress began to make statements in opposition to the sale.[88] The president's science adviser, D. Allan Bromley, broke with the administration by writing to the Pentagon with his concerns about the acquisition. Opponents hoped that enough political pressure might lead Nippon-Sanso to back out of the deal as Fujitsu had. Ultimately, the Justice Department decided to block the sale, alleging that the Japanese firm was trying to circumvent competition in the American gas cabinet market by buying out its competitor.[89] The trial occurred in March 1991, almost a year after the sale agreement was announced. In the end, the court denied the Justice petition. Ironically, in his decision the judge cited the testimony of semiconductor executives, who said they would not want to deal with a Japanese supplier because of the sensitive nature of gas distribution technology; thus, the court's reasoning went, there was no need to worry that Nippon Sanso would win an unfairly high share of the market.[90] The deal was finally closed in early May, and Sematech, as promised, canceled its contract with Semi-Gas.

Just as the Semi-Gas purchase was completed, Sematech publicly accused six Japanese firms of purposely and routinely delaying shipments of critical wafer processing equipment needed at American plants and charging up to a 30 percent premium over the price paid by Japanese consumers. Senator Lloyd Bentsen (D-Tex.), who chaired the Senate Finance Committee, initiated a General Accounting Office investigation of the charges. The Japanese equipment suppliers vehemently denied the allegations and attributed any delays to the difficulties of supplying follow-up service abroad. They also argued that close customer-supplier relations were simply more common among Japanese firms. These ties, however, were precisely what concerned Sematech and led it to support domestic ownership. Interestingly, however, executives at semiconductor companies who were supposedly being victimized did not publicly back the consortium's charges. Although an executive vice president for Intel testified at the Semi-Gas trial that the semiconductor industry was put at a general bargaining disadvantage as the equipment industry came under foreign control, Intel, TI, and Motorola all denied having any problems with foreign suppliers.[91] Another Intel vice president voiced understanding of the Japanese firms' motives: "We all have key customer supplier relationships. When we introduce a new device, people like IBM and Compaq get access to it first." Domestic suppliers also hedged their reactions. The president of SEMI/Sematech (representing U.S. suppliers) was less than supportive of Sematech's charges: "Some of the stories about preferential availability have significant truth in them. Some of them are half-truths. And some of them aren't true at all. . . . The issues related to timely availability are really issues between individual suppliers and individual consumers, and the depth of the partnering agreements between them."[92] When the GAO report was released in September, it drew even more criticism for its reliance on anonymous officials at unnamed U.S. firms. The study was unable to document any actual examples of discrimination. Sematech's president, William Spencer, tried to shift the terms of the debate: "The real argument is not whether the Japanese withheld technology or not, but the need to put U.S. technology in a position of strength. Then instead of complaining, the U.S. will have sources for that technology in this country."[93] Sematech officials ascribed the lack of support from the industry to fears on the part of American companies that any statements could jeopardize business relationships. The suppliers were similarly worried, according to one official, about offending their customers, especially given how difficult it was to obtain a toehold in the Japanese market.[94] Sematech itself, however, dealt exclusively with U.S. companies and so did not share these concerns. The consortium also found it useful to press these charges to convince the public, Congress, and a skeptical Bush administration of the critical national interest in maintaining government funding of Sematech.

Throughout all these the controversies over IFDI in the SM&E industry, a consistent pattern of political conflict emerged. The chip industry expressed some concern about the implications of the takeovers but did little to stop them.[95] In fact, the industry was reluctant even to voice support for blocking foreign acquisitions. However, Sematech took a harder line. In addition, SM&E executives advocated stronger IFDI restrictions, seeking to revise the Exon-Florio criteria so that CFIUS would take into account "economic security," calling for a moratorium on further foreign acquisitions in industries with a negative trade balance (to be lifted when the capital costs for foreign companies were the same as they were for domestic ones), and unlike the SIA, expressing support for the Bryant amendment (which would increase reporting requirements for foreign investors).[96]

The Semiconductor Industry: Conclusion

Overall, the demands of the semiconductor industry with regard to IFDI and the treatment of foreign-owned firms in the United States were ambivalent and contradictory. For a globalized sector, the chip producers favored a surprisingly restrictive IFDI policy. On the other hand, their demands were often put forth in an indirect or low-key way. There was no direct FDI counterpart to the industry's demands for contingent trade protection, even when such a policy was necessary for the effectiveness of its trade policy strategy. The pattern of demands seems to have little economic logic.

What appear to be contradictory policy demands make sense when one looks at the political context in which the issue arose. Since the industry had a number of options for pursuing its underlying preferences, firms made a calculation about the benefits and costs of presenting various demands. In many of the instances in which one would have predicted strategic investment demands, they did not appear because the costs were too high. For example, the absence of an institutional mechanism that could regulate IFDI and a legitimate argument for doing so increased the costs of opposing the Fujitsu bid for Fairchild as it reduced the probability of success. With the passage of the Exon-Florio amendment an institutional channel was in place that could reduce the costs of demanding a less open policy. But because this institution gave so much discretion to an unsympathetic president, the law only slightly increased the probability of achieving a more stringent FDI regulatory regime, thus keeping demands for restrictions costly. This was even truer with respect to greenfield investment, despite the fact that such activities undermined the STA and the 1987 trade sanctions. With economic incentives pointing in contradictory directions, industry actors formulated their policy preferences in terms of what was politically feasible. Policy demands that were considered legitimate and that could be addressed through existing institutional channels were more likely to be heeded, and thus they were more likely to be made.

As for the SM&E acquisitions, the Global Industry hypothesis would explain the chip industry's reluctance to oppose IFDI in vertically related sectors as a result of its fear that regulation would backfire either by encouraging FDI restrictions in foreign countries or by increasing their own input costs. However, industry actors did not cite these reasons in explaining their positions. Instead, many executives expressed opposition to the sales for precisely the reasons suggested by the Strategic Industry hypothesis.[97] More important, although individual semiconductor firms and the SIA failed to oppose the takeovers, they made a conscious decision to delegate the issue to Sematech. The consortium played a very active role lobbying for a more restrictive IFDI policy. Sematech repeatedly testified against the acquisitions in congressional hearings and before CFIUS, it threatened to cancel contracts with U.S. suppliers that were bought by foreigners or to make them compensate Sematech for the value of the technology the consortium funded, it advocated tightening the Exon-Florio amendment by directing CFIUS to consider "economic security" as a relevant factor and to weigh the cumulative effect of IFDI, and in some cases, it actively tried to enlist American buyers to put up capital to outbid foreign companies. All these actions had the full support of the member firms, which included the largest and most internationalized producers in the industry.[98]

The delegation of this issue to the consortium allowed the industry to take positions it otherwise would not have taken. First, Sematech did not deal with international companies and so had no reciprocity fears. Second, collective action costs were lower than they would have been to obtain the agreement of every member firm for every political decision Sematech made. Most important, Sematech's relationship with the Defense Department enabled it to assert that national security could be compromised if the sales were allowed, an argument that was perceived as a more legitimate reason to regulate IFDI than simply the protection of domestic producers or even putting pressure on the Japanese government for reciprocity. "We let Sematech speak for us," one executive said, because its raison d'être was to focus on strengthening the domestic electronic infrastructure; thus it was "appropriate and adequate" that Sematech take the lead.[99] Although the consortium's original focus had been on the manufacture of leading-edge chips, it had come to concentrate almost all its attention on sustaining the viability of the SM&E sector.[100] Sematech's organizational mission was to support domestically owned suppliers. MRC, Monsanto, and Semi-Gas, for example, were all major Sematech contractors. Their acquisition by foreign companies would affect the extent to which they could participate in Sematech programs; the acquisitions imposed direct costs on the consortium (and therefore on U.S. taxpayers).

THE AUTOMOBILE INDUSTRY

IFDI in the U.S. automobile industry led many would-be patriotic consumers to puzzle over what exactly constituted an "American" car. Did it depend on where the car was assembled? How much local content it contained? Where it was designed and engineered? Where the profits from its sales went? The "Big Three" domestic auto companies—General Motors, Ford, and Chrysler[101]—confronted a more concrete challenge: how to respond to the competitive threat posed by foreign subsidiaries. The U.S.-owned companies had already been pounded by import competition during the 1970s.[102] In response, U.S. companies and labor groups put enormous pressure on Washington for help. Shortly after President Reagan took office, his administration averted a congressional quota bill by negotiating a voluntary restraint agreement (VRA) with Japan limiting the flow of vehicles into the United States. As a result, Japanese imports flattened out and eventually began to decline. For Detroit, however, what trade policy gave, IFDI took away. By the early 1990s, the total Japanese share of cars and light trucks had risen to 30 percent, and of the Japanese nameplate vehicles sold in the United States, 60 percent were produced by "transplants." One out of every four cars produced in the United States came from these subsidiaries.[103]

The Production Profile hypothesis would predict that as transplant production replaced imports, U.S. automakers would demand policies to regulate IFDI or to discriminate in favor of American-owned producers in the United States.[104] The financial situation of the domestic industry fluctuated throughout the period under consideration, experiencing a severe downswing in the early 1980s, a recovery in profitability during the middle of the decade (though relative market share continued to decline), another interval of financial distress in the late 1980s and early 1990s, and a recovery beginning in 1993. Variation in demands for restrictions on IFDI should reflect this variation in economic circumstances.

The Global Industry hypothesis would predict that the international ties of American auto companies—mostly in the form of outward FDI rather than exports—would constrain the industry from demanding restrictive policies on IFDI. U.S. auto companies have long fought against foreign government FDI restrictions as well as attempts at home by organized labor to limit their outward investment activities. U.S. firms would refrain from seeking a more restrictive IFDI policy, more so than they would with trade policy, out of fear that these demands might eventually be turned against their own overseas activities. American producers varied in their outward orientation, and the Global Industry hypothesis would predict that their IFDI policy preferences would likewise vary.

Finally, the Strategic Investment hypothesis would predict that U.S. firms would demand restrictive polices targeted against Japanese producers in order to put pressure on Japan to allow reciprocal access for vehicles produced by U.S.-owned companies. From the standpoint of domestic producers, the Japanese market was inaccessible to exports or FDI because of informal barriers such as the country's inspection and certification system, commodity taxes, and existing distributional networks. Auto executives protested that Japan's closed market gave its producers a "sanctuary" from which it could earn excess profits and thereby subsidize its sales in other, more competitive markets.[105] However true these accusations, U.S. producers saw little prospect of success in the Japanese market (where most consumers favored smaller cars) and during this period did not expend much effort trying to increase market share there. Unlike with semiconductors (characterized by significant scale economies), exclusion from the Japanese market did not impose huge costs on the U.S. auto industry. The real battle was over the American market.[106]

Although the Big Three did not export much to Japan or produce cars locally there, they developed important ties with many of their Japanese competitors. Early in the 1980s U.S. firms in effect decided that they could no longer produce competitive small cars but still wanted to provide their dealers with a complete line of vehicles.[107] Therefore, they subcontracted with second-tier Japanese manufacturers (in which they purchased a minority share of equity) to produce cars that were then imported into the United States and sold under a domestic nameplate; often consumers did not even realize that these "captive imports" were foreign-made. GM had an arrangement of this sort with Isuzu (holding a 34% ownership share of the Japanese company which later rose to 40%) and Suzuki (5%), Chrysler with Mitsubishi (24%), and Ford with Toyo Kogyo, also known as Mazda (25%).[108] In the case of Chrysler-Mitsubishi and Ford-Mazda, actual joint venture subsidiaries were set up in the United States—the Diamond-Star plant in Bloomington, Illinois, and the AutoAlliance plant in Flat Rock, Michigan—in which the partners shared in selling the output.[109] The Global Industry hypothesis would expect these joint ventures and outsourcing agreements to lead domestic firms to support liberal commercial policies since restrictions could harm their own operations or disrupt their supply of captive imports. But this welcoming attitude would not necessarily extend to greenfield IFDI, where Japanese firms entered as independent competitors. Furthermore, the equity Detroit held in these second-tier auto companies did not give U.S. firms much influence in their management or access to Japanese consumers. Thus the alliances provided only a weak incentive for U.S. producers to seek liberal policies.[110]

In sum, the economic interests of the auto industry were ambiguous. The Production Profile approach expects U.S. firms to extend their demands for import protection to the output of Japanese transplants. The Global Industry explanation suggests that extensive outward FDI, as well as outsourcing arrangements with Japanese automakers, would lead Detroit to favor an open IFDI policy. The Strategic Investment hypothesis emphasizes contingent demands for restriction based on exclusion from the Japanese market, though it is questionable how important that market was to U.S. firms.

By contrast, foreign market access and economies of scale had much more relevance for the upstream auto parts industry.[111] Because of the long-standing ties between the Japanese automakers and their suppliers, U.S. parts producers faced great obstacles in their attempts to increase exports to that market. They had even less success in the Japanese after-sales market.[112] When the Japanese auto firms began shifting production to the United States, domestic parts makers saw their best chance yet to increase sales. Location, in conjunction with the Japanese reliance on "just-in-time" production methods, would serve as a competitive advantage for

U.S. parts firms. But as detailed later, domestic parts makers had as much difficulty selling to the transplants as they had trying to export to Japan, and they ascribed these problems to unfair Japanese practices, namely the replication of the keiretsu system in American territory. Thus it was the parts makers rather than the auto companies that had an incentive to put forth strategic demands for trade and investment policy.

Early Encouragement of IFDI

The VRA limiting the number of Japanese vehicle imports intentionally excluded any mention of components, subassemblies, or "knock-down kits," thus providing an incentive for the Japanese firms to relocate production to the United States if they wanted to maintain market share.[113] The United Auto Workers (UAW) regarded this as a major benefit of the VRA. UAW chief Douglas Fraser traveled to Japan, where he emphasized to policy makers and auto executives the importance of their creating American jobs in order to reduce trade friction. Once Japanese companies had made substantial investments in the United States, the UAW argued, the export restraints could be lifted.[114]

Domestic auto companies took a similar position, repeatedly demanding that Japanese companies relocate production to the United States.[115] Labor's position reflected its concern with alleviating unemployment, but the enthusiasm of the Big Three auto companies for IFDI is more puzzling. If firms were interested in maximizing market share and profit, why would domestic companies want to replace imported Japanese vehicles with locally produced Japanese vehicles? The answer rested on two assumptions—both of which turned out to be mistaken. First, U.S. executives doubted that the Japanese would actually respond by making large investments.[116] Second, these executives assumed the Japanese automakers could not maintain their competitive advantages in an American setting. Detroit welcomed greenfield investments because the domestic firms believed that relocation would impose higher costs on Japanese automakers and thereby reduce their U.S. market share.[117] Only later would the success of the transplants—in terms of both production quality and sales—demonstrate that the Japanese edge lay not in wage disparities, tax advantages, or exchange rates but in firm-specific management and production methods that could be transferred to foreign subsidiaries.[118]

Interestingly, many Japanese automakers shared this pessimistic assessment of their prospects for U.S. production. These firms feared that their production system, with its distinctive style of industrial relations and close communication between suppliers and customers, would not travel successfully to the United States. The exception was Honda, which, after opening a motorcycle plant in Ohio in 1979, began U.S. production of Accords in 1982. But Nissan and Toyota (the number one and two Japanese producers, respectively) repeatedly expressed great reluctance to invest abroad.[119] It was only after the adoption of the VRA that the Japanese reconsidered. At that point FDI was seen as the only way to hold on to American market share.[120] Following Honda's lead, in 1983 Nissan began producing trucks in Tennessee, followed by automobiles in 1985. The rising value of the yen after 1985 only hastened this trend.

The NUMMI Joint Venture

In February 1983 GM and Toyota announced that they would jointly build 200,000–250,000 subcompact cars a year for up to twelve years at an old GM plant in Fremont, California, which the two companies later dubbed New United Motor Manufacturing, Inc. (NUMMI). Although each of the companies would pay half the cost and supply half the components, GM would sell the entire output through its Chevrolet subsidiary. The benefit for GM was that it would learn how to build a competitive small car, using Japanese production methods, while saving more than $1.5 billion by not having to design the vehicle from scratch.[121] It hoped to appeal to young import buyers and, as with captive imports, cement in them a brand loyalty to GM. For its part, Toyota saw a low-risk way to find out if it could transfer its Japanese production system to the United States, at the same time soothing trade friction.[122]

The other domestic auto companies, however, strongly opposed the deal. Chrysler's Lee Iaccoca said of the arrangement, "It's not right and I will do everything in my power to see that the American public gets a clear picture of just how wrong it is."[123] There was not much, however, that he or anyone could do to block the joint venture. The only regulatory obstacle the companies faced in gaining approval for the investment was the antitrust review. Chrysler pounced on this issue, taking the lead in seeking a permanent injunction against the venture. Ford and AMC subsequently joined in, calling for the Federal Trade Commission to withhold its necessary approval. The FTC provisionally approved the venture in December 1983, and Congress held hearings in February 1984, at which opponents hoped to shoot the deal down before its final acceptance.[124]

Although the auto firms emphasized antitrust in their motion to the FTC, they publicly highlighted other reasons for their opposition. Chrysler noted that the venture would allow Toyota to evade the VRA. So too would recent investments by Honda and Nissan, which Chrysler had encouraged. The difference, according to NUMMI opponents, was that here Toyota was investing without building its own plant. The output, according to Iaccoca, would be "designed and, for all practical purposes, built in Japan. At least half of its components—and probably all of the most sophisticated parts—are going to be shipped from Japan." This was "Trojan-horse tokenism" that would "satisfy and pacify" Washington without constituting real investment.[125] The underlying goal of the other domestic companies was to induce greenfield investment by Toyota so the company would then face the high costs of American production.

Both Ford and Chrysler owned stakes in Japanese companies but argued that these second-tier Japanese companies did not pose the same threat to the U.S. industry; both U.S. companies also said they had no objection to a GM alliance with either of its other partners, Suzuki or Isuzu. Such an alliance would contribute more to total IFDI, according to Ford's testimony, since these smaller Japanese companies were less likely than Toyota, in the absence of a joint venture, to have the resources or incentives to invest in a greenfield factory.[126] Chrysler threatened that if the deal went through, it would have no choice but to replace its Omni and Horizon subcompact with Japanese-made cars. And Ford added that if Chrysler did this, "it's basically no holds barred."[127] The FTC approved the deal in March 1984 but only after imposing further restrictions on production volume, product pricing, communication between the two companies, and the lifetime of the joint venture. Chrysler subsequently dropped its lawsuit, claiming it had really only "sought public debate on the issue and we had made our point."[128] Once the antitrust issue disappeared, there were no other grounds on which the deal could be blocked; no legislative tools existed that could prevent an international joint venture. No further objections were raised, and in fact Chrysler itself, just before ending the lawsuit, announced its Diamond-Star joint venture with Mitsubishi. Subsequently, Ford reached an agreement with Toyo Kogyo (Mazda) to share the output from assembly at the Flat Rock, Michigan, plant.

Domestic Content Legislation

The Fair Practices in Automotive Product Act, passed by the House of Representatives though not by the Senate, was designed to increase the required minimum percentage of U.S. content in all automobiles sold in the United States. Every company would face a rising minimum content level as its sales volume increased.[129] The bill's supporters (most prominently, organized labor) claimed the legislation would not inhibit trade but rather attract inward investment. "Content is not protectionism in disguise. It's job legislation, pure and simple," declared a UAW advertisement.[130] Opponents (the Reagan administration, auto dealers and importers, export-oriented industries, and large business organizations) countered that foreign firms could not possibly meet the proposed content requirements and so would be subject to the penalty import reductions. The American International Auto Dealers Association (AIADA) claimed that it would be "economic suicide" for the Japanese to try to meet the content targets. The Reagan administration agreed that the Japanese would not sacrifice their cost advantages by relocating. Therefore, they argued, the bill was essentially a quota combined with a prohibition on increased outsourcing by the Big Three.[131]

The effect the legislation would have on U.S. producers was the subject of some debate. The Production Profile approach would suggest that since the VRAs had not provided the economic boost many in the industry had hoped for, mandating IFDI would have appealed to domestic firms (given prevailing beliefs about the production cost differential between Japan and the United States).[132] Alternatively, if the Japanese were unable to meet the domestic content requirements and therefore faced further import restrictions, all the better. The Global Industry hypothesis, however, predicts that the auto firms would oppose the bill. Although the U.S. firms could satisfy the local content requirements as written, the proposed law might inhibit the increasingly popular use of foreign outsourcing for components, a strategy Detroit saw as essential for its own competitiveness.[133] The shift in policy might also provoke foreign retaliation or at least obstruct U.S. efforts to negotiate away foreign investment restrictions abroad. These arguments were emphasized by the U.S.-based multinationals in groups such as the Business Roundtable, the National Association of Manufacturers, and the Chamber of Commerce, which strongly resisted the bill.[134]

The auto companies themselves took varying positions on the legislation. GM, the most internationalized firm, was most consistent in its opposition, testifying that domestic content requirements would inhibit the company's effort "to rationalize production on a global basis" as well as possibly provoke foreign retaliation. CEO Roger Smith expressed support for the general principle that manufacturers "have an obligation" to produce where they sell; he emphasized, however, that private "business arrangements" would prove more effective in this task than a government mandate that was "inflexible and unpredictable in its results."[135] Ford executives stated that domestic content legislation could function "as an instrument of last resort to be considered when other measures to correct trade inequities and imbalances have been tried and have failed."[136] In its congressional testimony Ford expressed sympathy with the goals of the legislation, arguing that Japan had historically complied with local content laws in other countries and would do so if such laws were passed.[137] But when pushed to take a stand either supporting or opposing the legislation, a Ford vice president refused to respond directly, saying only "not now."[138] Chrysler's position was even more opaque than Ford's. CEO Iaccoca argued that the legislation would send a signal to Japan that the United States was "serious" about addressing trade friction.[139] Although the company relied on its 15 percent stake in Mitsubishi to procure the small cars necessary to fill out the product range for their dealers, Chrysler VP Robert Perkins contended that the Japanese probably would not retaliate because they were "born negotiators . . . and they do not like confrontation," especially with their largest market.[140] But Chrysler executives also claimed that domestic content bills are "almost impossible to administer in a way that not does not do damage to their intention." The better solution would be to attack the exchange rate and tax disparity problems directly.[141] When asked at a late 1983 hearing whether he supported the local content bill, Iaccoca replied, "No, not at all."[142] Instead, Chrysler executives announced they favored tighter quotas, though they conceded these measures were "not substantially different in approach" from local content legislation. If given the choice between local content or nothing, they testified that they "would far prefer local content."[143]

In sum, the Big Three were divided, with GM opposed (though not very actively) and Ford and especially Chrysler ambivalent. Domestic firms kept a low profile during the whole debate. Opponents of the bill seemed unsure whether the Big Three were allies or adversaries. Some of the industry's ambivalence resulted from the multiple effects of the legislation: the protectionist and IFDI-inducing effects were desirable, but the constraints on outsourcing were not. The VRAs were supposed to accomplish the first two goals while avoiding the third, and so, despite continuing deterioration in the Big Three's market share, Detroit maintained its preference for the negotiated quotas over domestic content laws.[144] An additional factor was the widespread recognition of the proposed legislation's poor chances of ever becoming law. Ford and Chrysler, at least, could avoid antagonizing the UAW without fearing the bill would actually pass.[145]

Besides labor, the big winners from the proposed legislation appeared to be the domestic auto parts manufacturers. But like their Big Three customers, these companies did not make this issue a priority. In fact, their trade associations expressed opposition to the bill. The Auto Parts and Accessories Association (APAA) testified, "We must export. We must have the opportunity to become original equipment suppliers worldwide, and by virtue of this, gain and maintain a healthy share of the global replacement market. In order to succeed, we cannot afford to be hamstrung by high local content demands here or elsewhere."[146] It did not matter for the parts makers, as it did for labor, whether auto production occurred in the United States or abroad; rather, they cared about who would supply these auto producers, wherever the vehicles were assembled. With remarkable prescience the suppliers feared the legislation would induce IFDI by Japanese automakers, in turn provoking IFDI by Japanese suppliers. Given the close ties inherent in the keiretsu system, the lion's share of any resulting increase in business would go to these new transplants, not the U.S. suppliers. Therefore, the APAA favored more directly protectionist measures, such as increasing duties on vehicle imports with remissions based on the proportion of U.S. parts and components.[147]

After domestic content legislation fizzled in the Senate, the subsequent upturn in Detroit's financial position lowered the pressure on Washington to enact further auto protection legislation. Between 1983 and 1988, aided by lower gasoline prices and improved demand for big cars, the combined profitability of the domestic producers exceeded that of any other U.S. industry.[148] During this period U.S. companies continued making profitable deals with Japanese producers to serve the American small car market. As a result, domestic producers relaxed their opposition to foreign imports. This shift contributed to the Reagan administration's decision to abandon the VRA in May 1985 (though Japan unilaterally maintained limits on its exports).[149]

Insofar as the domestic content proposals were designed to send a signal to Japan encouraging investment, the bills had their intended effect. During the mid to late 1980s the transplant presence grew rapidly. This "second wave" of Japanese transplant investment included startups by Mazda's Flat Rock plant (1987), Toyota's first greenfield transplant in Georgetown, Kentucky (1988), Diamond-Star in Illinois (1988), and a joint Subaru-Isuzu plant in Lafayette, Indiana (1989). Detroit could no longer complain that the Japanese refused to locate production where they sold cars.[150]

As a result of these new plants, however, many in the industry began to worry about overcapacity. By 1986 industry analysts were predicting that the next few years would see a major crisis for the domestic industry: plummeting Big Three market shares and the closure of maybe nine or ten existing assembly plants.[151] During the booming mid-1980s, however, these dire predictions still seemed a long way off. Overcapacity had not yet become a pressing problem, and the Big Three remained indifferent to the wave of Japanese IFDI that had begun to transform the Midwest into "auto-alley."[152] Organized labor, in contrast, had already become disillusioned with the transplants because of the UAW's difficulty in organizing foreign-owned plants.[153] Labor groups also expressed disappointment in the low level of domestic content used by the Japanese assemblers. As transplants continued to gain market share, labor groups claimed that the heavy reliance on imported parts meant that IFDI would end up reducing overall industry employment.[154] Low domestic content also became a pressing issue for the U.S. auto parts industry and later for the auto assemblers.

Auto Parts and Domestic Content

When the foreign automakers first began to relocate production to the United States, domestic parts makers saw an opportunity to finally penetrate the Japanese market. Later, when a disappointed parts industry started complaining to Washington about the low domestic content levels of the transplants, the Japanese carmakers responded with three arguments. First, they maintained that U.S. components did not meet their exacting quality and reliability specifications—a claim the parts makers vehemently denied. Second, the transplants maintained that they were newcomers to the United States, and as they became more familiar with American suppliers, their domestic content levels would rise accordingly; U.S. suppliers countered that they had heard such assurances before and that they wanted results. Third, the Japanese subsidiaries asserted that even with these disadvantages they did in fact have high domestic content levels—in some cases higher than Big Three vehicles, depending on how the term *domestic content* was defined.

This last point was the subject of great controversy. The transplants claimed that non-component-related expenses such as overhead, insurance, transportation, advertising, and so forth should be counted (as they were when the Environmental Protection Agency calculated domestic content for the purposes of Corporate Average Fuel Efficiency standards).[155] Using this more inclusive standard, Honda and Toyota said they were at 60 percent, Nissan said 63 percent, and Mazda 50 percent.[156] The next year, Honda bragged that its 1991 Accords qualified as "domestic" cars under the EPA rules.[157] By contrast, the U.S. parts firms focused on local sourcing of components. They pointed to a GAO report estimating that Japanese transplants had a 38 percent domestic sourcing ratio (compared with 88% for the U.S. makers), thus allegedly causing the loss of twenty-five thousand jobs in 1988. Parts firms also claimed that the components Japanese transplants did source locally were not the technologically advanced kind (engines, transmissions, and electronic parts) but rather the "energy-intensive" and "bulky, standardized, generic" products such as batteries, seats, glass, carpeting, dashboards, trim, paint, and steel. Significantly, most of these parts were absent from the lucrative replacement market.[158]

Another dispute revolved around whether the "domestic" in domestic content included components made by foreign-owned suppliers located in the United States. For example, the allegedly domestic Honda Accord sourced only 20 percent of its parts from "traditional" U.S. suppliers (i.e., U.S.-owned firms).[159] Figures reported by the Japanese Automobile Manufacturers Association used the location criteria and were therefore denounced as meaningless by the U.S. parts industry.[160] The domestic industry wanted U.S. trade negotiators to press for an agreement that would provide more differentiated information on sourcing by Japanese companies (in Japan and in the United States), broken down by the ownership of the supplier, a task the Japanese claimed was impossible.[161]

U.S. parts makers had opposed the earlier domestic content legislation precisely because they feared such pressure would lead more Japanese parts companies to build plants in the United States in order to be counted as domestic. Even after the content proposals failed to become law, IFDI in auto parts accelerated, so that by the end of the 1980s around three hundred Japanese supplier transplants had set up American operations.[162] Japanese auto manufacturers reported growing levels of American-*made* parts in their vehicles, but American-*owned* suppliers did not share in this business. According to U.S.-owned companies, the investments by Japanese parts makers were economically redundant. "The capacity to supply parts already exists in the United States," argued a spokesman from APAA. "It is not necessary for the Japanese vehicle assembly plants in the United States to also build a base of Japanese-owned parts suppliers." Instead, this FDI represented a "preconceived plan to eliminate U.S. competition in the motor vehicle industry."[163] Foreign-owned suppliers did not have to worry about market capacity because their keiretsu ties with Japanese assemblers in the United States guaranteed them a large market, risk-free. Sheltered in this market segment, the parts transplants could then launch a price offensive to capture the Big Three market. By the summer of 1987 the APAA was advocating contingent restrictions on IFDI. Transplants were called a "peril to the U.S. economy," and the wave of Japanese supplier relocation to the United States, according to the APAA president, posed "the gravest possible threat to the future of American-owned parts makers."[164]

In sum, the parts industry advocated what the domestic automakers never could bring themselves to support: "U.S. discouragement of further investment should be the corollary to our top objective of [transplant] market access."[165] Even here, though, there were no demands for actually barring investments or requiring government approval for greenfield transplants. In fact, industry representatives were ambiguous in their recommendations of what precisely the government should do. One suggestion involved legislation preventing state governments from using federal funds in incentive packages offered to foreign investors. The parts makers argued that these taxpayer-supported subsidies gave an unfair advantage to the investors, whose new plants ended up adding to overcapacity problems.[166] However, federal funds made up a small portion of these incentives, and in any case there was little the parts makers could do to prevent this practice.[167] The parts industry continued to attack IFDI, but its demands were constrained by the lack of existing tools for regulating foreign direct investment.

Meanwhile, by the late 1980s American auto manufacturers began to revise their indifferent attitude toward transplant production. This shift coincided with a severe downswing in the financial fortunes of the Big Three. After enjoying a record combined profit of $11.2 billion in 1988, the domestic automakers experienced a dramatic reversal, seeing their earnings fall by 25 percent the next year; 1990 was their worst year since 1983, and the downward trend continued until 1993. During this period, by contrast, the transplants were increasing their car production, mostly by expanding existing transplant facilities.[168]

The first hint of a new attitude on the part of U.S. manufacturers came in statements concerning trade policies. The Big Three suggested that Japanese producers were unfairly evading import restraints by assembling vehicles with low domestic content. "The number of imports on wheels has been declining but the number of imports in boxes is increasing," complained Chrysler president Robert Lutz. "People assume that if a vehicle is screwdrived together at an American plant it is an American car. . . . But no matter where final assembly takes place, those cars are essentially import products."[169] Industry executives suggested modifying the VRAs to take into account transplant production. In May 1987 GM chief operating officer F. James McDonald called for every car produced in the United States by Japanese subsidiaries to count as at least half a car against the restraints on exports, since, he claimed, their local content was less than 50 percent. Ford's CEO predicted that transplant output would soon exceed the entire Japanese quota (2.3 million units). He argued that Japanese FDI was not having the effect that Detroit anticipated because the transplants were "assembling 'made in Japan' auto kits in Tennessee, Kentucky or Ohio." He therefore recommended that because of this low domestic content, the export ceiling be reduced below two million (even though this would not affect transplant sales).[170] In July 1987 Senators Byrd, Dole, Bentsen, and Danforth wrote to Japanese prime minister Yasuhiro Nakasone expressing concern that Japanese exports had not declined along with the increase in transplant production and proposing that knockdown kits be counted in the VRA.[171] The Japanese refused, and the senators dropped the issue. In January 1991 Chrysler, Ford, and the UAW publicly urged further import reductions to compensate for increasing transplant production.[172] Aside from isolated statements by company executives, however, there was no serious political activity to back up this new attitude toward IFDI.

When in the early 1980s the industry perceived a threat from imports, it sought trade protection to gain some breathing room. But at the end of that decade, faced with a similar threat by the transplants, U.S. carmakers did not issue analogous demands to limit transplant production. Rather, they confined their focus to the local content levels of the Japanese subsidiaries. In economic terms this was an odd strategy. How would boosting the share of components from U.S. suppliers in transplant-produced vehicles help the domestic auto firms? Some argued that although screwdriver assembly would not sufficiently blunt the Japanese advantage, higher local content would. However, by 1986 the yen/dollar exchange rate had eliminated much of the Japanese price advantage, and by the early 1990s U.S. auto parts makers were arguing (in the context of negotiations to increase Japanese local sourcing) that U.S. parts were *more* price competitive than Japanese parts.[173] Yet if this were so, then auto manufacturers were only hurting themselves when they urged the transplants to increase their domestic content. Furthermore, the Big Three were simultaneously intensifying their own foreign outsourcing strategy.[174] Nonetheless, as the capacity and market share of the transplants increased, the automakers joined the parts makers in using the issue of domestic content to attack the transplants, and did so in the context of a number of issues that arose in the late 1980s and early 1990s.

Foreign Trade Subzones

The foreign trade subzone program allowed auto manufacturers to delay paying duties on imported parts until after they were incorporated into a finished product; as such, they were subject to the lower vehicle rate (2.5%) as opposed to the higher rate on parts (4–11%). Numbering nine in 1980, these subzones proliferated rapidly during the decade. Of the 116 subzones existing in 1989, 43 consisted of motor vehicle plants, but they accounted for 90 percent of economic activity under the program. Foreign and domestic automakers alike used this tariff break: GM had fifteen,

Ford twelve, and Chrysler eleven. Foreign manufacturers, although they had fewer subzones, imported more components and so enjoyed greater tariff savings; a GAO report estimated tariff and tax savings of up to $10 million a year for foreign makers and $1 million a year for domestics.[175]

In order to gain subzone status for a plant, a company had to apply to the Commerce Department's Free Trade Zone (FTZ) Board. The board was then required to post a notice in the *Federal Register* soliciting comments, though the applications were routinely approved. As the auto parts suppliers began to complain about the transplants, however, the free trade subzones (or, as the APAA derisively called them, "foreign investment subzones") came under attack.[176] In 1986, citing the low level of U.S. auto parts used by Japanese manufacturers, the APAA called for a moratorium on subzones until Congress could further study the issue.[177] Subzones, the group argued, added to the industry's overcapacity problems, injured domestic suppliers, and led to shutdowns of domestic assembly plants with high levels of American content. Lee Kadrich, the association's director for government affairs, declared, "Our position is that the Foreign Trade Zone Board should look at what effect a new plant will have on jobs nationally—not just locally. Is that plant really adding to the economy or is it simply displacing jobs somewhere else?"[178]

The parts suppliers sought a more stringent approval process, a time limit on subzone status, and periodic reviews to determine the economic impact the zones were having on the domestic parts industry. Another parts trade group, the Motor and Equipment Manufacturers Association (MEMA), proposed that subzone benefits apply only to vehicles that were actually exported, following the original intent of the program (that is, boosting exports), and that this criterion be applied retroactively; as it was, exports or transshipments accounted for only about a tenth of zone activity.[179] Unlike the proposal of Rep. Marcy Kaptur, who wanted specifically to bar Japanese companies from using foreign trade subzones (until there was "trade reciprocity in auto parts"), the parts makers recommended a nondiscriminatory approach. Still, they emphasized that the transplants gained disproportionately more benefits than domestic firms—two to four times as much, according to MEMA.[180] Along with lobbying for changes in the overall program, the parts makers mobilized against specific subzone applications. The APAA and MEMA (along with representatives of the steel industry) challenged Toyota's petition for its Kentucky plant, prompting an FTZ Board hearing. They also challenged Subaru-Isuzu's request for its Lafayette, Indiana, plant and Diamond-Star's application for its Bloomington, Illinois, plant.[181]

As mentioned, the Big Three themselves participated in the subzone program to a greater degree than the transplants; in fact, ten of their larger plants accounted for 60 percent of all subzone shipments in 1986. In 1989 the Motor Vehicle Manufacturing Association (MVMA) testified in favor of the FTZ program, arguing that because U.S. firms had to import locally unavailable foreign parts, the zones helped the domestic industry remain competitive.[182] Chrysler was the only dissenter from the pro-subzone consensus; when the parts firms contested Toyota's Georgetown, Kentucky, application, Chrysler sent a letter to the Commerce Department supporting domestic content requirements for all subzone users.[183] This was a surprising position, considering that in 1989 Chrysler was operating fourteen subzones and had three more applications pending (including one, at its Diamond-Star joint venture, to which the auto parts groups had filed an objection). Indeed, an annual report by the trade zone board noted that Honda (as well as GM and Ford) generally used a higher percentage of U.S. parts and materials than most Chrysler plants.[184] Chrysler vice president Robert Perkins asserted, "It has become obvious to Chrysler that we and other domestic manufacturers are being and will continue to be placed at a competitive disadvantage vis-à-vis foreign transplants unless some changes are made in the criteria for operating subzones." He added that of course the company "would expect to follow any new policies or standards the [Commerce Department] establishes for trade zones," including those in which Chrysler had an interest.[185]

As the transplant presence grew, the rest of the automakers eventually came around to Chrysler's position. In 1990 Nissan, which was planning to nearly double the capacity at its Smyrna, Tennessee, plant, submitted a request for expanded subzone coverage (by which it hoped to save up to $10 million a year). The parts makers immediately attacked Nissan for its low level of domestic sourcing, but this time the MVMA joined in and filed an objection on behalf of all three domestic automakers to the subzone application.[186] While the request was being considered, Nissan applied for a temporary increase in its vehicle ceiling, but the Big Three, along with the APAA, challenged that, too. The MVMA letter to Commerce stressed that the Nissan expansion (increasing its capacity from 250,000 to 450,000 vehicles per year) would exacerbate an already glutted North American industry.[187] The shift in the industry's position, however, coincided with two other developments. First, Detroit believed the incoming Clinton administration would be sympathetic toward the industry's problems.[188] Second, as a result of pressure from the domestic parts makers, the Commerce Department had instituted new rules requiring the FTZ Board to take into account the effects of subzones on national employment levels and the health of the domestic industry. This gave subzone opponents a new avenue for expressing opposition. The MVMA-APAA letter cited these new rules, as did industry executives.[189] With new tools to attack the subzones, automakers found it worthwhile to join the parts makers in opposing the transplants' applications.

Despite Detroit's optimism, however, the new administration did not respond favorably to the domestic industry's position. The Treasury Department maintained that denying the petition would lead to retaliatory discrimination against U.S. companies abroad.[190] With political support from Tennessee's governor as well as Vice President (and Tennessee native) Al Gore, Nissan finally obtained expanded subzone status in March 1993.[191] It proved difficult to persuade policy makers to put obstacles in the path of transplant capacity expansion, given the perception that the subsidiaries were directly creating American jobs. One auto executive remarked that despite Detroit's unhappiness at continued transplant growth, objecting to the proposed expansion simply would "make us seem ultraprotectionist."[192] The domestic automakers, though they maintained their position on transplant subzones, backed away from challenging a new Toyota subzone request for almost doubling the capacity at its Kentucky plant. One auto industry lobbyist conceded, "It didn't seem necessarily productive to go through the whole exercise again. There are other fish to fry."[193]

Rules of Origin

Negotiations on the North American Free Trade Area (NAFTA) agreement, and specifically the rules of origin (which determine local content requirements for duty-free entry), were another example of the evolution of the domestic auto industry's position toward a more antagonistic reaction to transplants. Rules of origin are used to prevent foreign firms from setting up an export platform in one country in order to gain access to another within the free-trade area. Like local content laws, rules of origin can be interpreted as both protectionist (in that they can restrict the movement of foreign goods) and pro-FDI (in that they encourage more extensive production within the free trade area). Japanese companies complained about the first effect, and Detroit emphasized the second. Ford's CEO claimed, "Every percentage point increase [in the rules of origin] translates into more investments in the North American manufacturing base."[194] Such tributes to IFDI were somewhat disingenuous since the Big Three were not in favor of bringing more Japanese production to the United States; rather, their interests lay in preventing the transplants from locating in Mexico to evade American trade laws.[195]

The auto industry's position toward IFDI had already begun to change in its approach toward trade with Canada. The 1965 U.S.-Canada Auto Pact had set a 50 percent North American content level in order for vehicles to be exported duty-free between the two countries. U.S. parts makers subsequently complained that Canada was trying to lure Japanese firms by offering them duty remissions (up to 100%) on parts they imported into Canada for assembly. U.S. firms had also benefited from this program, but in the mid-1980s they shifted their position and joined the suppliers in objecting to Canadian policy.[196] As a result, the U.S.-Canada Free Trade Agreement (FTA), negotiated in the late 1980s, had several features that disadvantaged the Japanese transplants. Corporate membership would now be limited to the original members (except for a GM-Suzuki joint venture called Canadian-American Manufacturing, Inc., or CAMI, which had just joined the pact).[197] After a phase-in period the transplants would be able to ship vehicles duty-free to the United States if they met a North American content requirement of 50 percent.[198] With content newly defined as the value of materials originating in each country and the direct cost of assembly in the exporting country, that 50 percent requirement was equivalent to 70 percent under the old rules.[199] The duty remission program was phased out, though the Big Three retained certain performance-based waivers.[200] In effect, the FTA created a "two-tier" North American industry that discriminated against foreign subsidiaries.

The U.S. government signaled an even harder line on this issue in 1991, when Customs launched an investigation of whether Honda had misreported the North American content of Canadian-assembled Civics imported duty-free into the United States. In March 1992 Customs ruled Honda's domestic content was 48 percent (rather than the 69 percent it claimed) and slapped a $16.5 million back-duty on the Japanese company. By disallowing labor, machinery investment, and safety/environmental investments, and by following FTA rules that "rolled up" parts that contained 51 percent domestic content to 100 percent and "rolled down" those with less than 51 percent to 0 percent, Customs calculated that the Civic's engine was foreign, even though the engine was cast, machined, and assembled in Ohio.[201] Congressional leaders called for an across-the-board investigation of every other Japanese carmaker in Canada (all of which had lower local reported content levels than Honda).[202]

As the debate over NAFTA began to heat up, much of the discussion focused on how the agreement would facilitate outward FDI by U.S. manufacturers to Mexico. The Big Three themselves, however, spent their energies lobbying about the treaty's automotive provisions affecting transplant production. Specifically, Detroit sought a stricter local content minimum for vehicles to be considered North American. Ford and Chrysler wanted a 70 percent regional content level, and GM asked for 60 percent (though only, GM added, if it and other U.S.-owned companies could average the content of all their product lines).[203] Parts makers were asking for 75 percent. The final agreement set local content at 50 percent, rising to 62.5 percent over eight years for cars, light trucks, engines, and transmissions. The auto industry also wanted to eliminate roll-up and adopt a stricter method by which individual parts were to be traced back to their source. NAFTA incorporated this change, effectively boosting the minimum regional requirement even further.[204] Finally, the U.S. automakers proposed that the two-tier system of the U.S.-Canada agreement be applied to NAFTA—a clear violation of the national treatment principle.[205] Tariffs and performance requirements would be eliminated immediately for the companies that already had plants in Mexico (the Big Three, Volkswagen, and Nissan), but newcomers would have to wait ten to fifteen years. Representatives from the transplants, who had wanted the local content level to stay at 50 percent and who had opposed the two-tier system, criticized the agreement as protectionist and "a giant step in the wrong direction."[206]

In explaining the industry's position on rules of origin, some have emphasized sensitivity "to their weakening competitive position vis-à-vis the transplants."[207] American companies believed that integrating their continental operations and taking advantage of cheap Mexican labor would give them a competitive boost. Preventing the transplants from doing the same would provide the U.S.-owned companies with a relative advantage.[208] But rules of origin would have no effect on investments within the United States. If anything, they would boost IFDI in the United States because Japanese transplants that were concerned about their content levels would invest in the United States in order not to risk losing access to the most lucrative market in North America. In fact, this is precisely what Canadian and Mexican negotiators accused their U.S. counterparts of trying to promote. The administration wanted to be able to sell the agreement as "creating jobs" and knew that high rules of origin would encourage risk-averse investors to shift production to the United States.[209] The U.S. automakers could not have been joyful about the prospect of creating more transplant capacity within the United States. If the rules were intended to "close the back door" to the U.S. market (i.e., prevent Mexico from being used as an export platform), the front door to IFDI remained wide open.[210] Strict rules of origin would certainly help the parts makers, but the gains for the Big Three were more questionable. There may have been some advantages to making Japanese companies pay the (2.5%) tariff on vehicles imported from Mexico, but this seemed a roundabout way to deal with the real threat: transplant production within the United States.

Nevertheless, the industry's position made sense in that directly restricting transplant production was simply not in the cards. No institutions existed that could provide this policy, and any demands for such restrictions could be portrayed as inhibiting job creation. By contrast, rules of origin were a much more politically promising (if less economically helpful) policy for the industry to pursue. Seeing that Washington already was pushing for these rules for its own reasons (to boost NAFTA's job-creation potential), the industry only had to push it further. Industry officials worked closely with American negotiators, helping them draft their positions on the rules of origin.[211] The policy preferences put forth by U.S. firms were the best they could realistically hope to achieve and would still hurt the transplants.

Exports to the European Community

The issue of corporate nationality arose again during a brief dispute between the Bush administration and the European Community. Specifically, the Europeans, after setting a quota that limited total Japanese market share, had to decide how to classify vehicles manufactured by Japanese companies in the United States. Early in 1990 the United States trade representative, Carla Hills, notified Brussels: "We would be remiss if we didn't stress how strongly we feel that a Japanese nameplate car made in our country is an American car."[212] The administration's position, just as in the rules-of-origin disputes, stemmed from its desire to maintain the attractiveness of the United States as a destination for Japanese FDI. If the EC counted a Honda Accord from Ohio as Japanese rather than American, Honda would have an incentive to shift production to Europe rather than expand its U.S. plant and create more American jobs.[213] Although domestic manufacturers concurred with the government that strict rules of origin were useful, they did not agree that counting U.S.-built Japanese cars as American was also a good idea.

Chrysler vice chairman Gerald Greenwald fired off a letter to Hills objecting that the Japanese should not be able to use the United States as "a Trojan Horse for their export efforts to Europe." However, he cast his argument in terms that addressed the politically popular job-creation argument; that is, that the USTR's position ("that the U.S. government considers any assembly in the U.S.—regardless of content—to be American") would *decrease* IFDI by removing pressure on the transplants to boost their local content level. More immediately, it would hinder Chrysler's efforts to get its partner Mitsubishi to augment the percentage of American content at Diamond-Star.[214] Ford's CEO also sent a letter to the administration protesting the policy.[215] Both Ford and Chrysler felt that the USTR ought to spend its time prying open the Japanese market for U.S. vehicles (i.e., those made by U.S.-owned companies) rather than the European market for Japanese vehicles (i.e., those made by Japanese-owned companies).[216] Beyond these public statements, however, the domestic companies did not do much to fight the administration's position. The Europeans quickly acceded to the U.S. government's position after deciding that the numbers involved were too small to justify risking a trade battle with Washington.[217] The mini-dispute came and went so quickly that it never had the chance to develop into a full-fledged issue.

The Trade Enhancement Act of 1992

At the end of 1991 Rep. Richard Gephardt (D-Mo.) and Sen. Donald Riegle (D-Mich.) introduced legislation that would, among other things, limit the U.S. sales of Japanese vehicles to their 1991 level (3.8 million vehicles) in 1992. The bill would reduce the limit by 250,000 a year unless the trade deficit with Japan fell by at least 20 percent. What distinguished this bill from previous protectionist efforts was that for the first time, the quantitative limits would include both imports and locally produced vehicles. The transplant limits would not apply, however, if "traditional" firms supplied half the value of components. In turn, "traditional" suppliers were defined as either wholly U.S.-owned or, if Japanese-affiliated, producing parts with 75 percent of their value from non-Japanese sources.[218] The bill also called for launching two Super 301 cases, one targeted against Japanese dumping of auto parts in the U.S. market and the other charging that keiretsu and other "anti-competitive" business practices—in Japan but also among the transplants—functioned as an unfair trade barrier to U.S. firms.[219] Applying Section 301 to firms in the United States was another unprecedented action; Nissan wrote to Congress complaining that "this kind of blatant discrimination overturns decades of U.S. policy of national treatment and non-discrimination among foreign investors."[220]

Chrysler was the first automaker to pledge its support for the bill; in fact, Chrysler executives helped draft the legislation.[221] GM, by contrast, announced its opposition. Ford conditioned its support on the results of President Bush's trip to Japan in January 1992. During that trip the American delegation, which included the Big Three CEOs, presented a demand for a 20 percent reduction in the $41 billion trade deficit. The Japanese responded with a number of commitments for U.S. auto parts purchases and imports of U.S. cars, but the American executives expressed disappointment at the results.[222] Although GM maintained its position opposing the measure, Ford chairman Harold Poling joined Iaccoca in endorsing the bill: "We prefer negotiation to legislation," he told Ford shareholders in May, "but given the lack of progress, we have concluded that passage of the Rostenkowski trade bill would be in the best interests of America."[223] Ford executives acknowledged that the transplant cap would cover the Ford Probes produced at the Mazda Flat Rock plant. The 1993 Probe (as well as Mazda's 626 and MX-6) all qualified as domestic under EPA guidelines but under the proposed bill were considered transplant vehicles.[224]

It is interesting to compare the industry's position on this legislation with its stand on the domestic content proposals that were debated in the early 1980s. As already discussed, those bills were part of organized labor's attempt to fight unemployment by encouraging Japanese IFDI and by placing restraints on Detroit's foreign outsourcing activities. Their primary emphasis was where auto production—and the jobs associated with it—would be located. By contrast, this legislation interpreted domestic content as referring to parts supplied by *U.S.-owned* companies; thus domestic parts makers—who opposed the earlier legislation because they rightly foresaw that it would lead to increased IFDI by Japanese parts suppliers—supported this legislation without reservation. Furthermore, this legislation was targeted specifically against Japanese manufacturers. The only purpose the domestic content criteria had in the proposed law was to determine whether a vehicle would count against the Japanese market-share limit. This difference made it much easier for Chrysler and Ford to support minimum domestic content levels. Another important difference, of course, was that Detroit no longer believed it had nothing to fear from Japanese plants in the United States. A decade after agreeing to the VRA, Tokyo tried once again to alleviate congressional pressure by reducing its export quota from 2.3 million cars per year to 1.65 million. But in a testament to how much had changed during the 1980s, all this reduction accomplished was to bring the limit into line with what the Japanese companies were actually exporting.[225] Trade protection no longer helped in an industry in which IFDI had replaced exports as the most important means of market penetration.

Ford and Chrysler maintained that the legislation would increase employment, but opponents of the bill repeatedly argued that the transplant cap would harm the interests of workers employed by foreign-owned companies. Even one of the bill's co-sponsors admitted that with the transplant clause "you really do pit American workers [at Big Three factories] against American workers [at transplant factories]."[226] Controversy over this issue threatened other industry goals (such as the effort to reclassify imported minivans and four-door sport utility vehicles as trucks in order to boost the tariff from 2.5% to 25%), so ultimately the transplant clause was dropped from the legislation.

MVMA Membership

A few weeks after the 1992 presidential election, the Motor Vehicle Manufacturing Association altered its membership rules, ousting Honda's U.S. subsidiary. This was not the first time the auto manufacturing trade association had tightened its participation criteria. In 1986 the MVMA had required its members to manufacture at least half their American sales within the United States (a grandfather clause allowed Honda and Volvo to remain members). At the time, the stated reasoning was that the MVMA wanted to focus on promoting the interests of manufacturers, not marketers. Thus in May 1988, when Toyota expressed interest in joining, it was rejected.[227] But Honda, the first Japanese company to build a U.S. plant, had long considered itself the most American of the transplants. The company had vowed to surpass 90 percent local content by 1996 and to do it by relying on traditional U.S. suppliers, mostly second and third tier.[228] Meanwhile, the rest of the transplants were also close to meeting the criteria for joining the group. Toyota and Nissan were expected to become eligible for membership by 1993. Once again, the MVMA altered its membership criteria, but this time the justification was that the group wanted "to focus on the common issues and interests that are unique to the domestic manufacturers." By *domestic*, MVMA president Thomas Hanna made it clear, the association meant those companies that were not "controlled from abroad."[229] Illustrating this intention, the group changed its name to the American Automobile Manufacturers Association (AAMA) and took over the duties of the U.S. Council for Automotive Research (which oversaw a number of Big Three R&D consortia on technologies such as electric-vehicle batteries, engine emissions, and safety features).[230] Finally, in a minor but symbolically important move, the organization also relocated from Detroit to Washington, D.C. "We'll be more active and aggressive in Washington than we have been," said the group's president.[231]

This shift in the lobbying group's approach received solid support from the Big Three; in fact, the usually internationalist GM argued most strenuously for the move. The industry was in the midst of battling Japan over minivan dumping and sport-utility reclassification. Although Honda itself did not manufacture those products, the company frequently expressed disagreement with MVMA positions.[232] Japanese firms interpreted the change as a turn toward nationalism on the part of the Big Three. "It's 1957 thinking in the 1990s," complained a Mitsubishi vice president. Toyota's U.S. spokesman said of the move, "This is stupid and absolutely schizophrenic. . . . [The Big Three] can't make up their minds whether to go global or to get into a bunker."[233] In fact, the industry was doing both.

Content-Labeling Bill

In the final days of 1992 Congress attached an amendment to a federal transportation funding bill requiring cars and light trucks with more than 15 percent foreign content to carry a label listing the domestic content of the entire vehicle, where the vehicle was assembled, the two countries that contributed the greatest value of parts, and where the engines and transmissions were built. Fearing that the bill could lead to a "regulatory quagmire," the MVMA's president initially argued that companies should be allowed to use the domestic content numbers devised for CAFE purposes, thus keeping administrative costs to a minimum.[234] However, two months later the newly named AAMA backed the measure, saying the law would counteract the "considerable amount of advertising by foreign and transplant automakers" that were falsely claiming that many of their products were as domestic as cars and trucks sold by the American auto manufacturers.[235]

Representatives of importers bitterly attacked the legislation; Honda called it "the American automobile mis-labeling act," and Mazda considered it "blatantly discriminatory." Indeed, more was involved than simply providing objective information to the consumer. The bill's formula for determining local content favored manufacturers that built their own parts (which, as it happened, were the Big Three); parts from unaffiliated suppliers that had less than 70 percent North American content would be rolled down to 0 percent whereas parts from wholly owned suppliers would be calculated at their actual domestic content percentage. Thus a component manufactured by GM-owned Delco Electronics with 69 percent domestic content would count as 69 percent in a Geo Prizm built at the NUMMI plant, but the same part in a Toyota Corolla built in the same plant would count as 0 percent. Second, the bill did not count labor costs as domestic content. Finally, vehicles of a single model line, no matter where they were built, would be lumped with a single domestic content figure (thus, for instance, averaging Honda Accords built in Ohio, Canada, and Japan). It is no wonder the transplants saw the bill (which became law in October 1992) as tilted toward helping the Big Three.[236]

Conclusion: The Auto Industry

Overall, the auto industry's behavior on issues related to IFDI and foreign transplants provides support for both the Production Profile and Global Industry explanations. At times, the domestic producers seemed oddly indifferent to the transplants, which, in Iaccoca's words, were "murdering" the Big Three. Their political demands seem unexpectedly tame given the severe industry downturn and the increase in transplant market share during this period. But at other times the U.S. industry put forth restrictive demands regarding the treatment of foreign-owned firms that seemed just as curious, in view of the fact that U.S. firms were multinational companies with extensive foreign investments and international alliances of their own.

The parts industry presents a somewhat simpler case. These firms opposed IFDI from the start. Indeed, they declined to push for local content legislation in the early 1980s precisely because they believed it would lead to investment by their Japanese rivals and subsequently to overcapacity in the industry. The attitude of domestic parts makers toward IFDI by Japanese *assemblers* was more complicated. In principle, domestic suppliers welcomed such investment because they saw an opportunity to finally crack the Japanese market. Moreover, they recognized that as an industry they needed to think globally in order to succeed; they had, for example, protested against rules of origin in the European Community which they perceived as excessive.[237] But once the domestic parts makers realized that the Japanese auto transplants would maintain their close ties with their own national suppliers, the domestic firms adopted strategic investment demands. They advocated restrictions on transplants: denying the plants subzone status, preventing duty-free movement of their goods within North America, and including transplant production in Japanese market-share quota. Their goal was to pressure the Japanese automakers to increase their purchase of components produced by American-owned firms, and the restrictions on the transplant assemblers were a means to this end. But even as this goal proved to be out of reach, the domestic parts firms maintained their hard line against IFDI, if only because they would benefit from protecting the market share of the Big Three.[238] The auto parts industry spoke out much more forcefully on these issues than did the Big Three and expended much more energy in pushing for stricter regulation of the transplants. Even here, though, there were no demands for formal IFDI restrictions.

By contrast, the Big Three domestic automakers did not initially carry over their protectionist trade demands to the realm of IFDI, for the simple reason that they did not perceive a threat from transplant production. By the mid-1980s the success of the Japanese subsidiaries and the resulting overcapacity became apparent to the domestic manufacturers. However, this outcome did not translate into actual political demands until the early 1990s, when the industry—sometimes all three makers, sometimes just Ford and Chrysler—demanded, among other things, denying subzone status to transplants, tightening rules of origin in regional trade agreements, limiting imports and transplant output, launching a Section 301 investigation against the transplants, and labeling the transplant vehicles in a way that emphasized their "foreign-ness." That these actions coincided with the severe industry downturn and increased transplant market-share gains lends support to the Production Profile explanation.

The Global Industry hypothesis would emphasize the role of Detroit's own exports and investments. This approach accounts for variations among the U.S. auto firms: the more global GM consistently took more liberal positions than did domestically oriented Chrysler. The auto companies targeted their restrictive trade policy demands against a country (Japan) in which the potential for retaliation against exports and FDI was low. On the other hand, Ford was also multinational, yet in the early 1990s it took positions like Chrysler's. Moreover, even GM lent its support to various protectionist initiatives such as the minivan antidumping case and the push to reclassify sport-utility vehicles as trucks.[239] GM also departed from strictly liberal policy demands on many of the transplant-related issues discussed in this chapter. GM executives explained this inconsistency by distinguishing between government mandates that restrict competition (which the company opposes) and government pressure to pry open foreign markets (which it supports), even though this latter approach may entail employing sanctions or restrictions. This behavior would be consistent with the Strategic Investment hypothesis. However, many of the trade and investment policies GM demanded were not designed to open foreign markets; its positions on issues such as subzones, rules of origin, and trade association membership did not include any linkage to Japanese market access. A more revealing distinction was made by a GM executive who noted that despite the company's general bias toward a liberal commercial policy, it was willing to support the government's use of those policy tools it already possessed in order to safeguard the industry's interests.[240] International ties may inhibit restrictive policy demands, but even global firms, when they face a serious competitive threat, will look for relief from the state; demands for protection or a restrictive IFDI policy are more likely when the relative chances for success are high, however, and that in turn depends on the political context.

The outsourcing agreements that domestic companies maintained with

Japanese companies, as well as their involvement in actual transplant joint ventures, did not constrain the U.S. automakers from voicing demands for restrictive policies. Often this had peculiar consequences. For example, Ford supported transplant limits even though they would affect production of the Probe at Flat Rock. Chrysler opposed subzone status for transplants even as its own Diamond-Star plant was in the midst of applying for it. GM favored stricter minimum content levels for rules of origin even though its Canadian joint venture with Suzuki had fought Washington over whether it was inflating its measurement of North American content. Just as in the semiconductor industry, domestic industry actors felt no cognitive dissonance in pursuing global alliances at the same time as they demanded restrictive policies and shrugged off the criticisms and accusations of inconsistency from their Japanese partners.[241]

Although the U.S. auto firms faced formidable barriers to exporting to or investing in Japan, they did not adopt strategic investment demands. It is true that the industry often couched its demands in calls for reciprocity.[242] Moreover, industry actors frequently complained about how the Japanese would use profits from their own closed markets to subsidize the creation of further capacity overseas, even during recessions.[243] However, the primary focus of the U.S. automakers (as opposed to the parts makers) was on U.S., not Japanese, market share. Their efforts to penetrate the Japanese market have been, until the late 1990s, minimal. That market has never been essential for survival the way it has for U.S. semiconductor manufacturers.

In sum, the domestic auto industry's demands on issues relating to IFDI and the treatment of foreign-owned firms in the United States are partly explained by the first two economic hypotheses. The industry's hostility toward Japanese transplants roughly followed its growing perception that these factories posed a competitive threat to the U.S. automakers' own economic welfare. This became clear in the mid to late 1980s, but it was only around the early 1990s—when the Big Three barely averted financial catastrophe—that the industry translated this attitude into policy demands.[244] The Global Industry hypothesis can help both to make sense of intra-industry variations in demands and to account for why the industry's demands on IFDI were always more muted than its trade policy demands. But the industry's demands fluctuated between reflecting competitive pressures and its global ties—a variation that the two hypotheses cannot by themselves explain.

Furthermore, neither of these explanations can account for the puzzling form industry demands took. Specifically, why did the automakers make *domestic content* the centerpiece of their campaign against the transplants? This was an issue on which the Big Three were themselves vulnerable because of their own foreign outsourcing. Neither the UAW nor the Japanese automakers ever tired of pointing out Detroit's hypocrisy on the nationalism issue; the importers' association noted that the Big Three accounted for 10 percent of the U.S. automotive trade deficit with Japan via their captive imports.[245] What makes these demands even more counterintuitive is that they did not address the problem of transplant manufacturing capacity, the real source of the domestic industry's predicament. Even if the transplants were to increase their domestic content (however the term is defined), it is unclear how this change would reduce the threat they posed to profits or market share of the Big Three. On the basis of the latter's underlying interests, it would have made more sense to lobby for a market-share cap on Japanese vehicles that included both imports and transplants. Such a move would not have been unprecedented; indeed, this was exactly the approach chosen by the European auto companies.[246] Transplant capacity was even greater in the United States than in Europe, but the Big Three never seriously lobbied for a similar kind of arrangement. At one point they floated the idea of counting transplant output as equivalent to a fraction of an import for the purposes of the VRA, but after the Senate drafted a letter to this effect and mailed it to the Japanese prime minister, the proposal was dropped and Detroit did not bring it up again. Similarly, Chrysler and Ford supported the Trade Enhancement Act of 1992 but did not expend much effort pushing for the measure. This legislation would cap transplant production only if the subsidiaries did not source 60 percent of their parts from U.S.-owned parts makers. Although this was good for U.S.-owned parts makers, it is hard to see how it would benefit U.S.-owned auto assemblers.

Ann Krueger, in her discussion of rules of origin, suggests one explanation. She argues that because of the characteristics of the Japanese production system, requiring Japanese assemblers to disrupt their tight relationship with previous suppliers raises their costs; therefore, tougher content requirements hurt Japanese assemblers relatively more than the same standards hurt U.S. makers.[247] All the better if, like the Trade Enhancement Act, the rules are aimed only at Japanese producers and not applied across the board. But this belief—reminiscent of the industry's views in the early 1980s—that inducing more intensive Japanese FDI would blunt its competitive advantage—became less tenable as time went on. With the improved performance by U.S.-owned parts makers and especially the dramatic increase in the value of the yen, transplant vehicles with more domestic content posed an equal if not greater threat to the U.S.-owned assemblers.[248] Industry actors continued to complain about the cost advan-

tages enjoyed by the transplants.[249] But whatever the real importance of
these advantages, it is difficult to see how requiring a 60 percent domestic
content level would reduce them.

Another possible explanation centers on the parts-making divisions of
the Big Three automakers themselves. After all, GM and Ford are respectively the first and second largest producers of auto parts in the world.
They use the components in their own vehicles but also sell to other auto
manufacturers. Thus they have a direct economic interest in pressing for
increased local sourcing by the transplants. However, this explanation falters in that GM, the largest parts maker, was the least active in pressing its
demands whereas Chrysler, which sources almost all its parts from outside
the company, was the most active. Some executives emphasized the overall importance of a healthy domestically owned parts industry.[250] But the
auto parts sector is less R&D-intensive than the semiconductor materials
and equipment industry, and the global structure of the industry does not
create the same kind of potential for wielding market power to disrupt the
flow of inputs to the U.S. automakers. Detroit has never expressed the
fears of becoming dependent on foreign suppliers that were so common
among chipmakers.

Ultimately, the best explanation for the nature of the industry's demands is a political one. The U.S. industry determined that limiting transplant market share was not a realistic policy demand. There was no existing institutional mechanism that could provide protection against
transplant production—no escape clause or antidumping duty in response
to IFDI as there was for imports. The goal was ideologically suspect and
would not have attracted political allies. After advocating Japanese investment for so long, Detroit would face public and congressional resistance if
it turned around and opposed the transplants directly. Despite the hostile
attitude of the UAW toward the transplants, most people believed that
IFDI created jobs, and this belief was an insurmountable ideological barrier. Unlike the semiconductor industry, auto manufacturers could not appeal to national security as a convincing reason for maintaining an
American-owned industry. Because of the auto industry's size and visibility, employment became the bottom line to which all sides in a political
conflict had to appeal. Thus the transplants, the Big Three, and the auto
parts manufacturers all put forth competing claims over how this or that
policy would create or destroy jobs.

From this standpoint, domestic content was a much more politically attractive campaign. First, the parts makers had already raised this issue
(though it took the automakers a while to join them). More important,
there were domestic political institutions in place that could supply this

kind of policy: Foreign Trade Zone Board regulations, NAFTA's implementation rules, trade legislation to which IFDI measures could be added. Ideologically, these demands could also be used to make the jobs argument work for Detroit. The Japanese had long emphasized the employment-creating aspect of transplants, and this argument had been extremely effective in preventing IFDI restrictions from gaining support among politicians. After President Bush's visit to Tokyo in January 1992 (for which the raison d'être, Bush said, was "jobs, jobs, jobs"), the Japanese intensified their public relations campaign, emphasizing the contributions the transplants made to the U.S. economy. This publicity crusade was successful enough (according to the domestic automakers) to convince the press, influential opinion shapers, and—most important—policy makers that the definition of an "American" car was ambiguous. The domestic industry, feeling that it had to "draw a line in the sand" and directly and publicly confront the issue of whether transplant vehicles were indeed domestic, focused on the low levels of parts from domestic (especially from "traditional" U.S.-owned) companies. We are not against foreign direct investment, industry spokespeople emphasized. But as a Chrysler executive complained, "If they they're going to have a PR campaign that says they're American, then be American."[251] The emphasis on local content, then, was a political tactic, designed to counter the effective deployment of the job-creation argument, which Japanese companies were using (successfully) in Washington to prevent the U.S. industry from achieving its political aims on trade and investment issues. The industry's reasoning is illustrated by a comment made by Ford's chairman and CEO, Red Poling: "I look at it from the standpoint of things we can control and things we cannot control. . . . So I say, focus on the things you have direct control over."[252] Political structures shape what things can and cannot be controlled.

FIVE

A Liberal Response
Machine Tools and Antifriction Bearings

Fighting import competition in the 1980s, the American machine tool and antifriction bearing industries both found that national security concerns could win them enough support in Washington to attain the protectionism they desired. Yet in each case foreign competitors subsequently jumped over import barriers by relocating production in the United States. The national security strategy that had proved so effective against imports ran into problems when the nature of foreign competition changed. Threats to economic security had traditionally been defined in terms of production location; it proved very difficult for U.S. firms to make government officials regard foreign ownership as a problem. Political institutions set up to address one issue could not easily be used to address another.

For machine toolmakers, the form of investment made it even more difficult to challenge IFDI. Unlike the semiconductor case, most of the IFDI in machine tools came in the form of greenfield plants and thus was not subject to federal rules regulating foreign mergers and acquisitions. Faced with a similar situation, the auto industry highlighted the transplants' low domestic content, arguing that foreign companies were not engaging in "real" investment and therefore not creating as many jobs as they were displacing. Toolmakers could potentially tie the content issue to national security: if transplants relied heavily on imported parts, IFDI would perpetuate the foreign dependence and undermine the intended effect of the quotas. But because much of a machine tool's value was embodied in its controller, foreign transplants were able to reach relatively high domestic content levels without too much difficulty by using domestically produced controllers. Although these components came from foreign-owned companies, they were manufactured in the United States. Once again, location was the relevant criterion for security purposes, and it became the standard for commercial policy as well. As a result, domestic firms found there was little they could do to persuade the government to regulate IFDI more strictly. The domestic tool industry did not oppose a controversial acquisition (Fanuc's buyout of Moore), nor did it press to exclude transplants from the "Buy American" procurement rules. It did support the exclusion of foreign firms from a government-supported R&D consortium, but that was because the project's mission was to address the dependence of U.S. firms on foreign controllers. Overall, however, the machine tool industry's policy preferences toward IFDI were not very protectionist, an outcome that is difficult to explain solely on the basis of the industry's economic interests.

The antifriction bearing industry experienced a similar situation. It also found itself under assault, first by imports and later, after obtaining anti-dumping relief, by the output of foreign-owned transplants. Again, domestic firms found it difficult to use the security argument (which had been so useful in winning import protection) to make a compelling argument for regulation of IFDI. When a Japanese company, Minebea, attempted to acquire New Hampshire Ball Bearings Company, U.S. producers had no available means to block the deal. Nor did they lobby for the government to alter its procurement rules in order to use ownership rather than location as the standard for buying "American." Because of the political context, the bearing industry did not play a major role in putting pressure on government officials to change U.S. IFDI policy.

THE MACHINE TOOL INDUSTRY

The machine tool industry accounts for only around 0.1 percent of U.S. GNP and less than 2 percent of U.S. manufacturing value added. It employs less than 10 percent of the number of workers in the automobile industry. Two-thirds of domestic tool builders employ fewer than twenty people, and more than four-fifths employ fewer than fifty.[1] Like the semiconductor industry, though, this sector has attracted disproportionate attention because it produces intermediate goods that are used by many different manufacturers. Since the industry makes the tools that firms use to produce other goods (including machine tools themselves), the competitiveness and technological position of the machine tool industry affects productivity in almost every manufacturing sector. As the president of the industry's trade association remarked, this sector is "the belt that holds up the pants of industrial America."[2]

The severe downturn in the domestic industry's fortunes during the 1980s therefore provoked widespread concern.[3] A number of factors contributed to this decline. First, the domestic market for machine tools was shrinking.[4] Alongside this trend, short-term cyclicality of demand persisted. Usually, when demand was at a peak, U.S. producers allowed orders to accumulate, which they would then fill when business slowed. Meanwhile, shortages would appear, and customers often had to wait months (or occasionally years) for delivery of new machines during these booms. As long as American producers were dominant, this approach had proved effective in helping smooth out the business cycle for U.S. tool-makers. But in the mid-1980s, when the U.S. economy was recovering from recession, the strategy backfired. The delays allowed foreign produc-ers (especially the Japanese, who had stockpiled a large volume of high-quality, low-priced machines) to jump in and supply impatient American customers.[5] Since the 1950s Tokyo had been pursuing an active industrial policy aimed at developing a Japanese-owned machine tool industry. This policy, combined with strong demand and constant customer pressure for technological innovation, resulted in the emergence of a fiercely competi-tive Japanese tool industry.[6] As in the semiconductor industry, Japanese producers concentrated for the most part on simple, standardized, mass-produced products, most often used by small shops producing relatively unsophisticated goods, whereas U.S. companies produced for high-perfor-mance niches. Unfortunately for the American industry, it was the former market segment, not the latter, in which most of the growth occurred dur-ing the 1980s and which generated the bulk of industry profits—profits that could be redirected to R&D in more advanced market segments.[7] A final factor contributing to these outcomes was impact of the strong dollar of the early 1980s, which made American products relatively more expen-sive abroad and at home.[8]

Given this precipitous decline, the industry's shift toward a more protec-tionist trade policy position came as no surprise. It quickly became clear, however, that trade protection, by provoking Japanese tool producers to relocate production to the United States, would not do much to help Amer-ican firms. The Production Profile hypothesis would predict that U.S. pro-ducers would then extend their protectionist trade demands to IFDI, favor-ing stricter regulation of foreign investment and deviations from national treatment. The demands for a more protectionist approach would be higher among the firms that were less competitive and more affected by for-eign competition and would also rise in periods when demand weakened.

Had the industry been internationally oriented, then according to the Global Industry hypothesis, firms would not have put forth these kinds of restrictive demands. In fact, however, even when the U.S. industry was at its peak, it exported little of its output; U.S. tools never made up more than 5 percent of foreign consumption.[9] A few of the larger producers such as Cincinnati Milacron and Cross & Trecker had overseas sub-sidiaries, mostly geared toward serving foreign markets in Europe. During the 1980s even these operations shrank while U.S. firms were preoccupied with holding on to their decreasing domestic market share.[10] Industry offi-cials had little reason for concern about the potential costs of foreign retaliation in response to any U.S. barriers.[11] The Global Industry hypothesis, then, would predict that if firms had reason to favor IFDI restrictions, there would be nothing to inhibit them.

Contrary to what the Strategic Investment hypothesis would predict, there was no effort to link domestic restrictions to changes in Japanese government policy.[12] That was not because access to the Japanese market was easily available. Foreign market share remained low even after Tokyo eliminated its trade and investment restrictions, partly because the Japanese industry itself was so competitive but also as a result of informal market barriers (notably, the restrictive distribution system and the keiretsu ties between Japanese customers and suppliers).[13] The industry did express concerns about the obstacles to penetrating the Japanese market, and to a certain extent U.S. government officials tried to address these access problems in negotiations over trade agreements.[14] But as the industry retrenched in the 1980s, exports and outward FDI became less important. Although the Strategic Investment hypothesis therefore does not have much to say about this sector, both the Global Industry and Production Profile approaches suggest that domestic firms in this industry would be likely to put forth restrictive IFDI policy preferences.

Trade Policy Battles and Japanese FDI

In 1982 Houdaille Industries, Inc., filed a petition under Section 103 of the Revenue Act of 1971, a seldom-used clause that prevents companies in the United States from applying the investment tax credit to imported capital goods if these imports result from unfair trading practices. The Houdaille petition argued that Japanese tool prices were 20 to 40 percent below U.S. prices despite efforts by the Japanese government to set floor prices for exporters that were supposed to preclude dumping.[15] The suspension of the credit would have increased the effective price of Japanese-made machine tools by around 15 percent. The case dragged on for two years, and though the other machine tool builders and distributors supported the petition, Houdaille itself spent more than $1.5 million in lobbying costs. Finally, in September 1983, after Japanese prime minister Yasuhiro Nakasone personally intervened, the Reagan administration denied the Houdaille petition.[16]

In March 1983, with the economic situation deteriorating rapidly, the National Machine Tool Builders Association (NMTBA) decided to file a petition with the Commerce Department seeking quotas on eighteen categories of machine tools, thereby restricting imports to 17.5 percent of domestic consumption.[17] But rather than point to unfair trade or use the escape clause, the industry filed its request under Section 232 of the Trade

Expansion Act of 1962, that is, on the grounds that the national security of the United States was imperiled by the current level of imports. For a Section 232 action, there is no requirement for the industry to show that trade competition is unfair; indeed, it is not even necessary to demonstrate that imports produced the conditions in the affected industry. All that has to be shown is that given the state of the industry, continued foreign competition would damage national security.[18] Houdaille's bitter experience led many industry officials to believe this route was more likely than an unfair trade petition to succeed in gaining protection for the industry, even though up to that point only two petitions had ever been successful under Section 232 (both involving oil imports).[19] The Reagan administration, however, avoided ruling on the 232 petition by negotiating a VRA.[20]

The industry's argument, detailed in the petition, emphasized the possibility of shipment interruptions in times of national crisis. Factories in Japan and Europe, the industry trade association argued, "would not be reliable suppliers of machine tool during wartime."[21] Because the industry was not very multinational, there was little concern on the part of domestic producers that U.S.-owned subsidiaries located overseas would be lumped with foreign firms. However, an unintended result of relying on this argument was that foreign-owned firms on domestic soil would not be considered a threat to national security, though they could still pose a threat to the profitability of American producers.

Just as in the automobile and steel industries, voluntary restraint agreements accelerated the internationalization of production in the machine tool sector. In fact, there was an even greater imperative to relocate production in this industry, independent of the VRAs, because of the advantages of establishing a presence close to customers in order to customize and service the complex manufacturing systems that were becoming increasingly common.[22] The weak dollar also proved powerful in luring Japanese manufacturers to produce in the United States. But as in the auto industry, the pace and timing of the investments, as well as statements by Japanese executives, suggest that the trade quotas considerably hastened the growth of FDI into the United States.[23] Though Japanese firms had previously built up inventory centers in the United States for stockpiling tools, the VRAs induced the establishment of foreign-owned assembly and manufacturing plants. By 1988 nine major Japanese machine tool plants were operating in the United States.[24]

Controversy over Domestic Content

In negotiating the terms of the VRA, government officials explicitly considered the question of what would constitute "domestic." In the negotiated limits on consumer electronics and automobiles the government had left the rules loose in order to encourage job-creating IFDI. In this case, however, security concerns led the administration to ensure that the VRA would restrict the imports of knock-down kits as well as assembled machines.[25] The undersecretary of commerce for international trade explained the U.S. approach: "Our concerns are U.S.-based machine tool capability, not necessarily U.S.-owned machine tool capability, and we have delivered that message to our Japanese friends. [However,] the need is there for sustainable manufacturing capability in the event of interruption of overseas supply, and that would suggest that if an assembly plant was totally dependent on foreign parts, it would be only marginally better than an offshore assembly plant."[26] In other words, high levels of domestic content in IFDI mattered to Washington not because it would increase U.S. employment, cut the trade deficit, or reduce the cost advantage held by foreign companies but rather because of the same national security considerations that led to the emphasis on location over ownership in the first place. The less integrated and more import-dependent a foreign-owned subsidiary was, the less valuable it would be to the nation's defense during a potential conflict.[27]

Some of the details in the agreement, however, were left ambiguous. Commerce officials claimed that the VRAs covered imports of assembled and "substantially complete machines" but denied that any specific percentage of local content was required. Rather, each transplant would be required to show that "a significant number of critical components" were being produced locally.[28] Industry executives indicated that their understanding was that in order to be excluded from the VRA, foreign machine toolmakers had to reach a level of 50 percent U.S. content.[29] Because the rules were vague, the administration essentially determined whether production was American or foreign on a case-by-case basis. This assessment involved actual trips to transplant facilities by Commerce Department officials.

For all this, however, Japanese tool builders that relocated production to the United States did not experience much difficulty in reaching high levels of domestic content. Starting with Mazak, six Japanese builders were able to have their transplant output certified as American production by the beginning of 1990.[30] The machine tool transplants made a deliberate effort to use domestic suppliers in order to avoid the political controversy that had plagued the auto transplants. But mostly, the toolmaking plants were able to reach these content levels simply because they were able to purchase numerical control devices domestically, and these components accounted for a significant portion of the total value added. Japanese firms, especially Fanuc, dominated the controller industry, but these companies had little problem shifting production to the United States in order to serve the tool transplants. In 1988 a two-year-old GE-Fanuc joint venture launched a $5 million modernization program at GE's Charlottesville, Virginia, plant to produce computer numerical controls that would qualify as domestically produced. Taking no chances, GE Fanuc consulted with U.S. government officials in order to ensure that their devices would be considered American-made.[31] Following Fanuc's lead, Mitsubishi Electric began assembling CNC controllers in a factory outside Chicago in 1983; the main beneficiary was its biggest customer, Mazak, which could then use Mitsubishi's devices and still win the "Made in the U.S.A." certificate from the government.[32] Though these "domestic" controller suppliers were wholly or partly foreign-owned, for the purposes of the machine tool VRAs the definition of content used to determine the nationality of the final product was based on location. In this case there was no influential U.S.-owned controller industry to make a political issue out of the definition of *domestic* the way the auto parts makers had. This in turn made it less likely that the domestic machine tool industry would use the content issue as a vehicle to challenge IFDI as the U.S. automobile industry had.

American machine tool executives, however, began to raise questions as to whether the Japanese transplants really had achieved the high levels of domestic content they were claiming. These concerns increased as a result of several well-publicized incidents in which foreign companies were accused of illegally evading the VRA limits. Since the trade agreement was supposedly voluntary, the enforcement mechanisms were left as ambiguous as the content requirements themselves.[33] The NMTBA warmly endorsed Commerce's newly aggressive approach but also proclaimed its general support for IFDI as long as it was "real" investment.[34] The industry couched its opposition to "screwdriver" operations in security terms. Only real investment with high levels of domestic content would ensure that the country had "a domestic indigenous production capacity to meet our mobilization needs."[35]

Eventually, industry and government officials recognized the need to reform the rules on what constituted U.S. production.[36] In early 1989 Commerce officials began deliberating a proposal to place tighter rules on transplant assembly. Rather than measure overall levels of domestic value-added, the new regulations would define content levels by the specific components a machine contained. Imports of unassembled components would be assigned points, and a specified quantity of imported components representing a complete machine tool would then be counted under the quota. The new arrangement was also designed to measure content in a way that would favor the domestic sourcing of "critical" components (e.g., numerical controls, spindle assembly, major castings, and fabrications).[37] In February 1990 U.S. and Japanese negotiators met to hammer out the point assignments. Shipments of parts that exceeded twelve points would be considered kits, which would be counted under the VRA as imported tools. After the United States accepted some Japanese suggestions about specific point designations and agreed that third-country components would not be counted as imported content, the two parties reached an accord.[38]

The domestic industry strongly backed these new rules.[39] Nevertheless, the new system did not impose onerous burdens on the transplant producers. Indeed, Mazak executives complained that the rules were not strict enough: "We've spent $50 million on new machining systems for our machines while the other builders are out-sourcing their parts," said one vice president. An official from Okuma also noted that his company's bottom line would not be significantly affected.[40] What the rules did was impose clearer guidelines to prevent screwdriver assembly. Foreign producers disliked the uncertainty of arbitrary VRA enforcement more than they feared the stricter measures.

The revised content rules encouraged a new wave of IFDI.[41] Some Japanese firms that had been assembling imported machine tool kits in the United States increased their level of manufacturing, and a number of medium-sized machine tool manufacturers also set up American units. Contributing to the increased level of IFDI was the fact that U.S. and Japanese negotiators in Tokyo had recently lowered the VRA export ceiling in certain categories in line with the depressed demand in the American market. By 1991 transplant production by Japanese subsidiaries exceeded imports from Japan. The transplants also stepped up export of excess machine tools produced in the United States to Europe, Canada, and Latin America.[42]

The Debate over VRA Renewal

The debate over the effects of the VRA began to heat up as the agreement's 1991 expiration date approached and Washington had to decide whether to seek a renewal. Many believed the trade barriers had come too late to prevent most of the industry's retrenchment. A Milacron executive complained, "The tragedy is that the 232 petition was not accepted in the early '80s. The VRA helped to usher in a market opportunity but many domestic makers found themselves without the capital to take advantage."[43] Many well-known producers (such as Brown & Sharpe, Jones &

Lamson, and LaSalle) had exited the industry. Nine of the top twelve producers had entered into mergers or were absorbed into conglomerates.[44] Still others, including Cincinnati Milacron and Cross & Tecker, had significantly scaled back their operations. By 1987 the number of U.S. machine tool companies had declined to 624—fewer than half the number of firms in 1982.[45] Employment, at seventy thousand workers in 1991, was down 40 percent from its level ten years earlier.[46] Even for the firms that remained, the VRA did not help nearly as much as many in the industry had hoped.[47] Some industry executives attributed the lack of discernible improvement to the large inventory backlog that foreign companies had amassed before the agreement went into effect. In 1988 fortunes began to improve, but by the beginning of 1990 domestic firms still held only about half the U.S. machine tool market—less than they had in 1987 when the VRA was first imposed. Few perceived any significant mitigation of the U.S. industry's suffering, partly because foreign penetration in uncovered product categories increased but mostly because of increased IFDI in the United States. By 1990 imports made up around 50 percent of the U.S. market, and transplant output accounted for another 12 percent; this total foreign market share was only slightly below what foreign market share had been in 1986 before the VRA (67%).[48] The VRAs worked in that they reduced imports, but IFDI diluted their impact considerably.

The domestic machine tool industry never seriously considered advocating government restrictions on IFDI, most of which was greenfield investment and thus not subject to the restrictions of the Exon-Florio amendment. Given the absence of any legislative precedent or other usable instruments, as well as the ideological difficulties of arguing in favor of blocking investment, tool producers did not perceive such restrictions as a promising strategy. The automobile industry had managed to attack greenfield IFDI by focusing on the domestic content issue. However, this approach was unavailable to the machine tool industry since foreign transplants in this sector had relatively high levels of U.S. content (at least if location rather than ownership determined what was "domestic"). Although industry representatives acknowledged the disappointing results of the VRA, most firms saw little alternative to renewing the measures. In 1991 the industry trade association launched a lobbying campaign to have the VRA extended five years. Since foreign companies had not completely shifted from imports to local production, trade protection would still be better than nothing.[49]

Not all U.S. machine tool firms went along with the official trade association position. A few firms expressed fears that the restraints would interfere with efforts of U.S. multinationals to compete overseas.[50] Also, upscale niche producers argued that the VRA had resulted in increased Japanese competition in many of the products not covered by the quota. Neither of these groups, however, put much effort into opposing the renewal. Nor did machine tool users mount any organized opposition to the quota extension. In large part, this lack of opposition reflected the VRA's flexibility—that is, the frequent negotiations to adjust the export ceiling depending on domestic demand—and the absence of machine tool price increases that could be clearly traced to the quotas.[51]

The most serious opposition to the renewal came from U.S. firms that imported components covered by the VRA. Hurco, a machine tool firm in Indiana, led this small but vocal group. Unlike the industry trade group, the Association for Manufacturing Technology (AMT), these firms drew public attention to the effect the VRA had in promoting Japanese FDI in the United States, arguing that the quotas ultimately did little to help American firms.[52] The solution these critics favored was not to tighten investment regulation but rather to eliminate the putative cause of this IFDI: the initial trade protection. This political strategy lends support to the Global Industry hypothesis. Hurco and many other companies had adapted to financial crisis in the 1980s by outsourcing. The quotas, Hurco admitted, had thrown a monkey wrench into this approach and had nearly forced the company into bankruptcy by preventing it from importing Taiwanese parts. More generally, the company argued that its business plan—combining low-cost "iron" from Taiwan, South Korea, Turkey, Mexico, and Poland with U.S. or European CNC technology—represented the most promising approach for the American industry in the 1990s, but one that the VRA inhibited. Thus the quotas had the "perverse" effect of favoring Japanese industry over American companies, Hurco argued, and the company noted that the Japanese industry's trade association had not spoken out against the VRA renewal.[53] Indeed, with booming demand in the Japanese home market and transplant production in the United States, the VRA was barely affecting Japanese manufacturers. The quotas hurt the Taiwanese more severely, and some Japanese executives believed the VRA might actually help protect their investments against competition from Taiwan.[54]

Not surprisingly (given the original justification for the quotas), the political battle over VRA renewal turned on the national security issue.[55] The pro-VRA forces, in their public statements and testimony before Congress, framed the debate as one about economic security and national defense. Industry officials pointed to the "vital role" U.S. machine tools played in the Gulf War and testified that dependence on foreign sources would mean U.S. manufacturers could obtain only the machine tools that foreign companies chose to deliver; the level of technology and timing of deliveries would be at the discretion of foreigners.[56] "This really is a national-security issue, not a free-trade issue," the AMT insisted. In the earlier debates over the original VRA these arguments had been applied to imports, but at a November 1991 industry press conference held at the Capitol to launch the campaign for VRA renewal, executives warned that if foreign-owned firms replaced domestic ones in the United States, "the high-tech machines produced in America will be produced with new technological advantages that will be developed overseas, not here. And that new technology won't be shared with American government and business."[57] Industry officials were now suggesting that ownership, rather than merely location, was the issue, but they did not take the logical step of advocating IFDI restrictions; instead, they confined their demands to limiting imports.[58]

The battle over the VRA continued through the fall and winter of 1991. The anti-VRA forces were able to effectively counter the industry's national security argument.[59] In the end, the Bush administration compromised. In December, stating his recognition of "the importance to U.S. national security of [a] viable domestic machine tool industry," the president announced he would seek to extend the quotas for two years instead of five, though non-computer-controlled machines would not be included in the new agreements. The AMT expressed satisfaction, saying the extension would help the industry restore its competitiveness and thus strengthen the country's "ability to go to war with leading edge technology."[60] A new agreement was reached with Japan in April 1991 and with Taiwan shortly thereafter. Japanese firms, for their part, publicly reaffirmed their intentions to continue shifting machine tool production to the United States.[61]

Domestic Content in Downstream Sectors

The domestic machine tool industry expressed some concern that Japanese FDI not consist solely of screwdriver operation, but because the transplants were able to source the numerical controllers from Japanese-owned firms located in the United States, and because of the absence of a domestic tool parts industry to make this an issue, the toolmakers never took up the domestic-content campaign. After the content rule change in 1989 this issue dropped out of sight. But the domestic machine tool industry continued pressuring transplants in downstream tool-using industries, specifically motor vehicles, to increase their local content.

During the initial phase of IFDI in the automobile industry the local Japanese subsidiaries had imported nearly all their machine tools for the newly built factories. Later, however, when the auto companies began expanding and retooling, domestic machine tool companies saw opportunities for selling machines to the transplants.[62] But as with auto parts, the reality proved to be disappointing. Albert Moore, president of the AMT, echoing the testimony of the auto parts makers, ascribed the situation to the Japanese transplants' discriminatory buying practices.[63] The AMT's position paper stated, "It is one thing for the Japanese keiretsu system, operating in Japan, to effectively freeze U.S. machine tools out of the Japanese market; it is quite another for the Japanese transplants to freeze U.S. machine tools out of a significant portion of the U.S. market by importing the keiretsu system to America."[64] The AMT endorsed many of the same measures the auto parts firms championed. For instance, Moore recommended amending Section 301 to enable the administration to use it not just against foreign countries that excluded U.S. goods but also against the transplants.[65] Still, the issue of market access to the auto transplants never attained the same importance for the machine toolmakers that it did for the auto parts producers. Nor did the machine tool industry argue publicly (as did the auto parts makers) for distinguishing "traditional" U.S.-owned suppliers from Japanese-owned suppliers that had relocated production to the United States. Again, U.S. producers seemed to accept that location rather than ownership determined whether a supplier was domestic.[66]

Fanuc's Acquisition of Moore

Around the same time the industry was engaged in the battle over the VRA, another conflict arose concerning a proposed acquisition by a Japanese-owned company. The prospective target was Moore Special Tool Co., Inc., which built precision machine tools such as jig-grinding machines and aspheric generators. The company's tools were well regarded, and it had a significant export position (indeed, it had higher sales in Japan than in the United States), but it lacked the capital to upgrade its plant and equipment in order to maintain its competitive position.[67] In 1990 Moore reached an agreement to sell 40 percent of its equity to Fanuc Ltd. for $10 million. A couple of American companies had expressed some interest in making a bid, but the Fanuc deal was the most attractive to Moore's management because it left the Moore family in control and gave it the option of buying out Fanuc if the company regained profitability within two years.[68]

The proposed acquisition immediately provoked a storm of controversy, as Moore supplied grinders and measuring devices to the Energy Department, which used them to produce nuclear warhead components. The parties to the deal had hoped to defuse this issue in two ways: by reaching an agreement that would exclude Fanuc from access to sensitive information and by removing a clause from the original agreement that would have given Fanuc the option of buying out the remaining interest in Moore after five years. Fanuc described its planned investment as "passive" and tried to argue that it was interested only in using Moore's technology for nonmilitary products. It also emphasized that Moore had no direct classified government contracts and that its subcontracting work for the Department of Energy consisted of only around 10 percent of its annual sales, which themselves were less than $50 million.[69]

A number of extraneous factors contributed to the level of critical scrutiny this deal attracted. First, the Defense Production Act, under which the Exon-Florio amendment operated, had expired in October 1990 and had not yet been reauthorized. The administration advised all potential foreign buyers to stay in compliance, as the reauthorization was expected to be easily approved and would apply retroactively. In congressional hearings held to review the amendment's track record, many legislators expressed dissatisfaction with the administration's IFDI policy and proposed measures to strengthen the law. The sale of Semi-Gas to Nippon Sanso the previous year had left many in Congress determined to raise this issue and tighten American policy toward acquisitions. Overall U.S.-Japanese economic relations were particularly strained at this time as well. As a result, the timing of the bid proved unfortunate for Fanuc and Moore.[70]

Although the Committee on Foreign Investment in the United States, believing that Fanuc's financial support was crucial for preserving Moore's technology, approved the deal, there was significant opposition from Congress.[71] An influential article in the *Washington Post* by former State Department official Kevin Kearns argued that the components Moore produced directly affected the explosive force of a nuclear weapon and the risk of accidental detonation: "If there was ever a clear national security case, even according to the narrow [Exon-Florio] definition, the Moore case is it. What could be more deeply involved in national security than the machines that produce the nation's arsenal?"[72] In February 1991 Fanuc finally withdrew its bid, citing the pressure of legislators who, the firm contended, had "seized upon this proposed investment as a vehicle for expressing their larger concerns."[73]

Throughout this controversy the domestic machine toolmakers did not play a major role in stoking opposition to the acquisition. The AMT took no position and, unlike the semiconductor makers during the Fujitsu-Fairchild takeover battle, also refrained from behind-the-scenes lobbying against the acquisition. Unlike Fujitsu, Fanuc had not been accused of predatory dumping, and the domestic machine tool industry did not see the proposed acquisition as the harbinger of hostile foreign takeovers. The indifference also contrasts with the semiconductor industry's opposition to the Nippon Sanso takeover of Semi-Gas the previous year. In that case chipmakers feared becoming dependent on foreign equipment and materials. Machine toolmakers had already become dependent on foreign controllers. Whether Fanuc acquired Moore or not, this fact would not change. The political resistance to the Fanuc deal came from political officials, not industry actors. In general, foreign acquisitions did not arouse opposition from domestic firms. In fact, the most prominent takeover—the Makino takeover of LeBlond—was cited by an industry official as evidence of the *positive* contribution FDI could make to the American industry.[74]

Government Procurement Regulations

Since the 1970s around 5 percent of U.S. domestic machine tool consumption has been a result of direct government purchase, and significantly more (around 20–25%, according to various estimates) of indirect purchases through government contractors.[75] These averages mask wide variations across firms in the extent to which they rely on government business and, therefore, concern themselves with policies regulating government procurement. Still, the industry has long endeavored to reserve as much government business as possible for domestic firms. The issue of foreign ownership became entangled in this campaign as IFDI increased and the determination of what constituted a domestic or foreign purchase became more problematic. Traditionally, government procurement policies discouraged public purchases of imports in favor of domestically produced goods and services.[76] Following the 1979 Agreement on Government Procurement reached at the GATT Tokyo Round, the United States, like other countries, moved toward a reciprocity-based system. However, procurements for "national security purposes" were explicitly omitted by the new agreement. Whether this exception applied to machine tools became a matter of conflicting interpretations.

Concurrent with the machine tool industry's economic problems in the 1980s, domestic producers stepped up their lobbying efforts for policies designed to force the government to favor American firms when buying tools. In the summer of 1987 the NMTBA (along with representatives of the bearing and precision optics sectors) testified that the U.S. government was becoming increasingly dependent on foreign sources of militarily important supplies, with serious consequences for the nation's security.[77] This argument fell on sympathetic ears on Capitol Hill. Over the late 1980s Congress had repeatedly attached procurement restrictions to defense appropriation legislation. In 1987 Congress approved a provision barring the Defense Department from buying twenty-three different kinds of machine tools that were built outside the United States or Canada. The Pentagon opposed the measure, especially insofar as the rule might lead to tensions with other NATO countries, but the NMTBA lobbied strongly for the bill.[78] The industry also argued that contracts going to foreign companies should mandate that a major portion of the production be subcontracted to U.S. firms and that companies engaging in "unfair trade practices" such as dumping or falsifying the domestic content of their products should face suspension or debarment from DOD contracts.[79] Congress subsequently attached provisions to various defense authorization bills and trade laws that tightened these rules.[80]

What counted as an "American" product under these rules? Back in 1954 the government established uniform guidelines for government agencies that defined domestic goods as any end items manufactured in the United States made up of components whose aggregate cost is at least 50 percent domestic.[81] This standard provided some guidance but did not say what factors should be included as "costs" and did not distinguish between location and ownership. In practice, however, the Defense Department had long defined domestic and foreign in terms of where the production facilities were located.[82] The justification was that in times of war, sea-lanes might be disrupted and foreign countries might be unable or unwilling to supply the United States. Moreover, serious problems could develop with equipment purchased from foreign distributors without any domestic support capability.[83] Accordingly, U.S. producers, in putting forth demands for discriminatory government procurement policies, tailored their arguments to this interpretation. However, given the transplants' high content levels, foreign-owned subsidiaries were able to claim their tools were "American." U.S.-owned producers, who had traditionally attempted to preserve this market for themselves, had no answer to this assertion. If the Pentagon itself had determined that location was the relevant criterion, then the industry could hardly challenge the policy on security grounds. Without the security argument the domestic industry had no way to confront the transplants on this issue.

A few executives tried to make the argument that technological dependency on foreign-owned firms posed a security risk. "We would receive machine tools of a technology that foreigners would choose. Deliveries would be on a schedule that *they* would determine, and we could be cut off at *their* discretion," industry executives testified.[84] However, the machine tool industry was not as vertically integrated or internationally concentrated as microelectronics, so the industrial organization arguments against foreign ownership were much weaker. An AMT representative also argued that national ownership mattered insofar as R&D is carried out in the parent country. If, for national security reasons, there needed to be quick alterations of machine tool designs, it might not happen if the capability did not exist in the United States.[85] But the government could address this concern by providing incentives for firms (of any nationality) to conduct R&D at U.S. facilities. And in fact, in 1992 Congress passed amendments to the Defense Production Act requiring the DOD to take into consideration the location of R&D activity in determining whether transplants qualified as domestic sources.[86] In the end, U.S. producers could do little to challenge the gradual encroachment into this market by foreign-owned transplants.

R&D Consortia: ManTech and the NCMS

The U.S. machine tool industry had been participating in government-funded R&D programs long before semiconductor producers came up with a similar idea. In 1947 the Air Force had created the Manufacturing Technology (ManTech) program to develop and improve manufacturing technology that would aid the productivity, quality, competitiveness, and responsiveness of the U.S. defense industrial base.[87] In 1986 the Reagan administration boosted ManTech's funding and directed it to establish machine tool development as a primary "thrust area." ManTech, however, had always been much more oriented toward military production than Sematech.[88] The next year, the administration created the National Center for Manufacturing Science (NCMS) to conduct research on machine tool design and share its findings with member companies. Antitrust regulations were waived, and the Defense Department provided funding that was to be matched by industry contributions. About 180 manufacturers—toolmakers and their customers—participated in NCMS-sponsored activities.[89]

Like Sematech, the NCMS excluded foreign-owned firms from participating.[90] More precisely, participating firms had to be at least 50 percent owned by U.S. citizens and do at least 50 percent of their R&D and manufacturing within the United States. However, unlike the case with Sematech, this was the government's decision, not the industry's. The criteria were also notable in their incorporation of ownership into the definition of domestic production.[91]

In 1988 the NCMS teamed up with ManTech to develop a next-generation controller that would challenge Fanuc's dominant position within this product market. The larger goal—designated one of the consortium's highest priorities—was to reverse U.S. dependence on Japan for these components by leapfrogging Fanuc's technology.[92] The president of

NCMS, Edward Miller, claimed that Fanuc was not selling its most advanced technology in the United States: "If you look at it from a strategic or security viewpoint, the U.S. is at the whim of a non-U.S. organization. You can't run a smart machine without a good controller on it, so there should be a U.S. base for the technology. The Defense Department agrees with us."[93] But Fanuc produced its controllers in the United States. Therefore, unlike other ManTech projects, this program was premised on the importance of U.S. ownership, not just location. Furthermore, firms in the industry wholeheartedly supported NCMS's discriminatory membership rules. In these cases, unlike the other IFDI-related issues that arose, the security argument could be used to discriminate against local transplants. And when that happened, domestic firms were quick to adjust their own policy preferences accordingly.

THE ANTIFRICTION BEARING INDUSTRY

One of the important suppliers to the machine tool producers—the antifriction bearing industry—was in a position very similar to that of its toolmaking customers. Indeed, the two sectors share many characteristics: both are capital goods producers, face highly cyclical demand, require close coordination with customers, depend in large part on the auto industry, and play an important role in national defense.[94] Both also suffered declines in their economic fortunes during the 1980s.[95] As with machine tools and semiconductors, the Japanese strategy had been to focus on low-cost, high-volume production of standard products, aggressively expanding capacity and focusing on process technology improvement to boost productivity.

The industry's initial reaction to the penetration of Japanese competitors was also similar to that of the machine tool producers: it sought trade protection, though initially with little success. Still, as early as 1971, after the industry lost a bid for protection, the Department of Defense issued regulations requiring domestic sourcing of certain ball bearings used in defense production. Combined with persistent trade friction—a succession of escape clause, antidumping, and countervailing duty petitions—this requirement prompted foreign companies to relocate manufacturing facilities to the United States. By 1986 ten of the fifteen largest manufacturers of bearings in the United States were foreign-owned.[96]

As with machine toolmakers, the Production Profile hypothesis would predict that domestic bearing producers would support a more restrictive IFDI policy. The bearing industry was moderately global in orientation:

the major companies sold between a quarter and a third of their output in foreign markets, and almost all had at least sales subsidiaries overseas.[97] The Global Industry hypothesis would predict that firms with a more global position (which tended to be the larger producers) would not support restrictive policies. (In fact, contrary to these predictions, internationalized firms such as Torrington, a subsidiary of Ingersoll Rand, took the lead in advocating trade protection.)[98] And as with the toolmakers, there was little effort to link restrictive policies at home to liberalization abroad; therefore, the Strategic Investment hypothesis is less relevant in explaining this industry's policy preferences.

Much of the IFDI in this industry took the form of greenfield investment and therefore, as with machine tools, did not provoke much controversy. However, one acquisition sparked some debate. In 1985 Minebea Company of Tokyo, the largest Japanese ball bearing producer, offered to purchase New Hampshire Ball Bearings, Inc., for $110 million. As Minebea already controlled around a third of the U.S. ball bearing market (while maintaining a significant presence in miniature ball bearings), members of the Antifriction Bearing Manufacturing Association (AFBMA) expressed concerns that Minebea would dominate the miniature bearing market.[99] The Justice Department declined to challenge the deal on antitrust grounds. As for the Defense Department, the fact that no classified production technology was involved in the deal and that the company was not a sole supplier of components led officials to take a benign view of the acquisition.[100] At congressional hearings DOD officials emphasized that their prime concern was that an adequate production base be preserved on U.S. territory. And under the Pentagon's Buy American procurement rules, as long as production occurred in the United States, NHBB's output would still be classified as "domestic." A Pentagon official concluded, "I think the rules that we have for domestic origin will be enough. There is also authority under the Defense Production Act necessary to keep production here if that is necessary. There are remedies available to us."[101] Ultimately, despite some suspicion and hostility among member firms, the AFBMA did not testify at the Senate hearing on the bid and took no official position on whether the government should block the acquisition.[102] Without the support of the Defense Department on the security argument or of Justice on the antitrust issue, there were no legitimate grounds on which the domestic industry could block the takeover.

The industry continued to focus its demands on procurement and trade policy. A 1986 report by the DOD's Joint Logistics Commanders concluded that import penetration had decimated the bearing industry "to the point where it now sits upon a precipice ready to collapse." Unless the government acted to reduce the import share of the domestic market, this situation would "jeopardize the maintenance of a defense capability."[103] In the spring of 1988 the Pentagon, prodded by Congress, issued rules for its contractors to buy only U.S.-made bearings for the next three years. The regulations defined domestic bearings as including the output of foreign-owned subsidiaries in the United States, with some exceptions. The Pentagon's underlying goals were "to protect and strengthen the domestic industrial base for an industry critical to national security."[104] The AFBMA president acknowledged that the new regulations might induce foreign firms to relocate production but argued that U.S. firms would nonetheless benefit.[105] The domestic industry strongly supported the new rules and later spent a considerable amount of time and effort complaining to the government that the Pentagon was not doing enough to enforce them. Although only 17 percent of the domestic bearing market consisted of defense purchases (with dependence on defense work varying by firm within the industry), industry officials hoped the Pentagon's concern would add weight to a pending petition for import relief by reinforcing in the minds of policy makers the close association between bearings and national security.[106]

In July 1987 the AFBMA, following the machine toolmakers' example, had filed a Section 232 petition of its own, asking the government to reduce foreign imports of ball bearings from 65 percent to 32 percent of the U.S. market and of roller bearings from 40 percent to 18 percent.[107] An antidumping petition was filed by Torrington just two days after the new procurement regulations were published.[108] At the end of that year President Reagan rejected the 232 petition on the grounds that existing governmental programs were "adequate to bring the domestic industrial base into an acceptable posture for national security purposes." The industry's financial situation did not enter into the decision. Ironically, administration officials pointed to the concurrent dumping case and the DOD's Buy American directive in arguing that further trade protection was unnecessary.[109]

The dumping case proved more successful. Late in 1988 Commerce decided to award Torrington duties ranging as high as 212 percent (but averaging around 60 percent) on several types of bearings from nine different nations. Hardest hit were ball bearings from SKF (a Swedish company) and from FAG, Minebea, Koyo Seido, and Nippon Seiko (all Japanese). The ITC confirmed the Commerce finding, at least on ball bearings, cylindrical roller bearings, and spherical plain bearings, clearing the way for countervailing duties to be imposed according to the Commerce dumping margins.[110] The decision provoked an immediate outcry from manufacturing industries that imported bearings as inputs. Domestic users, including Caterpillar, Deere, GE, Westinghouse, and Black & Decker, organized an ad hoc coalition (American Manufacturers for Trade in Bearings) and lobbied hard against any restrictions, citing the likelihood of shortages, delivery delays, and double-digit price increases. According to the users, domestic manufacturers did not produce a sufficient volume of commodity ball bearings to satisfy industry consumers. Bearing manufacturers responded that the users had become accustomed to buying imports at artificially low prices. Furthermore, they asserted that they would invest in expanding production if they could be sure of getting "fair market value" for the output rather than having to compete against dumped imports.[111]

The Japanese industry reacted nonchalantly to the dumping decision, in part because the duties also targeted European companies.[112] Japanese firms maintained their dominant position in mass-produced bearings. But the major reason for their lack of anger was the ability of foreign bearing producers to circumvent the duties via relocating production. First, as in the steel industry, trade barriers against one set of countries led to transshipment through other countries not covered by the duties. Imports suddenly increased from Turkey, South Korea, and Poland. Torrington accused SKF, for instance, of switching its production to Argentina, Austria, and Spain to evade trade regulation and pointed out that Hong Kong, which did not have any bearing plants, increased its bearing exports to the United States by 255 percent, to $2 million in 1989.[113] Still, the ITC decided not to extend antidumping duties to other countries.

Second, just as had occurred in the machine tool industry under similar circumstances and for similar reasons, foreign producers accelerated the relocation of production to the United States. This investment consisted mostly of greenfield plants and the enlargement of already existing facilities.[114] For instance, a vice president at Koyo Seiko ascribed its $130 million investment in South Carolina to the desire to evade trade protection.[115] Minebea spent $30–40 million boosting production at NH Ball Bearings. SKF, after being hit with large dumping margins in a preliminary Commerce finding, shifted production of bearings to its Georgia plant while launching a $35 million expansion. NSK Corporation and NTN Bearing Corporation from Japan and GMN Georg Mueller from West Germany were among other companies to announce expansions after the antidumping duties. The duties were meant to help the U.S. industry modernize, and in fact capital investment in the United States rose in the late 1980s and early 1990s—but almost all of it was foreign-owned. This production ended up accounting for more than half of all bearings consumed domestically.

Initially, U.S. producers expressed a welcoming attitude toward IFDI. Torrington's president remarked, "If offshore companies want to build plants in the U.S., I think its great."[116] And like the machine toolmakers, the industry trade association allowed foreign-owned subsidiaries producing in the United States to become members.[117] But in the years that followed, as IFDI increased in magnitude, the industry's outlook shifted to outright hostility. In a number of governmental hearings industry leaders argued that foreign subsidiaries were engaged in simple assembly rather than component fabrication and that these subsidiaries were furthering the predatory trade strategies of their parent corporations.[118]

In attacking IFDI, the industry initially attempted to link the issue to national security. The director of AFBMA, Steve T. Martin (also from Torrington), testified: "Perhaps foreign ownership is not an important issue in other industries. However, in an industry with as great a role in defense as bearings play, I cannot believe that is a positive long-term development."[119] With this argument the industry was trying to persuade Congress, the Pentagon, the ITC, and any other government body that made decisions affecting the bearings industry to distinguish between foreign-owned and U.S.-owned firms. But like machine tool producers, the bearings makers ran into difficulty trying to apply the security argument (which had worked for trade protection and Buy American procurement regulations) to issues relating to IFDI. As long as foreign-owned firms maintained production in the United States, IFDI was not seen by government officials as posing the same kind of threat to the industrial defense base as imports. The DOD report that had persuaded the Pentagon to tighten its procurement rules also concluded that Buy American regulations would encourage IFDI and that this result was a positive thing, though the report noted that "domestic firms may not see this as a benefit."[120] This was an understatement, given the bitter criticism industry officials directed at this feature of the law.[121]

Although the domestic producers expressed their negative opinions about IFDI to Congress, they failed to convert these concerns into concrete political demands for stricter regulation of IFDI or foreign-owned firms. Instead, U.S. producers intensified their demands for strengthening the policies they had received before (trade protection, favorable procurement rules) even though these were the very policies that had encouraged IFDI in the first place. Yet they were also the only policies the bearings makers believed they had a realistic chance of obtaining, given the existing political institutions and norms. And indirectly, these policies could address the challenge of IFDI by strengthening domestic firms so they could compete against the foreign transplants.

CONCLUSION

In both the bearing and machine tool industries, domestically owned producers did not devote substantial resources to making IFDI or foreign ownership a major political issue. This lack of concern regarding IFDI is somewhat surprising from the perspective of both the Production Profile and the Global Industry hypotheses. Foreign (and especially Japanese) producers were increasing market share both in the United States and abroad. In response, American firms sought and eventually obtained trade protection in the form of VRAs, but overseas firms that could not export to the United States relocated production to maintain their market position. When local production by foreign-owned subsidiaries replaced imports, however, the national security argument became less useful politically for domestically owned firms. Scenarios of sea-lanes blocked or product access denied did not clearly apply when the production facilities were located within U.S. territory. Whatever domestic firms may have favored, government officials concerned with safeguarding national security perceived foreign-owned subsidiaries as superior to imports.[122]

Like the machine tool and bearing industries, semiconductor producers played the security card. But the chipmakers also emphasized the unfair trade aspect, which provided a legitimate fallback argument when their security case was weak. Furthermore, in the semiconductor case there was a more legitimate fear of dependency based on the vertical integration of the Japanese electronics industry. By contrast, Japanese machine toolmakers were less concentrated and less tightly linked to Japanese manufacturing customers. This meant that a foreign takeover of an American firm did not pose the same kind of threat in terms of access to advanced high-tech products. The weaker argument for IFDI restriction reduced the industry's chances of gaining allies among other industries or within the administration (and especially the defense establishment).

Most important, the institutional context differed for the semiconductor industry and the machine tool and bearing industries. In the semiconductor case national security concerns arose in controversies over foreign takeovers. Because the takeovers of the SM&E firms had to be approved by the Committee on Foreign Investment in the United States, it was natural for the U.S. firms to focus on the dangers of foreign ownership—that was precisely the issue CFIUS was designed to address. By contrast, the context was much less favorable for bringing up ownership issues regarding the machine tool and antifriction bearing industries. For procurement, the DOD had long used location criteria, and the tool industry itself had made location the guiding criterion for the VRAs. The chances of changing government policy from emphasizing location to emphasizing ownership were low, and industry actors did not put forth these kinds of demands.

Even if the institutional configuration were different, however, the experience of the machine tool and bearing industries suggests that when U.S. firms could make an argument that accorded with prevailing norms (and national security is the one widely acknowledged exception to liberalism), they could dramatically increase the chances of achieving their policy demands, thus reducing the relative costs of pursuing that political strategy. By contrast, when the national security argument no longer held, then even if the industry would still benefit economically from certain policies, the perceived chances of success were lower and hence the demands were less likely to be put forth.

SIX

A Strategic Response
Airlines and Telecommunication Services

Throughout the 1980s, service industries became increasingly central in international trade and investment. U.S. airlines and telecommunications firms faced some of the same problems in dealing with foreign competition as their manufacturing counterparts. However, because of several unique features of service industries, the nature of this threat differed significantly from the cases considered in previous chapters. Unlike manufacturing firms, which can export their products or invest directly, many service providers cannot serve foreign markets without establishing a local physical presence.[1] Thus it becomes virtually impossible to regulate trade without simultaneously addressing FDI. Also, many governments have regarded certain service industries as politically sensitive. In sectors such as shipping, air transport, telecommunications, and financial services, state officials have maintained that a strong indigenous industry is essential for preserving the state's sovereignty and national security. As a result, most countries have an extensive system of institutions and legislation to regulate service industries to a much greater degree than manufacturing activities. Although widespread privatization and deregulation have begun to erode this institutional edifice, the process has been slow and halting, especially with respect to opening national markets to foreign competition. In most cases, even after liberalization, states have remained heavily involved in managing service industries in order to promote national goals such as ensuring competition or fostering innovation.

As a result of these two features, service firms that want to serve foreign markets are caught in a bind. They need to locate "production" overseas in order to serve customers and gain foreign market share, but at the same time, they encounter an array of regulatory obstacles to establishing a physical presence in other countries because of the importance that host governments attach to these activities. Technological hurdles compound the problem in some industries, such as the two examined here. It can be economically prohibitive for even the largest and most global MNC to establish necessary infrastructures (e.g., airport hubs or telephone networks) for a stand-alone subsidiary to function. One way to avoid these startup costs would be through acquisitions, yet most governments (including that of the United States) have imposed restrictions on foreign takeovers. However, foreign competitors were still able to establish a foothold in the U.S. market, usually through some kind of international corporate alliance (ICA) with local producers.[2]

Although there has not been much analysis of the politics around these alliances, those who have noted the trend usually argue that ICAs will diminish the importance of corporate nationality. In formulating their commercial policy preferences, domestic firms should be less likely to support policies that will hurt their own alliance partners since their interests are now intertwined.[3] Alliances also provide domestic firms with an alternative response to some of the problems (shifting competitive advantage, risky investments in specialized assets, problems gaining foreign market access) that have traditionally led to protectionist demands. In the manufacturing industries, domestic firms, no matter how loudly they complained about imports and IFDI, almost never raised objections to the formation of international alliances.[4] They preferred foreign-owned firms to form alliances with local companies rather than export or invest directly.

In service industries, however, these alliances provoked political opposition from domestic producers. This reaction is somewhat surprising since U.S. firms in these sectors were very competitive internationally (a result of, among other things, the scale economy benefits derived from the large U.S. market and early deregulation that forced noncompetitive firms to adjust or exit the industry). Furthermore, most of the large, politically active firms in these industries had extensive international interests. On the basis of both the Production Profile and the Global Industry hypotheses, one would expect these service providers to put forth liberal policy demands. Their strong support for multilateral accords on liberalizing service trade testifies to an interest in fostering international openness. At the same time, American firms have faced exclusion from or discriminatory treatment in important foreign markets. The Strategic Investment hypothesis suggests domestic producers would therefore have an incentive to press their government to apply pressure (backed by the threat of contingent restrictions on the home market) in order to pry open foreign markets.[5] When foreign market entry occurs via alliances, domestic firms (at least the ones not participating in the alliance) may oppose these arrangements when the foreign producer's home market is not perceived as open or contestable. Not only do nonparticipating domestic firms receive no benefits from the alliance, but they are also put at a relative disadvantage to the participating domestic firm that now has sole access to its partner's market. The firm also can gain first-mover advantages in the foreign market, and for the excluded firms, it may not be possible to respond by forming ICAs of their own; in countries with former national champions there may be only one or two firms that would make attractive alliance partners.

Alliances in these industries almost invariably require government approval to ensure that the arrangements do not violate antitrust or other regulatory goals. Domestic actors can use this procedure as an opportunity to derail the proposed alliance. Even if the left-out firms cannot stop an alliance, they can demand concessions in the form of reciprocal market access as the price for government approval. Being shut out of foreign markets, then, can give even competitive and internationally oriented firms the motive to adopt conditionally nationalistic policy preferences regarding ICAs. In manufacturing industries, by contrast, foreign firms do not need to form alliances to gain access to the domestic market; they can export or (if there are trade barriers in place) invest directly. Foreign service producers often have neither option. Thus with services the host government's threat of preventing an alliance is a much more credible source of leverage for local firms. This explains the more frequent opposition to ICAs in these sectors despite the international orientation of the industries.

In the airline sector there was some muted opposition by domestic carriers to an attempt by Dutch-owned KLM to gain U.S. access through an alliance with Northwest Airlines. A U.S.-Netherlands open-skies agreement kept local firms from raising the reciprocity argument. Although the agreement itself did little for domestic airlines (they were more concerned with gaining access to Europe rather than just the Netherlands), there were no grounds for opposition. By contrast, when British Air attempted to invest in USAir, domestic producers responded with active antagonism. Existing U.S. regulations meant that the deal required administrative approval; local firms thus had a means to block the arrangement if they could mobilize politically. They could make a legitimate case regarding reciprocity and could put forth restrictive policy preferences by tailoring them to address the antitrust implications of an alliance. These objections, however, often could be addressed by mandating certain pro-competitive actions, so they were not always an effective means to block international deals.

In telecommunication services as well, local firms used the reciprocity argument to fight against approval for international alliances. This strategy depended on the extent to which foreign markets were closed. U.S. producers had a better case against France and Germany than they did against Britain (whose telecom market was more open). Over time, however, more and more countries began liberalizing, whether via EU initiatives or multilateral agreements such as the 1997 World Trade Organization (WTO) telecoms agreement. As a result, it became increasingly difficult for domestic firms to find a means to resist the encroachment of foreign providers. Opposition to international alliances subsequently diminished over time.

In sum, the nature of trade in services—the blurring between trade and FDI as well as the dense regulatory structures governing these sectors—leads to the proliferation of international alliances. In turn, these alliances often face domestic political opposition from other local firms. This opposition is most likely to materialize when access to foreign markets is restricted (providing a motive for restrictive policy preferences) and when foreign firms have no other option but to form an ICA to gain domestic market share (providing the opportunity for local firms to block market access completely). The root of the difference between the policy preferences of manufacturing industries and service industries toward corporate alliances has less to do with economic variables such as competitiveness, export orientation, or scale economies. Instead, the main difference lies in the political context and the regulatory legacy of sectoral prohibitions on FDI at home and abroad.

THE AIRLINE INDUSTRY

For a foreign airline to gain access to the U.S. market is no simple matter.[6] International flights require bilateral agreements between the governments whose territory the trip connects. Some kinds of services are simply prohibited; a foreign airline cannot, for instance, pick up passengers in one U.S. city and transport them to another U.S. city (a practice called *cabotage*). Nor can companies evade these restrictions by becoming multinational; foreign direct investment in the industry is severely restricted.[7] These regulations, originally adopted to support the fledgling domestic industry as well as to protect perceived national security goals, forced foreign-owned companies that wanted access to the U.S. market to ally with domestic carriers.[8]

U.S.-based carriers also faced obstacles in seeking market access abroad. However, the U.S. had "open skies" agreements with certain governments, allowing each country's carriers to fly anywhere in the other's territory. Even then domestic carriers ran into difficulty trying to penetrate foreign markets, either for cost reasons (e.g., there often was not enough business to justify establishing local hubs) or space constraints (e.g., limits on capacity at airports such as Heathrow outside London).[9] U.S. firms found it difficult to gain foreign market share on their own, and they were unable to overcome these obstacles through FDI. As a result, alliances with foreign carriers were essential to establish an international presence. As soon as one domestic company formed an ICA, pressure increased on the rest of the industry to follow suit, since the allied carrier now had a competitive advantage over its domestic competitors through its ability to "code-share" with its foreign partner.[10] The number of potential partners in any given country was limited since most nations had only one or two major airlines.

Firms in the airline industry thus had both the motive and the opportunity to politicize alliances. They wanted expanded access to overseas markets, and since alliances were essential for domestic market access, they could ask Washington to link approval to foreign liberalization. Despite the fact that every major U.S. airline sought to develop a global presence and to form alliances with foreign carriers, there was nevertheless significant domestic industry opposition to attempts by foreign firms to gain access to the U.S. market through ICAs. The extent of opposition varied since the problem of overseas market access was more acute with some countries than others. And firms that opposed one alliance suddenly changed their minds when they found partners of their own. Still, although the industry did not act monolithically, the overall level of political conflict in this sector was high. There was some disagreement among domestic firms over tactics, however; the larger firms tried to use protectionist regulations as a crowbar to open foreign markets whereas many of the smaller (weaker) firms welcomed foreign ventures but still favored restrictive laws requiring foreign firms to link with (and thereby provide resources to) U.S. firms. Usually, less competitive firms within an industry want to keep foreign competition out; in this case, however, foreign competition could come only in the form of an alliance, and foreign carriers often preferred to ally with weaker domestic companies (over which they could wield more control). Thus, weak firms welcomed foreign market penetration. By contrast, strong airlines such as American worried that relaxing U.S. rules on FDI would end up allowing foreign capital to keep otherwise failing carriers alive.[11]

In 1989 the first major international alliance, between KLM Royal Dutch Airlines and NWA, Inc. (the parent of Northwest Airlines), ran into immediate trouble. Although KLM's investment did not exceed the statutory limit, Department of Transportation secretary Samuel K. Skinner suspected that NWA would be beholden to KLM, given the size of the (nonvoting) equity stake, the favorable price the Dutch company was paying, and Northwest's financial vulnerability.[12] He subsequently required the investment group that was organizing the takeover to reduce the stake held by KLM or risk having its U.S. operating license revoked. Skinner also suggested that the absence of open markets abroad influenced his decision, asserting that although he believed in the principle of open investment, "to extol the virtues of a free market for the flow of airline capital without reference to the highly restricted market in which international airlines operate would be to ignore reality."[13]

Over the next few years, however, the situation changed. First, the domestic industry suffered a crushing downturn. Rising oil prices in the wake of Iraq's invasion of Kuwait, combined with recession-induced declines in air traffic, resulted in a $2 billion loss in 1990 for major carriers.[14] Eastern, Continental, and Pan Am were operating under bankruptcy protection, putting additional price pressure on the other carriers. As a result, industry and government officials began to consider foreign carriers a valuable source of badly needed capital.[15] Skinner boosted the amount of nonvoting equity in a U.S. company that a foreign airline could own. A commission set up to study the industry's problems recommended raising the legal limits on foreign control of domestic airlines to 49 percent of voting stock, as long as the source country gave reciprocal rights to U.S. investors. Finally, the DOT also rescinded the 1989 directive that forced KLM to sell a big chunk of NWA. Shortly thereafter the two companies decided to intensify their alliance by combining their operations as though they had merged while formally retaining separate legal identities.[16]

The prohibition on FDI still stood; KLM could not buy Northwest, so in order to coordinate fares, scheduling, seat assignments, and promotions without being accused of fixing prices or allocating market share, the two companies requested antitrust immunity from the government. The other domestic airlines were disadvantaged by this deal, since Northwest could now book passengers to any of the eighty European and North African destinations KLM served from Amsterdam without passengers having (at least officially) to change airlines. Other domestic firms expressed their opposition to the government's granting antitrust immunity.[17] However, any nascent opposition on the part of other firms fizzled out after an open-skies agreement was concluded with the Netherlands in September 1992. The market access issue no longer justified the domestic firms' opposition to government approval of the deal. Some protested that the right to fly anywhere in the Netherlands was not a fair exchange for KLM's access to the huge U.S. market. But policy makers argued that they could use the agreement in order to pressure other European countries to sign similar accords. Overall, the active opposition to KLM's actions was negligible, and the arrangement with Northwest was quickly approved.

The situation was very different in July 1992, when British Air (BA) announced a $750 million investment in USAir. BA executives admitted that they would have preferred simply to acquire USAir outright had U.S. law allowed it.[18] Even the more limited investment still required government approval.[19] Initially, DOT secretary Andrew Card indicated he would approve the deal unconditionally, issuing a statement that "such transactions hold the promise of competitive benefits to carriers, to their customers, and to the communities they serve. The world's airline industry is clearly moving in the direction of cross-border alliances."[20] With the Bush administration's pro-market biases and the obvious political benefits of preserving forty-six thousand jobs, the deal appeared to be headed for easy approval.[21] Immediately, however, the rest of the domestic industry sprang into action; in late September, United chairman Steve Wolf called the chairman of Federal Express to propose forming a coalition with Delta and American Airlines to fight the deal. The result was, as the *New York Times* put it, "one of the most heated battles in aviation history."[22]

In light of the industry's financial difficulties, a consensus among most industry observers held that foreign capital should be welcomed. Therefore, BA and USAir tried to highlight this aspect and keep it separate from the reciprocity issue (the absence of an open-skies agreement with Britain), arguing that the investment should be seen as a "straightforward commercial transaction" between two private companies. Had the deal been judged on this criterion, it would most likely have been approved.[23] USAir mobilized its employees, as well as business and government officials from the regions in which the airline maintained hubs. Thousands of demonstrating employees holding signs favoring the deal met the Bush campaign in Pennsylvania and North Carolina. The company put a form letter into its e-mail system, urging employees to send messages to Capitol Hill and to the Transportation Department. The message of all this activity was that without the investment, tens of thousands of American jobs would be lost.[24] Opponents of the deal, USAir charged, simply wanted to weaken a competitor.[25]

By contrast, the opposition emphasized the reciprocity issue, organizing massive counterdemonstrations and mail campaigns that claimed allowing the deal would end up *costing* American jobs. A BA-USAir alliance would dominate transatlantic traffic because of its ability to code-share while using monopoly profits to lower prices on more competitive routes.[26] U.S. carriers estimated that they would lose more than $500 million worth of business a year, and American's chief, Robert Crandall, went so far as to threaten that his airline would be forced to sell itself to a foreign company if the deal was approved without significant concessions from London.[27] Opponents focused their lobbying efforts mostly on the executive branch (via a mail campaign to the DOT as well as direct communications from the participating CEOs to the president), and they also made sure to meet with the other presidential candidates. This strategy paid off when Ross Perot condemned the deal in a nationally televised debate and a week later candidate Bill Clinton remarked in an interview on CNN that he had "real problems" with the deal, given the lack of access to the British market.[28]

Ultimately, the DOT decided to reject the deal in December 1992. Immediately after the Clinton administration was sworn in, however, the British company constructed a less ambitious deal, keeping its ownership below levels that would require Washington's approval (though it would still need DOT's authorization for wet-leasing and code-sharing provisions).[29] The other domestic carriers were not placated; they argued that the $300 million investment, combined with BA's announced plans for future investments, was merely a repackaged version of the original deal "on the installment plan." But this time there was little they could do to stop the initial equity purchase, beyond calls for a public investigation and petitions with the DOT opposing the deal.[30] Unfortunately for the opponents, BA's reduced investment and relinquishment of veto power over major USAir decisions meant that control was no longer an issue; thus there was no legal impediment to the restructured deal. The other problem for the opponents was that the BA-USAir code-sharing arrangement fully complied with a 1991 United States–United Kingdom bilateral agreement (known as "Bermuda 2"). AA and Delta called on Washington simply to renounce Bermuda 2 and block any foreign investment until U.S. carriers received more rights to overseas routes; the other airlines, however, were reluctant to support such a drastic approach.[31] Nor did antitrust laws help in this case; as one AA executive ruefully remarked, "[The deal] is great from the consumer standpoint so long as it's OK to cede control of the global airline system to foreign carriers."[32] The institutional context mattered; opponents, however much they argued that approval was "naive and shortsighted," could no longer latch onto existing regulations to block the deal.[33] Clinton's secretary of transportation, Federico Peña, recommended approving the remainder of the deal in March 1993 on the technical grounds that the investment did not impair USAir's "citizenship." However, he announced he would not approve any additional investment unless and until Britain opened its market further.[34]

Given the vehemence of AA's opposition to British Air's efforts to enter the U.S. market, some found it surprising that in June 1996 American requested antitrust immunity for a strategic alliance with BA in which the two airlines would merge just about everything except equity.[35] AA claimed it was simply responding to the imperatives of globalization; indeed, referring to the grant of antitrust immunity to other alliances (Northwest-KLM, United-Lufthansa, and Delta-Swissair-Sabena-Austrian), one AA executive argued; "We are the last in line."[36] The company's first choice had been to expand its international service on its own with Washington using access to the U.S. market as a bargaining chip in order to press for British liberalization (specifically, expanding access to Heathrow). As Crandall explained, "I would prefer to compete independently with all the world's other airlines. We had that debate. We've lost that debate. Governments, after all, make the rules by which we all play. . . . We understand the new rules and we will play by them."[37]

Nevertheless, the announcement set off yet another political battle. In this case, competing firms pressed Washington to reject the alliance flat out. This position was presented in testimony at congressional hearings held in April 1997 and in a letter to President Clinton from the chief executives of Continental, Northwest, TWA, Delta, Tower Air, and United.[38] The letter complained about "significant barriers to competition that would exist with the BA-AA alliance even under a liberal air services agreement with the U.K.," given the size and strength of the two airlines. The executives asked Clinton to put off open-skies talks with the British until after the Departments of Justice and Transportation had finished studying the effect of alliances on competition.[39] The market-access question, in this case, went beyond open skies and centered more specifically on access to Heathrow. In fact, access and antitrust concerns overlapped since ensuring that effective competition on transatlantic flights would restrain a potential BA-AA monopoly required Heathrow access for other U.S. carriers.[40] AA, by contrast, argued that when the government considered the antitrust implications of the alliance, it should look at the projected market share of BA-AA in the hypothetical context of a liberalized transatlantic market under an open-skies agreement. In such a case the alliance would look much less imposing. "There are a number of carriers who are ready to enter this market once the shackles come off," an AA executive testified.[41] Ultimately, approval was made contingent on both an open-skies agreement and other airlines receiving a certain number of slots at Heathrow.

In sum, even in an industry in which domestic firms were competitive and pursued global strategies, attempts by foreign-owned firms to establish a presence in the United States faced political opposition. Problems with securing market access abroad led U.S. carriers to favor excluding foreign firms from the domestic market absent reciprocal treatment; when this problem was resolved (as with the Netherlands), there was no longer an acceptable argument for blocking international alliances. Antitrust violations were one potential avenue for opposition, but these concerns could be addressed by attaching various conditions to the partnerships. At the same time, foreign firms had no choice but to enter into alliances in order to gain U.S. market access; thus, domestic carriers could try to block these deals without worrying that foreign firms would unilaterally seek alternate ways to serve U.S. passengers. Domestic regulatory structures gave U.S. carriers the tools they needed to fight against foreign competition but also imposed limits on how far the domestic producers could go in their opposition.

THE TELECOMMUNICATION SERVICES INDUSTRY

Among telecommunications industry executives there was a conventional wisdom that firms had to become global to survive. The reasons included both scale economies and the perception that multinational clients preferred dealing with a single vendor that could offer a full array of services seamlessly linking telephone and computer networks between offices on different continents. Like the airlines, however, firms chose for the most part to pursue an international alliance strategy to extending their global operations. The reasons, again, were both technological and political.[42] First, investment costs were huge, and technology life cycles were short.[43] Obtaining market access through the existing network infrastructure required cooperation from local producers.[44] Acquiring local firms would allow companies to avoid these problems; however, until the late 1990s virtually every country in the world restricted the activities of foreign-owned producers within its territory. In the United States foreign companies were prohibited from owning more than 25 percent of an American common carrier.[45] The original rationale for these laws—preventing hostile countries from spreading propaganda or impairing the nation's ability to mobilize communications facilities in wartime—may not have convinced as many policy makers or experts as it once had.[46] Nonetheless, their existence forced firms to pursue joint ventures in order to gain market access.[47]

American firms, partly thanks to early deregulation, were extremely competitive internationally compared with the state-owned or sheltered providers in many other countries.[48] U.S. producers, then, had incentive and the competitive advantages to become globalized, but they were thwarted by foreign market barriers. U.S. telecom firms repeatedly expressed frustration at their inability to gain access to foreign markets, especially in Europe.[49] Of course, the U.S. market was closed as well. These home restrictions, combined with the size and desirability of the American market (where almost half the world's MNCs were headquartered) gave U.S. companies significant bargaining leverage in their efforts to gain foreign market access. Whereas the Production Profile hypothesis predicts liberal policy preferences, the Strategic Investment hypothesis predicts that domestic firms would support a policy of conditional closure when foreign competition came from countries with more restricted domestic markets.

In the summer of 1993 MCI, the second largest American long-distance provider, announced it would sell 20 percent of its equity—the maximum allowed by U.S. law—to British Telecom (BT) for $4.3 billion.[50] AT&T had opposed an earlier application by BT to the Federal Communications Commission seeking a common carrier license in the United States.[51] The new alliance represented a different approach that AT&T could only find even more objectionable; not only would BT now gain access to the U.S. market, but the capital from BT would strengthen AT&T's strongest domestic competitor, MCI, in its attempts to expand into new ventures such as local exchange or cellular communication.[52] Sprint also came out against the proposed investment.[53] But although AT&T and Sprint were unhappy about the deal, they found there was little basis on which they could oppose it. Every effort was made by MCI and BT to conform to FCC regulations regarding foreign ownership. The two companies emphasized that MCI would maintain its independence: an integrated management would have headquarters in both countries with joint chairmen alternating in presiding over board meetings on their home soil. Although BT would receive "investment protection" that would give it some veto power over certain business decisions by MCI, the deal also contained numerous safeguards to ensure that public shareholders continued to wield effective control.[54] In the end, AT&T and Sprint dropped their opposition to the investment, and the FCC approved the deal in July 1994.[55]

It was no easy task to persuade the government to block proposed investments or alliances once they had been announced, as long as the deal conformed to U.S. statute. AT&T therefore asked the FCC to establish a general policy requiring reciprocal access in exchange for permission for foreign-owned firms to operate in the United States.[56] In November 1995, in a striking departure from the national treatment principle, the FCC decided to adopt this approach.[57] Approval for foreign-owned firms to enter the U.S. market through alliances would now be conditioned on whether there were any legal or de facto impediments to U.S. firms' ability to compete in the foreign firm's home market. The so-called effective competitive opportunity analysis would take into account (1) legal barriers to entry, (2) interconnection factors, (3) safeguards against anticompetitive practices, and (4) the country's regulatory framework. The FCC also would consider various "public interest" factors such as whether the foreign carrier was government-owned, whether the country in question was in the process of liberalizing its market, how the alliance would promote competition in global markets, and any national security implications.[58]

Subsequently, in November 1996, BT offered to buy the remaining portion of MCI for around $22 billion, with the newly combined company to adopt the Concert name. Although there was some attempt to maintain the separate identities of each firm (for instance, BT and MCI would operate under their original names in their home markets), the deal clearly challenged U.S. ownership restrictions and would therefore require the FCC to waive the statutory restrictions. BT had reason to hope the government would approve the deal. In a 1995 speech Vice President Al Gore had proposed opening foreign investment in U.S. telecom services "for companies of all countries who have opened their own markets."[59]

AT&T expressed immediate opposition to the BT-MCI deal.[60] But AT&T did not have a strong case, certainly nowhere near as compelling as that of the domestic airline firms that had opposed British Air's investment in USAir. In telecoms, unlike in aviation, Britain was among the most liberal markets in the world. And in the years since the initial BT investment in MCI, the British government had continued to liberalize. It was difficult for AT&T to make a convincing argument for blocking the BT-MCI deal on the basis of reciprocity when, in fact, AT&T was already a full competitor to BT in the British market. Nor did Britain have restrictions on foreign ownership (though a full takeover of BT would be impossible because the remaining shares were owned by the British government).[61] U.S. companies (specifically, the regional Bells and cable companies) were able to offer local telephone service in Britain through cable wires, which was not the case in the United States.[62]

AT&T had to make a more subtle argument about the practical obstacles to increasing market share in Britain: "The fact that the English market is more open than others," explained the company's vice president for law and policy, "shouldn't be confused for openness."[63] AT&T complained, "BT controls 90% of telephone numbers in the U.K. They operate in a market that is not open and competitive by the standards by which we judge competition in the United States."[64] U.K. callers faced difficulty connecting with the carrier of their choice, and AT&T had to rely on BT facilities.[65] Finally, AT&T claimed that approving the deal would send the wrong message to the rest of Europe; that is, governments would infer that privatization and liberalization would be sufficient to win U.S. approval for entry into the U.S. market, whereas AT&T wanted foreign governments to take more proactive steps to facilitate the entrance of foreign firms, such as splitting privatized companies into separate long-distance and local businesses (as had occurred in the United States with AT&T).[66] But these demands went beyond the scope of what U.S. officials felt was an appropriate standard of reciprocity. MCI and BT filed an application to the FCC documenting the compliance of the United Kingdom with every element of the effective competitive opportunities standard.[67] It appeared increasingly likely the deal would be approved.

AT&T tried to raise the antitrust issue but found few allies.[68] Consumer groups hailed the merger as a way to boost domestic competition. The regional Bells also supported the deal; they saw an opportunity to convince regulators that long-distance companies were strong and therefore did not need Washington's backing in disputes over compensation for connection to local networks. AT&T resigned itself to the reality that the deal would be allowed and instead tried to win some concessions from the British.[69] After the Justice Department approved the deal (subject to some minor safeguards), AT&T reluctantly decided to drop its challenge, conceding that in the period since November, when the deal was announced, Britain had made "significant progress" in opening its market.[70]

At the same time that the BT-MCI merger was being debated, another transatlantic battle was heating up. In the summer of 1994 Deutsche Telekom (DT) and France Telecom (FT) agreed to purchase 20 percent of Sprint for $4.2 billion in order to form a global joint venture, dubbed Phoenix (later renamed Global One). This situation was very different from the BT-MCI deal; DT and FT were both government-controlled monopolies. Both of their home markets were significantly less open than the United Kingdom's. But at the same time, both governments had pledged to accelerate their steps toward liberalizing domestic telecom markets to comply with the European Commission's deregulation deadline of January 1, 1998. Nonetheless, AT&T immediately challenged the alliance, arguing that approval should be linked to French and German market access.[71] Although Sprint argued that the venture would help quicken the pace of liberalization, AT&T wanted liberalization first: "The price of entry has to be the reality of competition, not just the promise of it," a spokesperson said.[72] In its filing with the FCC, AT&T emphasized the monopoly status of DT and FT and the resulting differences between this deal and the Concert arrangement, which the agency had already approved. Subsequently, MCI and BT joined AT&T in opposing the plan (leading Sprint executives to complain that "AT&T and MCI don't want the competition from us against their ventures").[73] The Justice Department eventually approved the deal, as did the Committee on Foreign Investment in the United States;

opponents then focused their efforts on the FCC, whose chairman, Reed Hundt, had expressed skepticism about the alliance.[74]

It was during this battle that AT&T pushed for the establishment of the new FCC reciprocity standard just discussed. MCI, having already received approval for its venture with BT, expressed support for the new FCC policy.[75] Sprint voiced sympathy for the general goals of the new policy but argued that the rule exceeded the FCC's legal authority (Sprint threatened to sue the agency), that it was "ill-timed," and that it could lead to a backlash in which foreign governments would fear the appearance of buckling to U.S. pressure.[76] Once the new reciprocity plan was adopted, however, the FCC used it as a benchmark for the Sprint decision (which by that point had already been pending for a year and a half).[77] Sprint need not have worried; in the end, the FCC held that although the French and German telecommunications markets did not allow for effective competitive opportunities for U.S. companies, two public-interest factors counterbalanced the lack of reciprocity. First, both European governments had made commitments to open their telecom services and infrastructure markets by January 1, 1998. Second, the injection of capital, by boosting the position of Sprint, would increase domestic competition within the United States, and the establishment of Global One would boost international competition.[78] Therefore, the FCC decided to approve the sale, with strict conditions to ensure that the alliance did not exploit the current monopoly position in Germany and France and that the promised liberalization actually occurred. There was not much more the opponents could do; MCI criticized the FCC for making the "wrong decision," and AT&T urged "vigorous oversight and enforcement" of the conditions.[79] Beyond that, it was a done deal, and the next month Sprint and its European partners launched their Global One joint venture.

Finally, in the summer of 2000 Deutsche Telekom offered $50.7 billion to acquire VoiceStream Wireless Corporation. DT had earlier considered buying up the rest of Sprint but backed down in the face of intense opposition in Congress and veiled hints that the FCC would frown on such a merger. VoiceStream was a smaller target, and this acquisition promised to provoke less conflict. But debate soon erupted on Capitol Hill over the issue of the German government's remaining ownership shares of DT (amounting to 58% though falling to 40% if the deal were to go through). A bipartisan group of thirty senators urged the FCC to block purchases by foreign companies that were more than 25 percent state-owned, and legislation to that effect was introduced in both houses of Congress.[80] Such actions would have almost certainly contravened U.S. commitments made in the 1997 GATS (General Agreement on Trade in Services) telecom agreement and would have subjected the United States to WTO suits and retaliatory actions. Congressional aides claimed that many local firms had privately expressed their support for stopping the VoiceStream acquisition, but few came out publicly for legislation that would do so.[81] The aides attributed this reluctance to corporate interests in expanding abroad and in attracting investment in their own companies.[82] The Chamber of Commerce opposed both bills, and the Information Technology Association of America claimed the proposed legislation would "hamstring the robustness of the digital economy."[83] Verizon and SBC Communications were said to be "sympathetic" but publicly stated that "defensive legislation isn't the right answer."[84] Although the global ambitions of domestically based firms do not always inhibit their opposition to IFDI, in this case the chance of successfully blocking the deal was slight. The WTO agreement had shifted the political climate and precluded reliance on the market-access argument to block the deal. By choosing VoiceStream instead of Sprint, DT also made it much more difficult to use antitrust tools to stop the investment. The only viable argument was the large government stake in DT, and addressing this point, Germany pledged to reduce its holdings. With little perceived chance of success domestic firms did not jump on this bandwagon, and as a result the opposition efforts fizzled out. Ultimately, VoiceStream's local senator, Slade Gorton (R-Wash.), persuaded Senate Majority Leader Trent Lott to drop his support for the legislative restrictions.[85] Subsequently, the FCC approved the deal, and in the spring of 2001 CFIUS approved it as well.

Overall, the telecommunications sector presents a somewhat mixed picture. Despite the global orientation of domestically based telecom firms, there was considerable opposition from U.S. firms to efforts by foreign companies to form international alliances in order to penetrate the American market. However, the domestic resistance to telecommunications alliances was not as forceful as in the airline industry. In the latter sector, foreign market access was more clearly a problem. Global progress in liberalizing telecommunications led to a diminishing incentive for domestic firms in that industry to push for reciprocity policies. For instance, the effort against BT-MCI was hindered by the difficult case AT&T had to make in demonstrating that the British market was less open than it appeared. The French and German markets were clearly more restricted, but both governments had made credible commitments to liberalize, and FCC officials liked the idea of using Sprint as a watchdog to make sure DT and FT did not try to slow down the liberalization process.[86] In this situation potentially hostile domestic companies chose not to devote significant resources to a futile political battle. The WTO telecom pact of early 1997 made the whole reciprocity issue much less relevant in any case and in particular led domestic firms to mute their response to DT's acquisition of VoiceStream. International alliances provoked opposition from domestic producers, but as the 1990s drew to a close, the opposition faded away.

CONCLUSION: SERVICE AND MANUFACTURING INDUSTRIES

Service industries such as the ones examined in this chapter are among the most competitive sectors in the United States. These industries have been active in pushing the United States to negotiate rules governing trade in services to facilitate overseas expansion. For these reasons, it is surprising (at least from the perspective of the Production Profile and Global Industry hypotheses) that domestic firms, to varying degrees, lobbied the government to block foreign firms from gaining access to the American market. It is even more surprising that in fighting foreign competition, domestic producers extended their policy preferences to international corporate alliances. The conventional wisdom sees ICAs as diminishing protectionist pressures. Indeed, though globalized manufacturing firms have supported import barriers and discriminatory FDI policies, they have not raised any objections to international alliances. By contrast, globalized firms in the service sector have. Because of both the nature of trade in services (the need for a local presence) and the sector-specific regulatory structures in even relatively liberal countries, alliances are often a sine qua non for service providers to gain market access. This situation gives domestic service firms more leverage than their cohorts in manufacturing, for they can use the prospect of alliances to wring concessions out of foreign countries. In manufacturing industries, overseas manufacturing firms have a number of options (e.g., exports, greenfield investment, acquisitions), not all of which can easily be foreclosed by domestic producers. Compared with these other options, domestic firms actually prefer alliances, so it would make little sense to throw obstacles in their way.

In the service industries the extent to which firms adopted restrictive policy preferences varied. In the airline and telecommunications sectors opposition to international alliances arose when the country in which the foreign firm was headquartered did not allow for reciprocal market access. That was the case with British Air as well as the French and German telecommunication providers. Over time, many countries have liberalized these sectors, whether through unilateral actions on the part of formerly closed countries, bilateral agreements (open-skies treaties), regional agreements (the EU's January 1, 1998, telecom initiative), or multilateral agreements (the WTO telecom treaty). This liberalization removes the incentive for contingently protectionist policy preferences.[87] To the extent that such efforts contribute to the United States' reform of its own discriminatory institutions (as was the case with telecommunications), domestic producers will lose not only the motive but also the opportunity to use existing regulations for the purpose of inhibiting foreign competition. In the future, if domestic firms ever find themselves in a disadvantageous position, it will be too late to seek government assistance in keeping out foreign competition. And with a different political context, firms will formulate different policy preferences. In this case, then, political institutions changed over time, and that change affected societal policy preferences. The changes made it more difficult for domestic firms to seek discriminatory policies, but by fostering global liberalization, the changes also reduced the incentive for these firms to seek such policies in the first place.

SEVEN

Political Variables and Policy Preferences

Industry actors in the United States have responded to incoming foreign direct investment in some unexpected ways. Domestically based producers who had expended enormous efforts and political capital fighting for trade protection did not seek comparable restrictions on IFDI, despite the fact that this form of competition posed just as great a threat to their market share and profitability (if not greater). At the same time, many U.S. companies did support tighter regulations and deviations from national treatment on a number of issues relating to IFDI and foreign-owned firms. This was true regardless of their own extensive overseas interests in the form of exports, foreign subsidiaries, outsourcing arrangements, and international corporate alliances. Barriers to foreign market access sometimes motivated firms to adopt contingently restrictive policy preferences. At other times, however, firms refrained from putting forth these kinds of demands, although they had economic incentives to do so. Thus the policy preferences of firms varied not only between trade and IFDI policy but also with respect just to IFDI policy—across industries, among firms within industries, over time, and even across different IFDI-related issues.

The three hypotheses derived from producers' economic interests have difficulty accounting for these differing reactions. Unquestionably, producer positions on foreign economic policy issues were very much affected by economic incentives. But the experience of U.S. industries during the 1980s and 1990s as they faced the challenge of IFDI demonstrates that these economic factors alone cannot explain policy preferences. Firms usually have a number of different, sometimes conflicting, interests; as a result, hypotheses derived from these interests often lead to conflicting predictions for policy preferences. Will producers demand restrictive policies in order to protect the rents they have obtained through trade protection, or will they instead focus on the dangers such politics might pose to their own global activities and thus support more liberal IFDI policies, or will they seek something else altogether? There is no theoretical reason to expect one of these incentives to dominate the others, and the case studies accordingly reflect the inconsistent and ambiguous corporate responses to IFDI.

The domestic political environment shapes the translation of an actor's economic interests into policy preferences. In particular, domestic political structures—institutions and prevailing ideas—make up an essential part of the explanation for policy preferences. With a number of policy tools to choose from that would further their underlying goals, firms are most likely to adopt positions that are compatible with existing political structures because these positions are most likely to gain acceptance from government officials. Although many scholars accept the importance of political structures in shaping policy outcomes, few have recognized their important role in affecting policy preferences. The effect goes beyond simply influencing what tactics an actor uses to lobby for a policy; rather, the basic positions producers take—support for an open policy, for restrictions, for reciprocity, or for something else—result from a combination of economic and political incentives. This argument has wider implications for our understanding of foreign economic policy and international political economy.

VARIATIONS IN THE POLICY PREFERENCES OF DOMESTIC PRODUCERS

The case studies revealed that the policy preferences of domestic producers varied across several different dimensions. Aside from the comparison between trade policy and IFDI policy demands, there were also differences across industries. Within a single industry, variation existed among firms, over time, and across issue areas.

Trade vs. IFDI

From the standpoint of the national interest, there are several reasons to prefer IFDI to imports: employment creation, tax revenue, technology spillovers, and so forth. Thus the government's support of a more liberal IFDI policy than trade policy is understandable. One study emphasizes policy makers' belief that anything undermining foreign investor confidence would lead to a slowdown or reversal of foreign (direct and indirect) investment into the United States, adversely affecting interest rates and exchange rates.[1] Another early analysis of IFDI in the United States highlights the "ideological consonance" of a liberal policy with the criteria that were important to the policy makers. The authors point out IFDI's visible effect on domestic employment and the tax base, policy makers' commitment to an open international economy, their fear of provoking economic conflicts among Western countries, and finally the fact that the groups that gained from IFDI were concentrated and aware of the issue.[2] For all the argument over IFDI during the 1980s and 1990s, the issue ended up fading quickly from public attention. As one author concludes, "The lack of perceived problems for U.S. political and economic systems, the dominant liberal ideology, and the political significance of the large multinational corporations in U.S politics has made U.S. leadership more interested in promoting than controlling foreign investment."[3]

Indeed, there were many reasons for the government to adopt a liberal IFDI policy. But when one shifts the analysis to the demand side, and specifically to the reaction of those industries directly affected by IFDI, the variables just mentioned become much less important. Societal groups care about their own returns more than they do about the country's ability to attract foreign capital to fund the trade deficit or about the danger of causing foreign-policy problems among Western allies. The losers from IFDI can identify themselves as surely as the gainers. In fact, the main gainers from greenfield IFDI—workers at foreign-owned plants—did not even know who they were until after the investment had been made whereas the losers (domestic firms) could see the threat very clearly. As for ideological "consonance," business leaders for the most part clearly shared the prevailing liberal ideology. In principle, they all championed the freedom to relocate production or to buy and sell corporate assets. But in virtually every case these executives argued that there were unique circumstances—unfair trading or purchasing practices, lack of reciprocity, security considerations, and so on—requiring a policy decision that deviated from openness or national treatment.

Thus despite the incentives for policy makers to adopt liberal policies, the absence of opposition to IFDI from affected industry actors remains puzzling when compared with their response to import competition. In both cases producers saw their profits being reduced by foreign competition. In both cases the affected firms should demand policies that would increase their own profits at the expense of their competitors.[4] Furthermore, one would expect their reactions to be a function of the intensity of foreign competition. More specifically, as the Production Profile hypothesis predicts, firms would be more likely to put forth demands for a more restrictive IFDI policy when the extent of foreign market share (including local production by foreign-owned firms) was higher, when these domestic firms were less competitive themselves, and when economic demand was more depressed.

In every single case, however, industry actors put far more effort into seeking trade protection than investment regulation, even when IFDI undermined the effect of recently acquired import barriers. Obtaining these trade restrictions had not been easy. These industries had put so much effort into lobbying for trade relief that many analysts questioned America's commitment to free trade.[5] It is surprising, therefore, that U.S. producers did not object more forcefully when their protectionist rents dissipated as foreign producers evaded trade barriers through IFDI.

In lobbying for trade protection, domestic firms sometimes addressed IFDI-related concerns as well. Domestic semiconductor manufacturers testified to the International Trade Commission that the output of Japanese subsidiaries should be treated the same way as imports. The automakers asked Washington to count a transplant vehicle as equivalent to half an import. Demands for higher domestic content requirements in the auto and machine tool industries were presented as attempts to ensure that trade protection not be completely evaded via screwdriver assembly. These issues were secondary to the trade protection campaigns, however. None provoked extensive political activity, and overall, IFDI never became nearly as important an issue for domestic firms as import competition. The relative importance of the two issues can be illustrated by comparing the amount of time, money, and political capital the industries spent, by listening to what industry officials themselves said about their priorities, and by examining their strategic lobbying decisions.[6]

The Production Profile hypothesis would suggest that foreign competition in the form of IFDI never posed the same magnitude of a threat to the profits of domestic firms as imports did and so did not provoke a similar level of political action. It is true that local production never completely replaced imports (it came closest in consumer electronics), but IFDI certainly diluted the effects of trade protection. One cannot know what would have happened in the absence of IFDI; even absolute protection from foreign competition would most likely not have solved the deeper problems plaguing many of these industries. Still, it was no secret that IFDI made trade protection increasingly ineffective. When foreign producers attempted to evade import barriers in other ways—for instance, via transshipment through third countries—producers in the semiconductor, machine tool, and steel industries took action to address the problem. One would expect the same response to IFDI. In the long run, IFDI may benefit domestic firms in that they can learn from foreign subsidiaries and ultimately must innovate themselves. Many analysts ascribe the recovery of the automobile industry to the transplants.[7] Although a few managers may be farsighted enough to take this benefit into account, by and large firms still lobby for short-term rents. Whatever the long-term consequences, the immediate effects of IFDI on these domestic companies were real and deleterious.[8] Yet the political response to IFDI was much less forceful than it was with imports.

One possible explanation for this difference is that U.S. firms were accustomed to fighting *against* IFDI restrictions, not for them. In the postwar period (and through the period under examination) the United States accounted for the largest share of outward foreign direct investment in the world. Consequently, American multinational corporations consistently sought maximum freedom for their own overseas activities. This effort involved fending off attempts by labor to restrict outward FDI, as in the battle over the Foreign Trade and Investment Act of 1973 (the Burke-Hartke Bill), which would have curtailed tax credits and deferrals for MNCs, as well as lobbying for policies supportive of outward FDI.[9] Whether through bilateral negotiations or multilateral forums and institutions, U.S. firms have unfailingly urged foreign governments to allow unfettered movement of capital and to adopt national treatment. It stands to reason that they would want to be consistent in their demands regarding IFDI, since any home restrictions could boomerang and end up harming their own international interests. Because of outward FDI's important role in the strategy of U.S. MNCs, they abstained from following the example of Europeans, who took a harder line against IFDI (for instance, in the auto industry, demanding and eventually obtaining quotas that counted both imports and transplant output).[10]

In two manufacturing industries—steel and consumer electronics—global orientation helps explain the variation between trade and IFDI demands. In steel the industry supported trade protection for obvious economic reasons: import competition had devastated the domestic producers through the 1970s and 1980s. When the VRA was imposed, it stimulated Japanese and Korean IFDI in the form of joint ventures with domestic companies. This investment gave domestic producers access to badly needed capital and technology (and in some cases a chance to exit profitably from the industry). The beneficial linkages with foreign companies restrained the U.S. industry from transferring its protectionist demands to IFDI. In consumer electronics the effect was more differentiated among firms. That is, the same international interests that led RCA and GE to sit on the sidelines during trade disputes while Sylvania, Magnavox, and especially Zenith took the lead in fighting foreign competition also led to divisions over IFDI-related issues. Domestic content was low among foreign investors in this sector, supplying a potential target to opponents that might want to lobby for stricter regulation. But the locally owned industry (what was left of it anyway) also had very low domestic content. Its own global strategy meant that there was not much difference between U.S. and foreign companies that could be used for political advantage. Thus an international orientation led to demands for a liberal IFDI policy.

The Global Industry hypothesis, then, can account for the relative absence of restrictive IFDI policy demands in the United States. In general, seeking investment restrictions would have been difficult for U.S. MNCs, given their long-standing efforts to promote liberal FDI policies abroad. But can this outward orientation explain why firms would seek import barriers but not IFDI restrictions? For some American industries (such as automobiles), outward FDI was more important than exports in serving overseas markets; therefore, retaliation in the form of trade protection posed less danger than possible FDI-related retaliation. Firms with outward investment but little export or intrafirm trade activity had more at stake in maintaining a liberal international investment regime than a liberal trade regime. Trade restrictions would impose minor costs that could be avoided by further overseas production. This might explain why the automobile, machine tool, and consumer electronics industries were more likely to support open investment than free trade. There were no cases in which firms supported free trade but not a liberal IFDI policy. On the basis of the trade-IFDI comparison, the Global Industry explanation cannot be completely ruled out.

As pointed out in chapter 2, multinational firms that one might expect to adopt liberal trade policy preferences have at times sought contingent protection in order to pressure foreign governments to liberalize access to their markets. According to the Strategic Investment hypothesis, firms will extend those policy preferences to FDI by putting forth restrictive demands when foreign investors are headquartered in a country that does not offer reciprocal treatment of U.S. investments. This hypothesis makes sense of the near obsession Americans had with Japanese FDI in manufacturing during this period, compared with the relative indifference to European investment.[11] Some have ascribed racist motives to this double standard.[12] There may have been elements of this sentiment in the public reactions to some prominent takeovers, but industry actors had concrete economic reasons to treat Japanese investment differently. European firms did not pose the same kind of competitive threat in semiconductors, automobiles, consumer electronics, and machine tools. European steel companies, which competed successfully with U.S. domestic producers, lacked the firm-specific skills that were prerequisite to investing abroad, and so the complaints of U.S. firms were confined to the trade and subsidy policies of the EC. Except with service industries, the reciprocity issue did not arise with respect to European IFDI.[13]

Despite the fact that Japan was singled out as the villain in political debates over IFDI, demands by U.S. firms for a strategic investment policy were not put forth as frequently as strategic trade demands were. When foreign firms circumvented import barriers or trade sanctions, thus rendering them ineffective as instruments of political pressure, domestic firms did not seek to plug these loopholes with demands for a more restrictive IFDI policy. The most notable example of this reluctance occurred in the semiconductor industry following President Reagan's 1987 sanctions; after relocating production of the affected electronic products, not one Japanese firm ended up paying duties on goods that were included in the sanctions. In the automobile industry U.S. producers were more concerned with the domestic market than the Japanese market during the period under examination, though they joined the parts makers in their campaign to pressure the transplants to purchase more U.S.-made components. These efforts ended up inducing foreign-owned part makers to relocate production as well. Subsequently, domestic parts firms sought a range of policies that would mandate higher domestic content and, significantly, define *domestic* as U.S.-owned production. These were strategic demands in that they were designed to put pressure on Japanese firms to increase the percentage of U.S. components they purchased. Eventually, the U.S. automakers joined this campaign, although their motives were different. Transplant domestic content levels were less important to the U.S. companies than was the political need to draw a sharp distinction between U.S. and Japanese companies. With machine tools, bearings, steel, and consumer electronics the focus of industry efforts was almost entirely on the home market, so the reciprocity issue did not become relevant.

Asymmetric treatment of FDI—the fact that for a variety of reasons, U.S. firms had so much difficulty investing in Japan—also could have provoked strategic investment demands. However, although industry representatives raised this point from time to time, they did not base many policy demands on it. There was no example of a restrictive policy demand that was contingent on Japan's easing of barriers to foreign investment.[14] Partly this is because these barriers to IFDI in Japan are informal and thus somewhat impervious to governmental pressure. When firms faced this problem with trade, they supported results-based agreements (e.g., mandating that a given share of the Japanese market consist of imports), but this solution was less practical with foreign direct investment, given the complexity and the costs of investing abroad.

Inter- and Intrasectoral Variation

Even though demands for tighter regulation or for discriminatory policies on the basis of nationality did not match pleas for import protection, producers still sought more restrictive IFDI policies and deviations from national treatment. These demands varied across sectors and, within sectors, over time and across different IFDI-related issue areas. Each of the three economic-interest hypotheses provides explanatory variables that purport to account for both intersectoral variation and three kinds of variation within a single industry: among different firms, over time, and across different policy issues related to IFDI.

The Production Profile explanation has a mixed record in accounting for intersectoral variation. Partly, this variation results from case selection. The manufacturing industries chosen for analysis were ones that had suffered from foreign competition, had sought and received trade protection, but had seen the value of that protection fall as foreign firms shifted from exports to FDI. Thus according to the Production Profile explanation, all these industries should have been more likely to favor IFDI restrictions or deviations from national treatment compared with firms that competed more successfully against foreign rivals. U.S. chemical companies, for instance, had no reason to support restrictive policies, despite high levels of IFDI. Nor of course, does one see these policy preferences from industries in which little IFDI occurred. Usually, foreign producers in these sectors lacked the transferable firm-specific advantage (e.g., product or process technology, superior management, a brand name, etc.) that is a prerequisite for foreign investment, as with textiles or agriculture.

But the extent to which domestic firms in the industries analyzed sought restrictive policies varied, and the Production Profile hypothesis has difficulty explaining that variation. Why would the semiconductor industry react more vigorously to IFDI than the machine tool industry when, if anything, the latter faced tougher economic conditions in terms of red ink, falling market share, or firm mortality? U.S. firms in the airline and telecommunications industries enjoyed a stronger competitive position internationally. Nonetheless, the policy preferences put forth by firms in the service industry were not more liberal. In fact, unlike the manufacturing firms, service providers mobilized against foreign producers' entry into the U.S. market via international corporate alliances.

The Global Industry hypothesis suggests that policy preferences will vary on the basis of global orientation. Yet the case studies show that this correlation does not hold. The more global industries—semiconductors, airlines, and telecommunications—were the more vigorous proponents of a stricter policy toward IFDI. By contrast, the machine tool and bearing industries were not very globalized yet did little to oppose transplant production. As mentioned earlier, the hypothesis does succeed in explaining why the consumer electronics industry reacted the way it did as well as why the steel industry was so welcoming of IFDI: the dominance of joint ventures over greenfield investment had the effect of buying off potential opposition.

Finally, the Strategic Investment hypothesis looks at variation in the policies and characteristics of the countries in which foreign investors were headquartered. Barriers to access in foreign markets were necessary but not sufficient for U.S. producers to adopt more restrictive policy preferences. Automobile and machine tool producers could barely stay afloat in the U.S. market. Though the domestic firms complained about Japanese barriers, they were in no position to make a serious effort to penetrate overseas markets and therefore would be unlikely to turn foreign market access into a political issue. In the semiconductor industry it is less obvious why domestic firms did not extend their strategic trade demands to IFDI. The incentive to do so was there, especially after the 1987 sanctions. The two service industries, on the other hand, did put forth strategic investment demands to keep foreign firms from establishing a presence in the U.S. market unless their home states took steps to make their own markets more accessible.

Overall, these broad interindustry comparisons are not terribly informative. There are too few sectors to allow us to draw any definite conclusions about the relative merit of the different hypotheses. Even more important, these demands varied not only over time and among firms but also over different policy issues related to IFDI. This is precisely why this book has defined its cases not as overall industry positions but as the policy preferences put forward (or not put forward) by particular firms in a particular policy episode.

The least problematic variation involved broad changes in policy preferences over time. It is no surprise, and consistent with the Production Profile explanation, that industry actors did not demand restrictive IFDI policies until the presence of local subsidiaries reached a critical mass such that they would constitute a competitive threat. In many sectors domestic firms initially encouraged IFDI because they believed it would reduce the competitive advantages held by their foreign rivals; each time, however, they were wrong. There was thus an element of learning involved; domestic producers required time to understand the nature of the threat from IFDI and the range of actions they could take to address it.[15] In the case of automobiles, even after transplant production had become a significant source of competition, domestic firms did not put forth restrictive policy preferences until their economic fortunes plunged in the late 1980s. During the subsequent recovery in the early to mid-1990s their attacks on the transplants decreased in frequency and intensity. In consumer electronics the Global Industry explanation works well in explaining variation over time. The firms that were most adamant in protesting IFDI at the outset gradually dropped the subject as they increased their own overseas position (or as they exited the industry). In airlines and especially telecommunications domestic producer attitudes toward foreign firms—in terms of alliances as well as ownership restrictions—became more liberal over time as foreign markets became more accessible to U.S. producers, just as the Strategic Investment hypothesis would suggest. On the other hand, in semiconductors and steel the variation over time either did not occur or did not occur in any patterned way (so it did not correspond to the economic variables emphasized by the three hypotheses).

There were also variations in intrasectoral policy preferences. The Production Profile approach does not have too much to say about these differences. As a rule, few firms in the beleaguered industries escaped the economic ills that afflicted the sectors as a whole. To the extent that some firms were doing better than others within a sector, this disparity was not translated into different demands on IFDI policy. The Global Industry hypothesis sheds light on some interfirm variation. For example, in the automobile sector the least multinational company, Chrysler, took the most restrictive view toward IFDI. As already mentioned, the Global Industry hypothesis also accounts for interfirm variation in the demands of the consumer electronics industry (GE and RCA vs. Zenith, Sylvania, and Magnavox). Finally, steelmakers who had made the decision to outsource their slab steel production did not, for obvious reasons, join the campaign against the importation of slabs by foreign-owned companies. On the other hand, the most global firms within the semiconductor industry were no less vigorous in their restrictive demands than the rest of the industry; they controlled Sematech and therefore oversaw Sematech's active role in lobbying against IFDI. With bearings the most internationalized firms, took the lead in what antitransplant activities there were. In automobiles GM and Ford (though more liberal than Chrysler) took policy positions that were decidedly nonliberal, despite their own extensive global ties. Ford supported the Trade Enhancement Act of 1992 even though it covered the Ford Probe, and Chrysler opposed granting foreign trade subzone status to foreign plants despite the fact that Diamond-Star (the Chrysler-Mitsubishi joint venture) was simultaneously lobbying for that very designation. Finally, internationally oriented firms in the service sector, such as American Airlines and AT&T, took a leadership role in fighting foreign attempts to penetrate the U.S. market.

The most troublesome variation for the three economic-interest hypotheses is that across different issue areas relating to IFDI. The Production Profile explanation makes no distinction among different ways to achieve the goal of profit maximization; industries that are expected to demand stricter IFDI policies (to increase profits) should do so whether the means are domestic content regulations, R&D subsidies, procurement rules, or acquisition barriers. There is no reason to expect demands from the same firms to change without a change in economic circumstances. Similarly, unless a firm perceived some connection between a type of IFDI policy and the probability of foreign retaliation, one would not expect contradictory demands about different IFDI policies. Such a connection is conceivable; perhaps foreign governments view certain policies as acceptable and others as beyond the pale. But there is not much evidence that foreign governments made these kinds of distinctions or that there was a relationship between these perceptions and policy preferences. With the Strategic Investment hypothesis some policies may be seen as more effective instruments of pressure than others, so firms that are shut out of foreign markets may demand these kinds of policies. Again, however, there is nothing to indicate that this was in fact the case. Industry demands varied across issue areas in a way that cannot be understood with reference to any of the economic-interest hypotheses. It is important to emphasize that this variation was not just in tactics (i.e., how best to achieve a given policy outcome). Rather, the variation occurred in the policy positions the domestic producers took: liberal, restrictive/discriminatory, or something in between. It is true that these policies were all different ways of achieving the same ultimate goal (profit maximization), but policy preferences are precisely what this book is trying to explain. Nor was this variation a matter of differences in emphasis; rather, policy demands from the same firms in the same industry were radically dissimilar. These differences, combined with the other unexplained sources of variation just described, require an alternative explanation to make sense of industry demands.

The previous discussion makes clear that the three economic-interest hypotheses are not being rejected or invalidated. All three explanations are useful for making sense of different aspects of the variation in observed outcomes. In fact, one or another of the hypotheses can account for each and every case. But this is not a theoretically satisfying state of affairs because each of the hypotheses generates different, and even contradictory, predictions. We are left with no basis to accurately predict demands, and thus the supposed advantage of these parsimonious economic-interest theories disappears.

THE EFFECT OF DOMESTIC POLITICAL
STRUCTURES ON POLICY PREFERENCES

The fact that a single firm would adopt different, even contradictory, policy preferences unrelated to changes in economic circumstances follows from the fact that firms have a number of economic interests with respect to IFDI. They want protection against foreign competitors, against the possibility of retaliation against their own investment activity, and against the perceived injuries they sustain from existing foreign restrictions. Producers must decide which of these myriad, sometimes conflicting, interests to emphasize. At times the decision is not difficult because overwhelming economic incentives lead actors to give priority to obtaining one kind of policy. In such a case one can map political demands directly from economic circumstances; other factors may have some reinforcing effect, but the outcomes can be understood without adding analytic clutter. This was true to varying degrees for steel and consumer electronics.[16]

But when global industries faced competitive threats from foreign rivals whose own markets often were not as open as the domestic U.S. market, they confronted a dilemma as to which course to take. In formulating their policy preferences, firms assess the returns from each policy minus the costs of putting forth demands for that particular policy. Producers have finite resources—time, money, and political capital—and must choose approaches that make the best use of what they have. But making this kind of cost/benefit calculation is often extremely difficult, given imperfect information and inherent uncertainty. For instance, estimating the probability of provoking retaliation or of advancing foreign liberalization is a formidable task—for both the analyst and the societal actors themselves. Still, producers can make rough comparisons of their various options. Before these options can be compared, however, the returns have to be weighted by the probability that they will actually be received. If two policies generate similar returns but one is more obtainable, a rational producer will pursue that one. When the returns differ and the probability of success is equivalent, the producer will pursue the more lucrative policy. When both the returns and the probabilities differ (as is most often the case), the producer will make some kind of expected utility calculation and pursue the policy that comes out on top.

The difference between trade policy preferences and IFDI policy preferences stems, ultimately, from the varying likelihood that pressure from producers will succeed in influencing government policy. What makes some policy options more obtainable than others? The answer lies in the political environment. Rational forward-looking actors will pay attention to their political environment when translating their economic preferences into policy demands. Specifically, firms will seek only policies for which domestic institutions exist to channel their demands and supply the policy output; moreover, the policies must accord with widely held beliefs concerning the appropriate role of the state. The discussion in chapter 2 provided more detail about how and why these two political variables work;

the argument here helps make sense of the outcomes described in the case studies.

In the semiconductor industry, though the contradictory demands made by domestic producers appeared to have little logic, in fact the industry put forth restrictive policy preferences on issues in which institutions existed to channel demands and in which national security played an important role. Firms did not oppose greenfield investment even when it undermined the Semiconductor Trade Agreement or the 1987 trade sanctions. In some cases, such as the Fujitsu takeover battle, the existing instruments, set up to handle only security and antitrust concerns, could not be used to block a takeover that did not threaten these areas. After the Exon-Florio amendment was passed, demands opposing acquisitions were easier to make and thus more frequent. The existence of Sematech itself created an institutional channel for these kinds of demands and enhanced their legitimacy. Sematech's mission was tied up with national security goals, so domestic firms used it (starting with its membership rules) as a weapon against foreign firms and their subsidiaries. In sum, although opposition to IFDI was less vigorous than the industry's trade policy preferences, it was far more energetic than one would expect from such a globalized sector. The institutional and ideological preconditions were favorable for a certain type of restrictive IFDI demand.

In the automobile industry domestic companies favored a less liberal policy, but not one of straightforward restrictions; rather, they joined with the parts makers in attacking the transplants indirectly, demanding that the government deny these subsidiaries subzone status, toughen the rules of origin in NAFTA, require labels on their vehicles, and restrict their sales unless certain content requirements were met. This emphasis on content was puzzling, especially since the transplants' use of more domestic parts would actually increase the competitive threat to domestic producers. This strategy makes sense only in the context of what was considered politically acceptable. IFDI was seen as creating jobs for an industry that had suffered from massive unemployment (and had repeatedly played this unemployment card to gain trade protection). Thus the only legitimate way to attack the transplants was for the domestic producers to distinguish between "real" investment and screwdriver assembly. With regard to the specific policy issues, the existence of institutional channels such as the Free Trade Zone Board, the Customs Department, and the NAFTA negotiating process made it more likely that certain demands would be made rather than others for which no structures existed. In some cases the parts makers (with more at stake and fewer conflicting overseas interests to restrain them) took the lead in pursuing legislative strategies to which the automakers could attach themselves.[17]

With machine tools domestic content could not be used as a vehicle for restrictive IFDI demands for the simple reason that these content levels were already high (the result of IFDI by controller producers). The industry's demands reflected its reliance on the only acceptable argument it had: national security. But playing the security card meant that firms had to emphasize production location rather than ownership. Arguments about blocked shipping lanes and production cutoffs proved effective in obtaining trade protection and domestic subsidies but not in obtaining any policies that would discourage IFDI or deviate from national treatment. The institutional channels that could plausibly provide favorable IFDI policies (for example, those dealing with government procurement policies) were associated with defense, but historically, the bureaucracies involved had defined *domestic* on the basis on production location. By contrast, when nationality was defined on the basis of ownership (as with the participation criteria for R&D consortia), the industry supported deviations from national treatment. The story in the antifriction bearing industry is similar. Domestic producers expressed opposition to the wave of IFDI that was undermining their trade protection. But without a legitimate security argument to block it, there was little they could do.

The impact of institutional variables is also evident in the behavior of the airline and telecommunications industries. Here existing regulations— long-standing sector-specific limitations on foreign ownership—provided the vehicle for domestic producers to battle foreign firms. When foreign firms sought to overcome these restrictions by forming international alliances, nonparticipating domestic firms pressed the government to block the ventures or make their approval conditional on foreign liberalization. These policy preferences hinged on the existence of regulations (for instance, antitrust laws and FCC regulations) that would provide channels for political activity. In some cases (KLM's alliance with Northwest, BT's alliance with Sprint) domestic producers found there was little they could do to translate their economic interests into political demands. Interestingly, those in both industries who favored restrictive policies did not base their appeals on the national security reasoning that lay behind the original adoption of the IFDI barriers. At least in the telecom case the contemporary relevance of this argument was questionable. The airline industry (like the auto industry) relied mostly on the employment issue whereas telecom providers emphasized fairness and reciprocity.

The two cases in which economic interests alone best explain policy preferences are the steel and consumer electronic industries. Both these sectors were experiencing extreme economic distress, and they were also the first to face the arrival of IFDI. Financial incentives were thus powerful, and uncertainty surrounded possible political options for dealing with the new form of competition. As a result, producers in these two industries responded in a straightforward manner to IFDI. Though domestic political institutions still played a role in shaping policy preferences, producers in these sectors adopted demands that closely mirrored their economic situation.

These two industry cases underline the extent to which political factors supplement rather than replace economic incentives in an actor's calculation of policy preferences. Still, these political variables explain variation at many different levels, making sense of seemingly contradictory demands within a single industry across different issue areas. They can also account for the consistent contrast between demands for trade policy and demands for IFDI policy. The institutional framework for dealing with IFDI in the United States is much less developed than the one that addresses import competition. With trade policy the procedures and arguments used by industries that want protection are well known and accepted. By contrast, producers who seek to limit IFDI have nowhere to turn unless institutional channels to address the situation happen to exist—for instance, acquisitions that pose a threat to national security as defined by the Exon-Florio amendment or that have negative antitrust implications. It is also much more difficult for firms to win public support for policies that restrict IFDI than it has been to argue for restricting trade. Investment is seen as creating jobs and (as in the machine tool and bearing industries) as posing less of a threat to national security than import dependence. Thus the institutional and ideological environment for demanding restrictive trade policies is much more favorable in trade politics than in IFDI politics. With IFDI, where restrictions already existed (as in the service sectors), the economic interests of U.S. firms were reflected in government policy. Other advanced industrial countries have had more experience in the twentieth century with IFDI and consequently have a better-developed institutional and ideological context that is more favorable for its regulation. Still, even in the United States, IFDI has become politicized and conflictual under certain circumstances: when the existing domestic political structures provide opportunities for adversely affected groups to take effective action. Looking at the domestic political environment, then, helps us determine how economic interests play out in the policy-making arena.

POTENTIAL OBJECTIONS

There are several potential objections to the argument presented here. First, at times economic interests may be compelling enough to make the political context less relevant. Firms may have relatively few important global ties or be under such economic pressure that their policy options are narrowed. For example, the auto parts producers were less reluctant than their Detroit customers to oppose IFDI because, being less global, they had less to risk from pursuing restrictive demands. In the steel industry domestic firms suffered similar constraints and benefited from the joint-venture form of IFDI. Consumer electronics firms were so noncompetitive that they ended up exiting the industry, at which point any demands for IFDI regulation were dropped. But when industries have a number of conflicting interests—when they face foreign competition but are themselves globalized and also encounter market barriers abroad—the economic-interest hypotheses will generate multiple predictions. Industry actors will then determine which policy demands to put forth in response to political factors such as institutions and ideas about legitimacy. To the extent this situation is becoming more common, the usefulness of the political approach will become even greater in the future.

Second, this book argues that domestic political structures shape policy preferences, but if these structures are the result of societal pressure, then one will have overestimated the importance of the political structures. It is certainly true that powerful groups will have an interest in shaping political institutions so that they produce favorable policy outputs. As discussed in chapter 2, however, the collective action obstacles involved in altering or creating institutions are formidable. To the extent producers succeeded in affecting the institutional context, such success occurred on a sectoral level, where the free-rider problem was less severe. One notable example is Sematech: the existence of this quasi-official body had an important effect on the demands of the semiconductor industry, yet the industry itself influenced the creation of the consortium (though the intent was not to affect IFDI policy). Another example involved the auto parts manufacturers' attempt to alter the procedures for granting subzone status to foreign automobile subsidiaries. A third example involves the efforts by telecommunications firms to press the FCC to adopt reciprocity guidelines in its approval of mergers and alliances. Mostly, however, producers treated domestic political structures as exogenous. Institutions are costly to create and alter; in the short to medium term they tend to resist change and are sticky.[18] In the long run societal actors play a role in the construction of domestic institutions, but such a role does not preclude these institutions from subsequently influencing the actors and their preferences.

Another objection to the argument presented here involves the loss of theoretical parsimony. There is no question that the conventional approach—the academic division of labor in which political scientists rely on economic theory to explain what groups want—allows for the development of more parsimonious policy-making models. By contrast, delving into the political origins of societal preferences makes it more difficult to produce simple and generalizable predictions of how groups respond to the international economy. For those who are committed to developing spare models of the policy process, deducing preferences will continue to be a more attractive approach. This book has argued that producers have multiple and conflicting interests. Deducing their policy preferences from their economic situation will lead to ambiguous predictions and incomplete explanations. It will be difficult to make progress in understanding policy outcomes and state behavior if we cannot explain where societal preferences come from. A given policy outcome, it may be claimed, illustrates the power of state actors to overcome societal pressures. But other analysts could respond by arguing that although it may seem as though powerful groups were unable to prevail, if one properly understood their preferences, it would be clear that they were in fact successful. The observed behavior of these actors could then be characterized as strategic misrepresentation or a result of environmental constraints. To determine how much power societal actors had, one must have a complete understanding of what they were trying to achieve.

The analytical challenge is to improve the "terms of trade" between the parsimony of the economic-deduction models and the empirical grounding of the more inductive political approach. We want to enrich the explanation of policy preferences while sacrificing as little theoretical rigor as possible. We need not abandon theoretical deduction. However, political scientists especially should expand the range of theories they use beyond those of economics. Societal preferences are not just *inputs* to politics; they are themselves the *product* of political processes. In order to understand them, analysts need to incorporate the vast body of scholarly work regarding the policy-making process rather than rely so completely on economic theories.

IFDI POLICY AND IFDI POLICY PREFERENCES

This book has confined itself to explaining the demand rather than supply side of the political market. In truth, the demand and supply of policy have a mutually interactive effect; neither can be understood in isolation.[19] When faced with this kind of iterative cycle, however, the analyst has to break in somewhere; this book analyzes the demand side, as it has received much less attention and, in the case of IFDI, presents more anomalies. Ideally, a unified model would simultaneously incorporate policy demand and policy supply. With a few exceptions work in IPE has yet to integrate analysis of both sides of the political market.[20]

The model one adopts for explaining policy supply has important implications for the discussion of policy demands. In a crude interest group model in which policy simply results from the demands of social groups, the political explanation will not provide much insight. That is, if powerful actors can secure any policies they want, their demands will mirror their underlying economic preferences and will not be affected by whether domestic political factors make one or another policy more obtainable (since anything is obtainable). By contrast, if policy is determined solely by domestic institutions, the ideology of decision makers, or international factors, then a political explanation will be able to account for demands but the findings will be inconsequential (since these demands will have little or no effect). Of course, the truth is most certainly between these two extremes, and the trick, as always, is to specify to what extent and how the policy preferences of social actors come into play relative to these other influences. This task cannot be adequately accomplished without a fuller explanation of policy preferences.

In addition to integrating analyses of policy demand and policy supply, future research should entail more comparative study of IFDI policy (and foreign economic policy more generally). This book's focus on the United States may limit the confidence with which one can generalize the findings. But multinational comparisons demand a solid knowledge of the political structures in each country. For instance, in order to know beforehand how ideological concerns will affect policy preferences, we must be familiar with the widely accepted beliefs, norms, and causal ideas that occupy a prominent place in that nation's history. Armed with this background knowledge, we can then test how important these ideas (as opposed to the more direct economic interests of producers) were in affecting industry demands for IFDI policies. The same holds true with political institutions. After making this assessment in various contexts, we can then step back to draw the kind of international comparisons that are necessary to determine how generalizable these conclusions are. Such an exercise would improve our understanding not just of incoming foreign investment but also more generally of how societal actors respond to the challenges of globalization in all its myriad forms.

The political approach laid out in this book represents the beginnings of a synthesis of a deductive, parsimonious, rational-choice orientation and a more accurate, context-sensitive, historical institutionalist approach. The main ideas behind such a synthesis are neither terribly complicated nor surprising. In formulating their policy preferences, actors calculate an *expected* utility incorporating not only the returns from various policies but also perceptions of the probability of various states of the world holding true (including the probability that they will be able to obtain certain desired policies). This calculation includes such factors as their ability to overcome collective action obstacles, defeat rival societal coalitions, and persuade policy makers to adopt their policy preferences. As elementary as this insight may seem, it has not been incorporated into the voluminous and ever-growing IPE literature on how foreign economic policies are made. Scholars have simply deduced the demands of social actors directly from their economic interests and then moved on to attempting to explain policy supply. One might respond that this approach represents a worthwhile sacrifice for theoretical parsimony. But with IFDI this method leads to an inability to explain which of many conflicting interests producers will favor. Ultimately, these economic-interest approaches are unable to predict or even explain a seemingly contradictory array of policy demands. Recent work suggests that a similar situation exists in other foreign economic policy issue areas such as trade and monetary policy, and the approach in this book could be profitably extended to these issues as well.[21]

Notes

1. THE CHALLENGE OF INCOMING FOREIGN DIRECT INVESTMENT

1. On the early history of foreign direct investment in the United States, see Wilkins 1989.

2. At the beginning of the 1980s the stock of IFDI in the United States was around $83 billion. Twelve years later it had risen to $420 billion. Graham and Krugman 1995, 14–15.

3. For the former, see Tolchin and Tolchin 1988 and 1992; Kearns 1992; Frantz and Collins 1989. For the latter, see Woodward and Nigh 1998; Graham and Krugman 1995; Kudrle 1991; Yamamura 1989.

4. In 1987 economist Paul Krugman predicted, "The political issue of the 1990s isn't going to be imports; it's going to be the foreign invasion of the United States." Cited in *Wall Street Journal* 7/24/87. For a contrasting prediction, see Stockman 1991. As for the public's concern, a 1988 poll showed that 78% of those questioned supported restricting IFDI in business and real estate. Cited in Kudrle 1991, 398. On the executive branch's position toward IFDI, see DeSouza 1994. On state and local officials, see Yanarella and Green 1990.

5. Reich 1989, 582. See Mundell 1957 and McCulloch 1991 on how trade barriers provoke compensating factor flows. On the connection between trade protection (or the threat of trade protection) and FDI more specifically, see Nicolaides and Thomas 1991; Ray 1991; Salvatore 1991; Bhagwati et al. 1992; Blonigen and Feenstra 1997.

6. McCulloch 1985, 147–48.

7. Encarnation 1992, 3.

8. See, for instance, Pierson 1993.

2. POLITICAL RESPONSES TO FOREIGN INVESTMENT

1. Morrow 1994, 19; Frieden 1999, 40; Moravcsik 1998, 24.

2. Frieden 1999, 44. Theoretically, it is possible that one's actions could lead directly to a given outcome. Thus Robert Powell (1994, 319) notes that the distinction between preferences over outcomes and preferences over actions is meaningful only in situations of strategic interdependence. In the political world, however, that encompasses enough of reality to make the preference/strategy distinction a useful one.

3. Rational choice theorists (e.g., Clark 1998, 246) claim that a "semantic misunderstanding" of this distinction lies behind the criticism often leveled at the theory: that it is unable to account for actor preferences. The critics, in this view, have confused (stable) preferences with (changing) strategies; the latter, in fact, can be explained with rational actor models. Powell (1994, 319) sees this same confu-

sion as being at the root of the relative-gains debate in international relations theory between neorealists and institutionalists.

4. In their survey of the interest-group literature Baumgartner and Leach (1998, 162) define *tactics* as referring to "the individual external activities in which groups engage" whereas *strategies* are "combinations of tactics used in particular situations" by which groups hope to attain their goal. But the term *strategy* can also be used to refer to the substance of what groups want (in order to satisfy some more basic preference) as well as the way they go about trying to obtain it. Some have also distinguished between *interests* and *preferences*. Steven Vogel (1999) defines interests as *objective* values that an outside observer can derive from economic theory or some other criterion. Preferences, by contrast, are *subjective* and can be gleaned through survey research or observation. The strategies that actors select in order to attain their preferences, according to Vogel, may not necessarily serve their underlying interests. The point of this distinction is to emphasize the role that norms and ideas play in leading actors to adopt preferences that, objectively, seem irrational. Thus the title of his article, "When Interests Are Not Preferences," refers to situations in which actors pursue goals contrary to what would maximize their economic returns. The problem with this formulation is, as I argue later, that it greatly underestimates the difficulty of determining an actor's "objective" interests. And though it is true that preferences are subjective, the analysts cited above (Frieden, Morrow, Powell) would object to the assumption that these preferences can be measured empirically, separately from strategies.

5. Frieden 1999, 46; Clark 1998, 263.

6. Frieden 1999, 53; Kimura and Welch 1998, 213.

7. Snidal 1986, 41–43; Clark 1998, 247; Frieden 1999, 52.

8. Frieden 1999, 60; emphasis in original. In this case, the theories are from the field of economics. Also see Snidal 1986, 42.

9. Snidal 1986, 41; Kowert and Legro 1996, 484.

10. On the public's trade policy preferences, see Scheve and Slaughter 2001.

11. Kimura and Welch (1998, 239), for instance, conclude that IR scholars should give up trying to derive national preferences. Pointing to recent research that emphasizes the importance of historically rooted norms, ideas, cultures, and social structures, they argue that states are not fundamentally like units: "What states prefer is always an empirical question, and there are no grounds for being optimistic that we can find robust patterns in interest-specification." Also see Zürn 1997, 299.

12. Frieden (1991, 436) points out some problems with applying international trade theory to the analysis of capital movements, but his arguments apply more to financial capital movements (where expectations are important in determining asset prices) than to FDI.

13. Gourevitch 1986, 55–56. This statement assumes that factors are relatively immobile across sectors, at least in the politically relevant short to medium term. See Frieden 1991, 436. If that were not the case, a factoral approach such as Rogowski 1989 would be more appropriate. On the debate between advocates of factoral vs. sectoral approaches, see Alt and Gilligan 1994; Alt et al. 1996; Frieden and Rogowski 1996.

14. Marks and McArthur 1990, 109.

15. Low barriers to exit dampen this effect since firms that can easily exit an

industry have less incentive to demand relief from the government. See Aggarwal et al. 1987, 350.

16. Goodman et al. 1996.

17. Lavergne 1983; Marks and McArthur 1990.

18. McKeown 1984.

19. Eden and Molot 1993c, 33, 39, 59.

20. Gourevitch 1986, 56.

21. Helleiner 1977; Milner 1988, 23; Pugel and Walter 1985. Firms that are both multinational and big exporters are the biggest free-trade advocates, and those that neither export nor invest abroad are the most protectionist. The intermediate cases are more ambiguous; multinational firms that export little and lack substantial intrafirm trade will, Helen Milner (1988, 24–25) argues, seek selective protection against their stronger competitors and are therefore more protectionist than domestic firms that depend heavily on exports. However, domestically based MNCs will oppose protection if they re-import the goods produced abroad back to the home country (whether through arms-length or intrafirm transactions). Firms that exclusively export care more about opening foreign markets and see home market opening only as a means to that end.

22. Destler and Odell 1987.

23. This is true even if they buy these inputs from domestic firms, since if domestic suppliers are shielded from import competition, they can easily raise their own prices. Destler and Odell 1987, 43–49.

24. IFDI will increase local competition if the investment is undertaken via greenfield entry (that is, through the establishment of new production capacity) but will not if it takes place through the acquisition of an existing firm. This generalization will not hold, however, if the greenfield investment drives domestic firms out of business or, on the other hand, if an acquisition prevents the demise or exit of the purchased firm. Since these effects are difficult to observe, the effect of IFDI on industrial concentration is a controversial topic. See Caves 1996.

25. Brander 1986.

26. Milner and Yoffie 1989.

27. For some of these critiques, see Krugman 1987 and Grossman 1986.

28. Producers are more likely to succeed when lobbying for strategic trade policies than for standard protectionist measures. The former usually involve industries perceived as competitive and entail arguments that appeal to norms of fairness and to the desire to expand rather than restrict trade. See Milner and Yoffie 1989, 271; Stegemann 1989, 99.

29. In some cases, in fact, MNCs prefer that foreign markets be closed to trade; that way, they can gain rents from their presence in a sheltered market the same way domestic firms can. Goodman et al. 1996; Nolt and Maxfield 1991.

30. Milner and Yoffie 1989, 246–47.

31. Edward Graham (1992) formally demonstrates the deleterious effects of asymmetric FDI policies on firms in the country that is shut out. John Zysman (1989, 108–9) also argues that asymmetry of access matters for the competitiveness of local firms.

32. Encarnation 1992, 36, 192.

33. Shoenberger 1985, 249; Flaherty and Raubitschek 1990.

34. Dennis Encarnation (1992, 34), looking specifically at the American-

Japanese relationship, argues, "In the U.S. market, with the Japanese taking advantage of unequal [FDI] access, the Americans have faced the discouraging prospect of being driven out of producing at home."

35. Milner and Yoffie (1989, 245) have argued that MNCs in industries not characterized by large economies of scale do not require centralized facilities and therefore could respond to overseas protection by investing directly in the foreign country or moving offshore to reduce costs. The first option, however, depends on the foreign country's being open to FDI (which is not always the case). The second option may not be sufficient to overcome the competitive disadvantages of being shut out of an important market. See Graham 1978 and Yoffie 1993a, 434, on the harmful effects of asymmetric market access in internationally oligopolistic industries.

36. Bergsten and Noland 1993, 72; Lawrence 1993, 90–93. A keiretsu is a loose network of Japanese companies, often organized around a single bank and sometimes tied by shared equity.

37. Brouthers and Werner 1990; Prestowitz 1988, 102–3.

38. Dani Rodrik and Chang-Ho Yoon (1989, 23) conclude that "there is a strong case for policy intervention when a home firm purchases intermediate inputs from its oligopolistic rival abroad."

39. Borrus and Zysman 1992, 26–28.

40. This will be true if externalities are not only localized geographically (which would be an argument against relying on imports) but also contained within national industry communities. See Cohen and Zysman 1987, 240; Tyson 1992, 40–41.

41. Ulrike Wassmann and Kozo Yamamura (1989, 139) find, "In effect, U.S. firms wishing to sell products to Japanese firms must overcome an additional hurdle not encountered in selling products to firms of other nations."

42. Kang 1997, 306.

43. On this point, see Gowa 1987, 19, on the allegedly "esoteric" nature of international monetary policy. But also see McNamara (1998, 59), who argues that "uncertainty translates into inaction on the part of domestic interest groups . . . lending more space to the role of interpretation by elite policy makers."

44. This argument applies to other issue areas as well. On trade politics, see Alt et al. 1996, 709, and Nelson 1988, 813. On monetary policy, see McNamara 1998, 35–36.

45. Kevin Grier et al. (1994, 915), in their study of corporate PAC contributions, conclude that "differences in the costs of collective action are the key variable in the choice to seek political influence." Also see Alt et al. 1994, 695. The endogenous tariff literature has devoted considerable attention to the collective action issue, though without necessarily reaching a consensus. Following standard Olsonian reasoning, most analyses (for instance, Anderson and Baldwin 1987, 22–23) claim that there will be more pressure for protection when there are fewer firms in an industry or when an industry is more concentrated. In contrast, empirical investigations (Milner 1988, 238; Lavergne 1983; Baldwin 1986) have cast doubt on the importance of industry concentration in explaining protection.

46. Rents will also be higher in concentrated sectors since they will not be eroded by competition. Milner 1988, 237–38; Gilligan 1997.

47. Uriu 1996, 15–16.

48. Other organizational characteristics also affect the cost of obtaining policy outcomes. For instance, after groups have paid the fixed costs of organization and have established political access channels, the marginal costs of action will be low and one should expect to see more political action even when the stakes are minor. Alt et al. 1994, 696. For a similar argument at the firm level, see Martin 1995.

49. Technically, the utility of an outcome (itself the product of some action and some state of the world) is multiplied by the probability of each state occurring. Summing these products over all possible states of the world yields an expected utility that we can then compare with others to explain actions. See Morrow 1994, 23.

50. Verdier 1994, 6.

51. See Garrett and Lange 1996 for an overview related to IPE. G. John Ikenberry (1988, 227) defines institutional structures as having three levels: "1) administrative, legislative, and regulatory rules and procedures; 2) centralization and dispersion of power within the state; 3) normative order defining relations between state and society." I emphasize the first and third components. The centralization variable is more useful in cross-national or cross-issue comparisons such as Katzenstein 1978.

52. Thelen and Steinmo 1992, 8; emphasis in original.

53. Clark 1998, 252–53.

54. Katzenstein 1978; Ikenberry 1988. See note 51 for Ikenberry's definition of domestic institutional structure.

55. Garrett and Lange 1996.

56. Alt and Gilligan 1994. Majoritarian institutions in which numbers matter tend to reward large mass movements, so coalitions tend to organize among factors or economic classes. Institutional arrangements that are insulated from popular pressures will reward small groups and lead to sectoral demands.

57. Rogowski 1999, 133–34.

58. Wendy Hansen (1990, 37–38) and Wendy Takacs (1981, 692) make a similar argument about corporate efforts to obtain administered protection.

59. See Sen 1986 on individuals and Katzenstein 1996 on states.

60. Goldstein and Keohane 1993, 13–14; see also Goldstein 1993, 10–12. For other examples, see McNamara 1998 on European Monetary Union and Hall 1989, 369, and Weir 1992, 190, on Keynesiansim.

61. See Vogel 1999 on the distinction between objective "interests" and subjective "preferences." Barbara Jenkins (1986, 159) shows that Canadian oil companies opposed discriminatory IFDI regulations, despite deriving substantial material benefits, because the regulations violated free-market principles that the firms valued. Their reaction was not completely a function of ideology; local firms worried about a precedent of government regulation that could subsequently be extended to their own activities. For a similar argument in the context of Argentine development policy, see Sikkink 1991.

62. Goldstein 1993, 235. These institutions in turn embody the norms that prevailed at the time of the institutions' formation.

63. On the domestic institutions of IFDI, see Graham and Krugman 1995, chap. 6; Jenkins 1992, chap. 3; Kudrle 1991; Glickman and Woodward 1989; Gordon and Lees 1986; Kang 1997; Safarian 1993; and Saxonhouse and Stern 1989. On U.S. policy toward outward FDI, see Bergsten et al. 1978.

64. On the subnational level, state governments have a variety of tools (tax incentives, subsidies, etc.) that they use to *encourage* IFDI.

65. These sectors include transportation (shipping, air transport), communications (radio and television broadcasting, telecommunications, satellites), and energy resources (mining, hydroelectric and geothermal power, nuclear power) as well as some state restrictions in real estate, banking, and insurance. See Wilkins 1989 for background. Restrictions in the telecommunications industry have recently been relaxed.

66. Under this law, parties to an acquisition or merger with a foreign company must notify the Committee on Foreign Investment in the United States (CFIUS). If this interagency body finds that the investment poses a threat to national security, the president may opt to block the deal. In practice the law has not had much effect owing to the executive branch's narrow interpretation of the statute. See Graham and Krugman 1995; DeSouza 1994; *Business Week* 5/2/94. For an alternative viewpoint, see Kang 1997.

67. Odell and Willett (1990, 38) argue, "Even if they do not stand up to rigorous scrutiny, the appearance of some type of public-interest argument—such as national security considerations or unfair foreign competition—substantially helps a rent seeker secure protection." But without political clout, they note, even an objectively strong case is usually insufficient to win substantial protection.

68. Kudrle and Bobrow 1982; Kraus and Reich 1992; Jenkins 1992.

69. Frieden and Rogowski 1996, 28.

70. Destler and Odell 1987, 109–19. Douglas North (1981, 32) also points to free-rider problems as inhibiting institutional innovation; this is why, he says, institutional innovation will come from the actions of rulers rather than from constituents.

71. The domain of industry cases includes only sectors in which IFDI undermined trade protection. In sectors (such as chemicals) where IFDI occurred but where domestic firms were competitive and therefore did not seek import barriers, there would be no reason to expect demands for a more restrictive IFDI policy. In sectors (such as textiles) where domestic firms did demand trade protection but where IFDI did not occur (because the foreign competitive advantage, cheap labor, was not firm-specific), one of course would not expect to see opposition to (nonexistent) IFDI. The case selection, then, does not allow for a true test of this first hypothesis. Still, some information can be gained by comparing the observed outcomes with the outcomes that the hypothesis suggests should occur.

72. Goldstein 1993.

3. AN ECONOMIC RESPONSE: CONSUMER ELECTRONICS AND STEEL

1. Textiles, apparel, and footwear, for instance, all faced formidable import competition in the decades after World War II. With respect to consumer electronics, the analysis here focuses on color television producers. In the early 1970s, in response to the rise of Japanese imports, U.S. producers shifted production of radio receivers, audio equipment, and monochrome televisions abroad and decided to focus their attention on producing color TVs, where their relative position, they believed, was stronger. Experience with VCRs later followed a similar pattern. Milner 1988, 136; Prestowitz 1988, 351.

2. *New York Times* 7/18/95.

3. Graham and Krugman 1995, 51; Reich 1991, 162.

4. Howell et al. 1992, 95. Michael Borrus and John Zysman (1992, 32–33) argue that "a cumulative knowledge gap" in the U.S. electronic industry has negatively affected U.S. manufacturing capabilities in newer consumer products (such as camcorders, hand-held TVs, and portable faxes), which in turn "drive the development, costs, quality, and manufacture of technological inputs critical to computing, communications, the military, and industrial electronics."

5. Aggarwal et al. 1987, 356; Moses and Pugel 1986, 125; U.S. Congress Office of Technology Assessment 1983; Baranson 1981, chaps. 5–9.

6. Nevin 1978; Choate 1990, chap. 6.

7. Destler 1992, 170. As discussed later, not all companies were equally active in these efforts. Zenith, Sylvania, and Magnavox, along with component manufacturers and unions, were the most energetic proponents of government action to protect the domestic industry.

8. Detailed discussions (albeit with a strong pro–U.S. industry point of view) can be found in Curtis 1994 and Schwartzman 1993.

9. Yoffie 1983, 216.

10. First, they thought the figure too high, though it represented something of a compromise between the industry's demand for a limit of 1.2 million units and the initial Japanese offer of 2 million (Meltzer 1987, 434). Second, the petitioners feared an inflow of imports during the month and a half before the OMA took effect on July 1. *The Washington Post* (5/19/77) reported that Japanese companies planned to "export almost everything they have in stock before June 30." Third, the OMA was linked to settling the antidumping, fraud, and countervailing duty issues. Apparently, U.S. Trade Representative Robert Straus sent a letter to the Japanese ambassador in Washington with assurances that the USTR would support Treasury's effort against these petitions. Yoffie 1983, 216. But many in the industry believed the only hope for the domestic producers to stay in the game involved neutralizing the alleged price advantage from Japanese dumping. *Washington Post* 5/31/77.

11. *Electronic News* 5/23/77.

12. Cited in *Electronic News* 3/28/77.

13. Millstein 1983, 135.

14. *Electronic News* 3/28/77.

15. *Electronic News* 5/23/77.

16. Yamamura and Vandenberg 1986, 263.

17. Burton and Saelens 1987, 287.

18. *Weekly Television Digest* 7/6/81. The share of the U.S. market served by these foreign-owned subsidiaries grew from 5% in 1974, to 22% in 1976, to 30% in 1978. Goodman et al. 1996, 573.

19. At first, this plant mostly assembled imported components, but after the OMA it increased the proportion of local parts while substantially boosting production. Baranson 1981, 45.

20. Moses and Pugel 1985, 130.

21. Though Philips did not face the OMA restrictions, it decided that producing in the United States was necessary in order to counter the Japanese moves into the American market.

22. Baranson 1981, 79; Moses and Pugel, 1985, 131.

23. Hitachi's decision to join forces with a relatively strong U.S. company was partly due to the Japanese company's earlier difficulties in running a plant in San Bernardino, California, which it set up in 1973 but closed in 1975.

24. Yoffie 1983, 83; Meltzer 1987, 438.

25. Millstein 1983, 109; *Electronic News* 6/25/79.

26. Aggarwal et al. 1987, 357; Yoffie 1983, 217–18.

27. *Electronic News* 10/9/78; *The Economist* 12/16/78; Yoffie 1983, 218; Aggarwal et al. 1987, 357.

28. Milner 1988, 135–36.

29. Aggarwal et al. 1987, 357.

30. Milner 1988, 139.

31. Aggarwal et al. 1987, 357.

32. Aggarwal et al. 1987, 357; Milner 1988, 142; Walter and Jones 1981, 45–46.

33. Milner 1988, 133.

34. Nevin 1978, 167. In 1976 of the five million television sets sold in Japan, five hundred were imported. The only way to earn money in the Japanese market, U.S. producers asserted, was to license technology, as RCA did in 1962. *The Economist* 12/16/78.

35. Nevin 1978, 175.

36. Though Matsushita "won" the battle, it was a pyrrhic victory. Quasar continued to lose market share and, according to industry analysts, gave the Japanese company "indigestion." *Business Week* 9/29/75.

37. *Electronic News* 12/4/78.

38. A similar suit had been filed four years earlier by National Union Electric Corporation (formerly known as Emerson Radio Co.). When Zenith filed its suit, the two were combined.

39. *Electronic News* 4/6/81.

40. *Washington Post* 5/31/77.

41. *Electronic News* 1/17/77.

42. *Electronic News* 3/28/77.

43. Graham and Krugman 1995, 52. See *Business Week* 3/12/79 on the product quality gains made by U.S. companies taken over by the Japanese.

44. U.S. House of Representatives 1986c.

45. Goodman et al. 1996, 574.

46. *Electronic News* 3/10/80.

47. *New York Times* 7/1/80.

48. *Electronic News* 7/7/80.

49. Goodman et al. 1996; Yoffie 1983.

50. *Electronic News* 10/31/77, 4/3/78.

51. See Burton and Saelens 1987, 289–92. The authors conclude (192) that "Japanese CTV plants [in Europe] are considerably smaller than those in the USA. The major reasons—restrictive licenses, ceilings on output, high local content ratios and minimum price 'guidelines'—have distorted the strategy and structure of subsidiaries and induced sub-optimal operations."

52. Robin Gaster (1992, 100) cites an estimate by the American Electronics Association of 28% for Japanese companies in the United States.

53. Jack Baranson (1981, 77) says U.S. value content of TVs sold by U.S.-owned companies dropped from 62% in 1972 to 30% in 1978.

54. Baranson 1981, 95.

55. *Washington Post* 9/29/77.

56. Florida and Kenney 1992a, 242.

57. *Weekly Television Digest* 10/19/81; Baranson 1981, 79.

58. *Weekly Television Digest* 10/19/81. There were also indications that Sharp and Toshiba were expected to seek subzone status for their own plants.

59. *Weekly Television Digest* 3/22/82. The government ultimately resolved this particular case by mandating that Sanyo pay full duties on imported tubes for TVs that were sold in the United States but pay reduced duties for TVs that were exported. This ruling, consistent with the original aim of the subzones (encouraging exports from the United States), pleased COMPACT, whose members were mostly worried about the domestic market, though it did not address RCA's concerns about exports. *Weekly Television Digest* 8/16/82.

60. *Television Digest* 10/21/85.

61. *Television Digest* 2/3/86.

62. *UPI Wire* 1/6/83. In 1982 162,144 tubes were imported in this form; by 1985 the number had risen to 1,094,048. U.S. House of Representatives 1986c, 698.

63. U.S. House of Representatives 1986c, 704.

64. They added that the bill sent "a message to all potential foreign investors that tariff structures critical to their U.S. operations are subject to sudden drastic changes that directly contradict both established Customs policy and the GATT obligations of the United States." U.S. House of Representatives 1986c, 708, 712.

65. *Television Digest* 2/10/86.

66. They also cited new subsidiaries in Southeast Asia and China that were "poised to launch another assault on the U.S. market." U.S. House of Representatives 1986c, 160.

67. *New York Times* 8/16/90; *States News Service* 8/15/90.

68. *BNA International Trade Daily* 3/19/91.

69. Zenith, which was the most active TV producer in joining the COMPACT campaigns, had a large enough captive tube operation that (along with RCA) an increase in imported tubes would not seriously affect production costs. By contrast, GTE and N.A. Philips worried that continued loss of tube sales could eventually drive them out of business. *Television Digest* 4/4/93.

70. Goldberg 1986, 185.

71. U.S. steelmakers were slow to adopt new process innovations such as continuous casting and instead tended to make "rounding out" investments rather than undertake the wholesale modernization that would have been necessary to regain competitiveness. See Goldberg 1986, 165–246; Crandall 1981; Dertouzos et al. 1989, 278–87.

72. U.S. Senate 1984b.

73. From 1969 to 1974 a voluntary restraint agreement limited imports from Japan and the EC. After the agreement lapsed, the mid-1970s saw a collapse in industry profitability and widespread plant closings, leading the industry to file Section 301 and antidumping petitions. President Carter responded with the trigger price mechanism (TPM), setting minimum prices on imports based on Japanese

production costs. In 1982 the TPM was suspended after a flurry of antidumping and countervailing duty petitions by U.S. firms, particularly against the EC. The EC and the United States reached an agreement in 1982. For details, see Howell et al. 1988, 517–27; Jones 1986; Borrus 1983.

74. The industry's actions in that year consisted of (1) an escape clause petition by Bethlehem Steel and the United Steelworkers union; (2) a push by the whole industry for a quota to limit imports to 15% of the domestic market; and (3) "a tremendous number" of antidumping and countervailing duty cases designed to make life miserable for foreign producers so that, according to US Steel's David M. Roderick, "all players of substance in the import game . . . would be very pleased to enter into quotas in a negotiated manner." Technically, agreements were made with twenty-seven countries, but the other signatories were allotted a total market share of only 1%. Cited in Destler 1992, 159; also see Hogan 1991.

75. *American Metal Market* 8/29/84. Some of this investment occurred (or was planned) before the final terms of the VRAs were decided on, though foreign producers fully anticipated some kind of trade restriction. Trade protection was not the only reason Japanese firms invested in the United States: other important factors included the rising yen, shrinking demand in Japan, and the prospect of serving the Japanese automobile transplants (which were encountering problems getting high-quality galvanized steel on a just-in-time basis). Florida and Kenney 1992b; *Chicago Tribune* 5/1/89.

76. *American Metal Market* 10/5/92.

77. Levinson 1987, 44.

78. Cited in *American Metal Market* 5/21/87.

79. See U.S. House of Representatives 1986a; Howell et al. 1988, 533; and *American Metal Market* 4/10/86, 12/31/86.

80. *American Metal Market*, 12/11/84, 4/10/86.

81. Jones 1994, 187.

82. Aggarwal et al. 1987, 360.

83. USX (as U.S. Steel was later called) sold its stake in a Spanish and Italian steel producer in the late 1980s. That left Armco as the only major steelmaker with any foreign equity presence (specifically, some minor operations in Spain, Latin America, and Australia). *American Metal Market* 10/7/91.

84. U.S. Senate 1984b.

85. *American Metal Market* 4/26/84; Hogan 1991, 210.

86. Hogan 1991, 210.

87. *American Metal Market* 8/23/84.

88. *American Metal Market* 4/26/84.

89. Gordon and Lees 1986, 84. In its defense the Justice Department argued that the NKK investment differed in being a joint venture rather than a merger and in not raising the level of domestic market concentration on particular steel products. *American Metal Market* 5/4/84. Subsequently, the LTV-Republic deal was allowed.

90. *American Metal Market* 4/26/84; U.S. House of Representatives 1984b.

91. *American Metal Market* 10/17/84.

92. The executive, Dennis J. Carney, insisted he had no problem with foreign ventures as such; rather, he objected to the size of this particular venture. *American Metal Market* 5/2/84.

93. Glickman and Woodward 1986, 48; Hogan 1994, 23.

94. *Financial Times* 4/27/90.

95. Florida and Kenney 1992a.

96. Nisshim initially bought a 10% share of W-P as part of a plan to build a $50 million coating plant in West Virginia that would make corrosion-resistant steel for automotive parts, appliances, and construction products. After W-P went bankrupt in April 1985—even before ground was broken on the proposed joint venture plant—the relationship was restructured, and Nisshin increased its share in the plant to 67%. *American Metal Market* 12/31/85; Gordon and Lees 1986, 102.

97. The owner of the other 50%, a California businessman, subsequently sold his share to Kawasaki, making the operation wholly foreign-owned. Since the Kaiser mill was about to close permanently, the Japanese and Brazilian interest was warmly welcomed by government and union officials, even though the mill, which had been an integrated plant, would now make only rolled steel out of imported unfinished slabs. From employing around 9,000 workers, the Fontana mill decreased the payroll to about 825 jobs. *American Metal Market* 7/18/84, 10/19/84; Glickman and Woodward 1986, 145.

98. This venture provided a way for USS to source high-quality, low-cost slabs from Posco's new integrated plant in Kwangyang, South Korea. Although the investment provided tangible benefits for U.S. Steel, workers at its Geneva, Utah, plant protested bitterly. Congressional hearings were held in April 1986 at which labor representatives blasted USS for its plan to import raw steel instead of modernizing its own "hot end" operations. The company defended itself by claiming it had no choice: "We could either exit the Western steel market, as Kaiser did, as Armco did, as Bethlehem did, as J & L did, as Bliss & Laughlin did. We chose to remain." U.S. House 1986b, 22; *American Metal Market* 7/23/85, 12/17/85, 12/23/86. The only other significant steel producer on the West Coast was the Japanese-Brazilian CSI, which already relied on imported slabs.

99. Hogan 1991, 209. For their part, USS executives believed that entering a joint venture was a prerequisite for winning business from the Japanese auto transplants. On this basis, a second joint plant was announced in Leipsic, Ohio, to serve the transplants. *Chicago Tribune* 5/1/89; Hogan 1994, 20.

100. With the Japanese putting up much of the $400 million required for construction, the mill cut the time it took to produce a coil of steel from twelve days to around one hour. *American Metal Market* 3/25/87; *Chicago Tribune* 3/11/90; Hogan 1991, 208; Reich 1991, 215.

101. Hogan 1991, 208.

102. The next year, the Japanese company invested another $350 million, boosting its stake to 50%. Armco's parent pulled out of the flat-rolled carbon steel business in 1994, leaving Kawasaki as the largest shareholder in the second integrated steel company (besides NKK-National) controlled by a Japanese company. *New Steel* 3/94; Florida and Kenney 1992b, 156; Glickman and Woodward 1986, 123.

103. Hogan 1991, 210.

104. Florida and Kenney 1992a, 156.

105. Even Bethlehem had a licensing agreement with Nippon Steel and had obtained some $200 million in loans from Japanese banks to help modernize two

new galvanizing projects. *American Metal Maker* 10/7/91. In 1992 Bethlehem and NKK-owned National agreed to a joint venture in Mississippi making galvanized steel.

106. *American Metal Market* 10/7/91; Florida and Kenney 1992b.

107. The speaker was Donald H. Trautlein, chairman of Bethlehem Steel Corp. Cited in *American Metal Market* 5/22/86.

108. Crandall 1986, 203.

109. See the AISI position paper ("Fair Trade Act Vital for Survival of Steel"), reprinted in *American Metal Market* 1/13/84.

110. Scheuerman 1986, 161–62.

111. *America Metal Market* 8/8/84. As discussed in chapter 4, this attitude was widely held among U.S. semiconductor firms.

112. Both quotations in *Chicago Tribune* 5/1/89. The Inland executive, Frank Luerssen, noted that the Japanese (and the Europeans) enjoyed a lower cost of capital than did American companies. "So if you can't beat them, what you do is join them, and that is what we have done. Today we can get capital in Japan. We have the Industrial Bank of Japan as a partner." *Chicago Tribune* 3/11/90.

113. *Ward's Auto World* 9/89.

114. Cited in Kenney and Florida 1992a, 158.

115. Encarnation 1992, 10–12.

116. Richard Florida and Martin Kenney (1992a) cite interviews with Japanese managers to this effect. A representative statement comes from the president of Sumitomo, who remarked, "We will consider investing in the U.S. only when the initiative comes from the American side, when we are asked to participate." Otherwise, he worried, Japanese FDI would create political friction. Cited in *American Metal Market* 10/5/84.

117. The Nippon Steel–Inland, USX-Kobe, and Kawasaki-Armco ventures all posted their first profits in 1994. That year the NKK-owned National earned profit for the first time in four years. Altogether, from 1984 to 1990, NKK earned a paltry 2.5% annual return on its investment in National. Meanwhile, Wheeling-Pittsburgh and LTV, both with Japanese partners, had sought Chapter 11 protection from creditors. *Nikkei Weekly* 12/26/94; *Japan Economic Newswire* 12/24/94; *American Metal Market* 10/7/91.

118. *American Metal Market* 10/3/86.

119. Florida and Kenney 1992a, 156, 161–62, 187.

120. Goodman et al. 1996, 579.

121. *New York Times* 7/1/92. According to one trade publication (*Iron Age* 11/92), these firms continued to provide data and general support for the petitions by the rest of the industry. Some Japanese companies expected their investments would shield them from the unfair trade complaints: "Having shown cooperation and support in both trade and investment, we are astonished that these efforts are being totally ignored by U.S. industry," said Yoshitaka Fujitani, the president of NKK's American subsidiary.

122. Scheuerman 1986, 178. The front-end slab production was the most labor-intensive part of the steel production process, so labor was loath to see it relocate overseas. U.S. House of Representatives 1989c, 1989e; Lima 1991.

123. The two domestic companies admitted that they themselves could not supply those slabs but insisted that Commerce reject the request as unjustified. *American Metal Market* 11/6/86, 1/8/87.

124. *American Metal Market* 11/24/86.

125. *American Metal Market* 12/16/86. In response, USX offered to sell semi-finished steel to CSI or any other company that would otherwise import slabs. The offer was rebuffed amid accusations that USX was attempting to sell domestic slabs at "prohibitive" prices since, according to the VRA, Commerce could not approve offshore purchases if a domestic supplier agrees to furnish the slabs at any nonprohibitive price. *American Metal Market* 3/10/88, 3/18/88.

126. U.S. House of Representatives 1989e; Lima 1991, 148.

127. U.S. House of Representatives 1989c, 172.

128. Bethlehem chairman Walter F. Williams acknowledged that finishing operations would have to be closed (a process he called "weeding the garden") and imports of semifinished steel increased, which would lead to closer international joint ventures; as he put it, "We are learning to trust one another and that we can live together." *American Metal Market* 6/29/87.

129. Jones 1986, 2.

130. Christelow 1995, 143.

4. AN AMBIVALENT RESPONSE: SEMICONDUCTORS AND AUTOMOBILES

1. Yoffie 1993b. In 1990 Japanese semiconductor manufacturers in the United States provided only about 7% of U.S. employment in the industry. Christelow 1995, 167; Graham and Krugman 1995, 43; Tyson and Yoffie 1993, 68; Angel 1994, 78.

2. Prestowitz 1990, 121; National Advisory Commission on Semiconductors, 1989, 5.

3. Borrus (1988, 39–40), for instance, argued that importing chips could not substitute for the "dense technology diffusion interconnections characteristic of technical spillovers from a domestic industry," especially as chips become more complicated and analogous to systems themselves. And based on the experience of consumer electronics and automobiles, he claimed, Japanese parent companies tend to keep their overseas subsidiaries a generation behind Japanese state-of-the-art technology. Also see Cohen and Zysman 1987, 123; Borrus et al. 1983, 143; Malerba 1985, 11; National Advisory Commission on Semiconductors 1989, 14.

4. Graham and Krugman 1995, 118; Moran 1990; Ziegler 1991; Dallmeyer 1987; Irwin 1994, 37; Green 1996; U.S. Senate 1987c, 175; 1987d; 1989.

5. Angel 1994, 26; Yoffie 1993b, 219; Irwin 1994, 7; Pugel 1987, 211.

6. On the rise, decline, and subsequent recovery of the U.S. semiconductor industry, see Howell et al. 1992; Borrus 1988; Borrus et al. 1983; Langlois et al. 1988; Malerba 1985; Warshofsky 1989; Wilson et al. 1980. On the industry's political activities, especially related to trade policy, see Milner and Yoffie 1989; Prestowitz 1988, chap. 2; Tyson and Yoffie 1993; Yoffie 1988; Coleman and Yoffie 1987; Denzau 1989; Flamm 1996.

7. The Oki Electric official is quoted in *Electronics* 5/12/86; also see *Electronic Week* 6/10/85; *Electronic News* 4/28/86. NEC claimed to have planned independently to increase U.S. capacity. *Electronic News* 8/11/86.

8. David Angel (1994, 80) suggests that IFDI actually "enhanced the ability of Japanese firms to capture market share, providing just-in-time delivery and local service support to the U.S. computer industry and other major users of DRAM circuits."

9. Yoffie 1993b; Milner 1988, 124. Most of the U.S. companies' overseas in-

vestment occurred during the 1960s and early 1970s and consisted largely of assembly and testing facilities in Southeast Asia, established to reduce labor costs, and fabrication facilities in western Europe, established to circumvent 17% tariff rates.

10. Milner and Yoffie 1989, 255; Pugel 1989. The extent to which the Japanese excluded U.S. semiconductor exports and FDI (which would provide the motive for strategic investment demands) was the subject of much controversy. Whereas some have argued that low U.S. market share reflected the lack of sustained effort or the product mix offered by U.S. firms, others have pointed to subtle barriers to access for non-Japanese firms, such as the Japanese electronic industry's vertical integration and cross-holding of shares among keiretsu members combined with a lax antitrust approach by the Japanese government. See Irwin 1994; Tyson and Yoffie 1993; Borrus 1988, 40–43, 121; Howell et al. 1992, 76–94; Encarnation 1992, chap. 2; Steinmueller 1988a, 39.

11. For similar reasons, downstream computer companies had reason to fear that Japanese firms would gain control over semiconductor production. Six Japanese companies—NEC, Hitachi, Toshiba, Fujitsu, Mitsubishi, and Matsushita—dominated chip production while also manufacturing consumer electronics, computers, and telecom equipment. If these companies were able to gain the market power to raise chip price, they could use the resulting rents to strengthen their end-product business. U.S. firms that bought foreign inputs would be subsidizing their competitors. There was also the possibility that Japanese manufacturers would gain a competitive advantage by virtue of their proximity and association with chipmaking operations; "design engineers on the systems side of Japanese companies would have an inside track on chips in development [and] . . . could be developing tomorrow's electronic products while their American counterparts were waiting for a chip's final specification." *Business Week* 9/4/89; Borrus 1988, 4; Pugel 1987, 215; Tyson and Yoffie 1993, 40; Irwin 1994, 19.

12. U.S. Department of Commerce 1986, 12.

13. Motorola, after making a similar argument in regard to Fujitsu, added a final twist: "Even if Fujitsu's U.S. subsidiary could otherwise be regarded as a domestic producer, it should be excluded from analysis as a 'related party.'" U.S. Department of Commerce 1986, 10.

14. Pugel 1989, 183.

15. Interestingly, the market share target included sales by American-owned firms, wherever these companies located production. Tyson 1992, 109; Bergsten and Noland 1993, 130.

16. In fact, slumping demand had recently led Fujitsu to shelve its plans for constructing a U.S. wafer fabrication plant in Oregon. Toshiba, Hitachi, and Oki had also postponed various projects that involved building chipmaking capacity in the United States. *Electronics* 11/11/85. The one company with existing U.S. capacity, NEC, did substitute production by its California plant for its exports from Japan. *Electronic News* 10/20/86.

17. Although the sanctions did not actually apply to semiconductors, the intended target of the sanctions—Japanese electronic companies—produced both chips and the covered products (such as computers, televisions, and power tools).

18. *Electronic News* 11/9/87, 12/17/87, 3/14/88.

19. *Electronic News* 9/14/87.

20. *Electronic News* 3/7/88; author's interviews with industry representatives, Washington, D.C., 1994.

21. *Electronic News* 11/2/87.

22. *Electronic News* 10/5/87; *Wall Street Journal* 8/26/87.

23. A letter from the SIA to the government stated that the decision to reclassify computer parts undermined support for the sanctions "by directing these sanctions at U.S. computer manufacturers in a fashion that was never intended when the sanctions were imposed." Cited in *Electronic News* 11/2/87.

24. Downstream computer and business equipment manufacturers were not indifferent to who owned their suppliers. During the DRAM shortages of the mid-1980s some firms expressed concern that Japanese chipmakers were favoring their long-time customers. This concern led several computer firms to begin raising funds to increase domestically owned chipmaking capacity. The project—dubbed U.S. Memories—eventually collapsed after the DRAM shortage ended and chip prices declined. *Business Week* 10/23/89, 10/29/89; Semiconductor Industry Association 1990, 70.

25. *Los Angeles Times* 11/30/87.

26. *Electronic News* 11/3/86.

27. *Business Week* 1/12/87; MacKenzie de Sola Pool 1988, 92; *Los Angeles Times* 11/30/87; interviews with industry officials, January 1994.

28. See Encarnation 1992, 124–26, for how this dynamic played out among foreign firms producing chips for televisions.

29. Quoted in *Electronic News* 12/1/86; also see *Wall Street Journal* 10/27/86; *Los Angeles Times* 11/30/87. *Zaibatsu* were the family-owned conglomerates that controlled much of the pre–World War II Japanese economy. Corrigan, a former Fairchild CEO, had a reason to take a leadership role. LSI Logic ranked second ($80 million), right behind Fujitsu ($85 million), in sales of gate arrays. Fairchild ranked fourth (behind Motorola) with $60 million. The sale would thus give Fujitsu a commanding lead.

30. Interview with industry officials, January 1994.

31. Intel executives also attended staff meetings of the Committee on Foreign Investment in the United States (CFIUS) and planning meetings of the Department of Defense in order to argue against the acquisitions. *Los Angeles Times* 12/1/87; MacKenzie de Sola Pool 1988, 4.

32. MacKenzie de Sola Pool 1988, 84; interviews with industry executives, January 1994. The SIA's aggressive approach to trade policy also casts doubt on two other motives for the industry's position on the Fujitsu acquisition (MacKenzie de Sola Pool 1988, 84): first, that U.S. companies were afraid of offending their Japanese joint venture partners and, second, that they worried about running afoul of antitrust law should they publicly advocate any policies to limit competition.

33. Fairchild was the sole source for a chip in the F-16, but according to Defense officials this fact was not due to any technological advantage; rather, no other company bothered to make the product. MacKenzie de Sola Pool 1988, 44; Dallmeyer 1987, 48; *Los Angeles Times* 11/30/87.

34. *Wall Street Journal* 10/31/86.

35. *New York Times* 11/3/86; *Electronics* 3/19/8.

36. *Electronic News* 2/9/87. The domestic industry could have bought Fairchild itself. However, such a move was unlikely because most American firms

had doubts about Fairchild's economic prospects. Interviews with industry officials, January 1994; MacKenzie 1988, 23; *Electronic News* 2/3/87.

37. Fujitsu said it planned to allow Fairchild to survive as a joint venture partner and to keep the new subsidiary "a completely American company," eventually selling public shares. Also, chip manufacturing technology would be provided to other companies in order to ensure supercomputer makers alternative suppliers. Finally, Fujitsu had agreed to a contract guaranteeing Cray a five-year supply of its most advanced chips. *Los Angeles Times* 12/1/87; *New York Times* 3/14/87; *Business Week* 11/10/86; Warshofsky 1989, 302; *Wall Street Journal* 10/27/86.

38. Quotes are taken from *Los Angeles Times* 12/1/87; also see MacKenzie de Sola Pool 1988; interviews with industry officials, 1994.

39. Yoffie 1993b, 210; also see *Electronics* 5/89.

40. *Electronic News* 3/23/87. Just to be on the safe side, the Japanese company had consulted with Defense officials on whether there would be any objections to a new $70 million wafer fab in Gresham, Oregon. "We were very welcome in the area. It was a very big difference from Fairchild," a Fujitsu executive remarked. Cited in Warshofsky 1989, 311; also see *Los Angeles Times* 12/1/87.

41. *Electronics* 4/2/87; *New York Times* 3/30/87; Pugel 1989, 194.

42. For example, NEC announced it would boost production of 256K DRAMs at its Roseville, California, plant by 60% in order to take advantage of the loophole in the STA and sell chips at a lower price. Hitachi announced in December 1986 that it would begin full wafer fabrication of 1-mb DRAMs in Dallas, allowing it to avoid the trade-agreement floor prices. Mitsubishi, Matsushita, and Toshiba subsequently followed suit. *Wall Street Journal* 11/24/86; *Electronic News* 12/29/86.

43. National Research Council 1992; *Business Week* 6/26/89.

44. Glickman and Woodward 1986, 271; Jenkins 1992, 104–5.

45. Interviews with industry executives, January 1994. One exception was the small, Idaho-based firm Micron Technology, which specialized in DRAM production. The company's CEO, Joe Parkinson, testified in favor of the bill, going so far as to advocate the prohibition of all foreign investment in the industry. As he put it, "It is against our whole ethic, our individual pioneer spirit, our free enterprise system, but that is the world economy we are dealing in today. . . . It is all-out war there." U.S. Senate 1987b, 34–35.

46. Washington was to supply half of Sematech's funding with the rest coming from member firms, each of which was expected to pay dues proportional to its share of the semiconductor market. Angel 1994, 168.

47. *Electronics* 5/28/87; Hart 1992, 275.

48. Industry officials expressed fear that formal legislation might later be used against the companies, for example by government controls on equipment exports for security reasons. U.S. Senate 1987d, 123.

49. *Electronics* 5/16/88; *New York Times* 8/15/88.

50. The quotations are from Mowery and Rosenberg 1989, 287, and Ziegler 1991, 166. Also see Reich 1991, 161.

51. Ziegler 1991, 166, 175; Bergsten and Noland 1993, 143.

52. Cited in Mowery and Rosenberg 1989, 287.

53. Interviews with industry officials, January 1994; *New York Times* 8/15/88; U.S. Senate 1987d, 123.

54. Sematech's funding was always politically precarious, and high-level White House aides in the Bush administration (specifically Budget Director Richard Darman and Council of Economic Advisors chairman Michael Boskin) made no secret of their hostility toward programs that smacked of "industrial policy." *Business Week* 11/27/89; *New York Times* 2/13/87; *Los Angeles Times* 3/26/87; interviews with industry officials, January 1994.

55. Alic 1991, 161.

56. *Electronics* 3/5/87; *New York Times* 8/15/88; interviews with industry officials, January 1994. Domestic firms maintained this position as long as the government was funding the consortium. When federal funding stopped in 1997, foreign members were allowed to join.

57. *New York Times* 8/15/88; *Business Week* 1/16/89. Robert Noyce, the head of Sematech, argued that alliances were not incompatible with Sematech's focus on bolstering the American industry. "It's not necessarily true that we can't pull ahead of the Japanese while working with them. The Japanese pulled ahead of the United States while working with us." *Electronic News* 1/16/89, 1/30/89. Also see *Electronic News* 9/18/92 and 5/3/93 on the SIA's attitude toward international alliances.

58. Stevens 1990; Cowhey and Aronson 1993, chap. 6; Steinmueller 1988b; *New York Times* 7/14/92; *Business Week* 4/2/87; *Electronics* 4/2/87.

59. *Electronic News* 5/29/89.

60. Stowsky 1989, 241; Angel 1994, 170.

61. U.S. Department of Commerce 1985, 67; Stowsky 1989, 243–48, 264; Steinmueller 1988b.

62. *U.S. News and World Report* 12/18/89.

63. Robert Costello, undersecretary of defense for acquisition, stated, "It is essential to keep the Perkin-Elmer technology in the U.S. under American ownership." *Electronic News* 5/1/88, 5/15/88.

64. Cited in Tolchin and Tolchin 1992, 119. Senator Jeff Bingaman (D-N.M.) had requested that the secretaries of defense, commerce, and treasury actively review the potential deal, and Rep. Jack Brooks (D-Tex.) had asked the Justice Department to examine the antitrust implications, arguing that the sale would cause the United States to become "wholly dependent on Japan for the technology needed to produce future generations of computer chips." *International Trade Review* 12/21/89. Senator Exon and Representative Florio wrote the administration that if Nikon made a bid for P-E, "there could be no more clear-cut case for use of your full authority under the Exon-Florio amendment." *New York Times* 12/2/89.

65. C. Scott Kulicke, in U.S. Senate 1989, 22.

66. Cited in Tolchin and Tolchin 1992, 118.

67. Admitting that, politically, this idea was "perhaps a little wild," he defended it by arguing that this extra charge would put the Japanese on a more even playing field with potential American bidders, who were handicapped by a higher cost of capital. U.S. Senate 1989, 124.

68. Noyce cited in *Electronic News* 7/10/88; *Reuters Newswire* 2/9/90.

69. *New York Times* 11/27/89; Tolchin and Tolchin 1992, 121; *Electronic News* 3/26/90; *Los Angeles Times* 3/20/90.

70. *Electronic News* 3/26/90; U.S. General Accounting Office 1990, 19; Semiconductor Industry Association 1990, 221.

71. Interview with industry executive, January 1994.

72. *Electronic News* 11/14/88.

73. According to one defense official, "Monsanto Electronic Materials hasn't hired an R&D engineer since 1980. . . . [Huels itself] is doing far more materials research in the U.S. at its R&D center in North Carolina." *Electronic News* 1/23/89.

74. *Electronic News* 1/16/89; Tolchin and Tolchin 1992, 53.

75. *Electronic News* 1/16/89. The quotation is from Sam Herrell, chairman of SEMI/Sematech, which was a subdivision of SEMI (Semiconductor Equipment & Manufacturing International), created in 1987 as an "interface" between SM&E producers and Sematech. The group, which provided funding and technical access to equipment companies winning bids on R&D projects, consisted only of U.S.-owned companies whereas SEMI itself, as its name suggested, included a number of foreign-owned firms, which could not participate in the consortium.

76. *Business Week* 6/12/89; *Electronics* 1/89; *Electronic News* 1/30/89.

77. *Electronic News* 12/12/88. Deputy Assistant Defense Secretary Robert McCormack expressed his frustration: "Only after . . . [the Huels bid] did some U.S. companies become concerned. They came running to the Defense Department, telling us, 'You can't let the Monsanto silicon operation go.' . . . I told them if they were so worried, then DOD would consider putting up half the money needed to buy the operation. When I asked the people in the room [at a meeting with industry executives] if anyone was interested, not a single executive put up a hand." Cited in *Electronic News* 1/23/89; also see *Electronic News* 12/19/88.

78. *Electronic News* 2/13/89.

79. *Electronic News* 11/13/89.

80. From 1987 to early 1991 there were almost forty acquisitions of domestic SM&E firms by foreign companies. Among the Japanese investors were Osaka Titanium (which bought Cincinnati Milacron's silicon epitaxial wafer production unit), Nippon Mining (which bought Gould, Inc., a company that produced 60% of the world's copper foil used in printed circuit boards), and Sony (which bought Materials Research Corporation, a supplier of target materials used in semiconductor production and a leader in sputtering and etching equipment).

81. *Business Week* 1/21/91.

82. U.S. Senate 1990b, 36; *Electronic News* 7/30/90, 8/6/90.

83. *Electronic News* 5/7/90, 8/23/90.

84. *Electronic News* 7/23/90.

85. *Electronic News* 6/18/90; *Financial Times* 7/18/90.

86. U.S. Senate 1990b, 53; *Electronic News* 5/14/90.

87. *Electronic News* 8/13/90.

88. Senator Albert Gore (D-Tenn.), at the time the chairman of the Senate Commerce, Science, Space, and Technology Subcommittee, held hearings at which he called the sale "an electronic Teapot Dome." Gore, however, was careful to distinguish FDI in general, which he praised for bringing jobs, from "unrestricted purchases of key technologies," which created minimal employment and harmed the country's long-run competitiveness. Senators Jeff Bingaman (D-N.M.) and Lloyd Bentsen (D-Tex.) also urged the Justice Department to block the sale, citing not only market-share considerations but also Sematech's concerns about compro-

mising confidential technical data. U.S. Senate 1990b, 3, 22; *Electronic News* 10/8/90.

89. Although some observers saw the Justice investigation as a sign of administration displeasure with the state of U.S.-Japan relations, according to a department spokesperson the suit "was purely an antitrust decision" and was not influenced by the White House. Cited in *Business Week* 1/21/91; also see *Electronic News* 1/7/91; *Washington Post* 10/23/90; *Financial Times* 7/18/90.

90. *Electronic News* 4/1/90.

91. *Electronic News* 3/11/91.

92. *Electronic News* 5/20/91.

93. Cited in *Electronic News* 6/17/91; also see *Electronic News* 9/30/91.

94. Interviews with industry officials, September 1994.

95. National Advisory Commission on Semiconductors 1991; *Electronic News* 1/30/89.

96. U.S. Congress, Joint Economic Committee 1986, 61.

97. Interviews with industry officials, January 1994.

98. If anything, the chipmakers were frustrated that Sematech could not do more. In its 1992 report the SIA praised Sematech's role but concluded: "While Sematech can grant R&D contracts to U.S. SME firms it can do nothing to prevent those same firms from being bought outright by Japanese producers. Sematech has opposed such foreign acquisitions, but . . . CFIUS routinely approves them, arguably to the long run economic detriment of the United States." Howell et al. 1992, 19. On the dominant role of large global firms in Sematech, see *Electronic Business* 5/1/88. The smaller firms often complained that the high dues (1% of the value of total chip sales, with a $1 million minimum) prevented them from participating.

99. Interview with industry official, January 1994.

100. Angel 1994, 169–74.

101. AMC, the fourth domestic automaker, had by this point effectively become a U.S. subsidiary of Renault and played only a minor role in industry politics until 1987, when it was acquired by Chrysler (which itself merged with Daimler-Benz in 1998).

102. Imports made up 1% of U.S. car sales in 1955, 15% in 1970, and 27% by 1980. For samples of the voluminous literature on the problems of the U.S. auto industry, see Altshuler et al. 1984; Womack et al. 1990; Dyer et al. 1987; Cole and Yakushiji 1984.

103. Destler 1992, 77; Rubenstein 1991, 116; *New York Times* 4/16/92; *Ward's Automotive Yearbook 1993*; *Wall Street Journal* 10/17/94. James Womack et al. (1990, 241) remark, "The speed and scale of this process are truly extraordinary. Indeed, nothing like it has ever occurred in industrial history. In effect, between 1982 and 1992 the Japanese will have built in the U.S. Midwest an auto industry larger than that of Britain or Italy or Spain and almost the size of the French industry."

104. Eden and Molot 1993a, 1993b.

105. Interviews with industry representatives, Washington, D.C., October 1994. In Europe and elsewhere, when U.S. automakers had faced foreign trade barriers, they were able to establish local subsidiaries to serve these markets. In

Japan this was nearly impossible. See Encarnation 1992, chap. 2; Mason 1994; Cole and Yakushiji 1984, 75.

106. *New York Times* 6/28/95; Gordon and Lees 1986, 133.

107. Conventional wisdom held that first-time buyers, who often opted for smaller cars, would remain loyal to the same brand when they were ready to buy larger (and more profit-generating) vehicles.

108. Cowhey and Aronson 1993, 115–19.

109. In October 1991 Mitsubishi bought out Chrysler's stake in Diamond-Star, and Chrysler subsequently reduced its equity share in Mitsubishi. GM and Toyota set up a joint venture in Fremont, California, called New United Motor Manufacturer, Inc. (NUMMI), which is discussed later.

110. Dunn 1987, 245; *Automotive News* 8/6/90.

111. Because the Big Three produced many of their own parts, the two sectors overlapped to a certain extent. GM was the most integrated, obtaining around 70% of its components from in-house divisions. Chrysler was the least integrated. Over the course of the 1980s all the American car companies moved toward purchasing more of their parts from outside suppliers in order to reduce costs. Womack et al. 1990, 139; Booz, Allen & Hamilton, Inc. 1985, 12.

112. Bergsten and Noland 1993, 112–13.

113. The other way Japanese firms adjusted to the VRAs was by moving upmarket, thereby increasing profit per vehicle sold. Although Japanese export volume remained relatively constant between 1981 and 1985, the value of these exports rose from $8.8 billion to $12.4 billion (although the yen had fallen by more than 10%). Nevertheless, Japanese firms found that they also could maintain their strong position in the low end of the market if they simultaneously shifted production to the United States. Aggarwal et al. 1987, 362; *Automotive News* 8/26/85.

114. *Automotive News* 5/7/84.

115. For examples of these demands by Chrysler, see Perkins 1983; by GM, U.S. House of Representatives 1982, 431; by Ford, U.S. House of Representatives 1982, 36; *Automotive News* 2/22/82; by AMC, *Automotive News* 11/8/82, 11/15/82; by the industry trade association, the Motor Vehicle Manufacturing Association (MVMA), U.S. House of Representatives 1982, 165.

116. GM's Roger Smith conceded that trade protection might lead to IFDI but argued: "I don't think that's the Japanese game plan, though, to build that much capacity. It would be the greatest thing in the world. . . . But . . . I think that is their long term game plan—protect the home market and ship overseas." *Automotive News* 12/9/85. By adopting this strategy, the Japanese could "export unemployment" to the United States. Ford's automotive group president agreed: "I don't think of transplants as exacerbating the capacity problem." *National Journal* 9/23/89; Goodman et al. 1996, 580; interviews with industry officials, October 1994.

117. Eads 1990, 219. Estimates on the magnitude of the cost advantage ranged from around $1,300 to $2,200 per car: Chrysler cited the latter figure; Ford's estimate was $1,800 and GM's $1,500. Cole and Yakushiji 1984, chap. 7. A study conducted by Chrysler asserted that the Japanese big Four (Toyota, Nissan, Mazda, and Honda) would have actually *lost* money from 1980 to 1984 without their tax advantages or the yen/dollar imbalance. Greenwald 1984.

118. Womack et al. 1990, 236, 240–43.

119. *Business Week* 8/2/82; Encarnation 1992, 130.

120. Cole and Yakushiji 1984, 71. In surveys of Japanese executives, trade restrictions were constantly cited as the primary motive in Japanese FDI in both the United States and Europe (though some firms also emphasized the proximity to customers in order to maintain market share). See Sazanami 1989, 110–11.

121. *Business Week* 2/28/83.

122. *Automotive News* 4/23/84.

123. *Automotive News* 1/1/84.

124. U.S. House of Representatives 1984a.

125. U.S. House of Representatives 1983b, 102. Because the jointly produced car would most likely replace GM's Chevrolet Chevette (which was 95% U.S. content), opponents argued that the venture would result in a net employment loss (which Iaccoca put at 50,000 jobs). *Automotive News* 2/21/83. Iaccoca remarked: "And I say to Toyota: Why do you not stop dipping your toe in the water? Take the plunge. Come build cars here on your own, instead of on the cheap." U.S. House of Representatives 1984a, 155. AMC's president agreed: "Toyota owes this country an automobile plant—and this isn't it." Cited in *Business Week* 1/9/84; also see *Automotive News* 3/21/83, 8/1/83.

126. U.S. House of Representatives 1984a, 378; *Automotive News* 1/16/84.

127. *Business Week* 10/31/83. GM officials replied that its competitors were already outsourcing through captive imports of Japanese-made small cars; at least there would be *some* local content in the cars GM and Toyota planned to produce. U.S. House of Representatives 1984a, 241; *National Journal* 2/25/84.

128. *Business Week* 4/15/84.

129. Kabashima and Sato 1986, 296–97.

130. *Congressional Quarterly* 9/11/82; U.S. House of Representatives 1982; Kabashima and Sato 1986, 298.

131. U.S. House of Representatives 1982, 192, 507, 543.

132. *National Journal* 6/4/83; *Ward's Automotive Yearbook 1984.*

133. From labor's standpoint, of course, this effect of the legislation was not accidental. A UAW official remarked, "We intended to write the bill to pressure the American companies to source more of their parts and production here." *National Journal* 7/10/82.

134. The Strategic Investment hypothesis does not apply to this case, as the bill was not designed to elicit market-opening concessions from Japan. Despite its sponsor's assertion that the bill's "most desirable result will be the removal of all trade barriers," nothing in the legislation tied U.S. policy to the removal of foreign barriers. Kabashima and Sato 1986, 310. *National Journal* 7/10/82.

135. U.S. House of Representatives 1982, 431–32, 438; Smith 1983.

136. U.S. House of Representatives 1982, 306.

137. U.S. Senate 1984c, 317; U.S. House of Representatives 1983a, 362.

138. This response exasperated the questioner, Senator Danforth, who called it a "non-answer." U.S. Senate 1984c, 241. *Automotive News* 1/17/83. Destler and Odell (1987, 148) place Ford with opponents of the bill, but Eden and Molot (1993c, 53) say Ford supported it.

139. *Automotive News* 11/7/83.

140. U.S. Senate 1984c, 247.

141. U.S. Senate 1984c, 235.

142. U.S. House of Representatives 1983a, 112. In February 1984 he testified, "I am against domestic content law, always have been, never supported it." U.S. House of Representatives 1984b, 177.

143. U.S. House of Representatives 1983a, 260. *Automotive News* reported on 3/8/82 and 11/5/84 that Chrysler favored the bill but on 5/28/84 that the company opposed it.

144. In 1983 GM broke ranks with the rest of the industry by coming out against the VRA. The immediate reason was that the company wanted to import more small cars from Suzuki and Isuzu. These two companies were adversely affected by Tokyo's reliance on previous sales figures in devising their formula to divide up the export quota among Japanese automakers.

145. Ikuo Kabashima and Hideo Sato (1986, 311) argue that the vote in the House owed a lot to this belief; they cite Rep. Gibbons: "I think that some of the Members voted for it because they figured it never was going to pass; they'd get a free ticket from Labor for having voted for it. . . . But most of them held their nose and came to me to apologize for having to vote for a piece of legislation that was so atrocious as this." Similarly, Chrysler's Greenwald concluded, "It is clear this approach will not succeed," and even many labor representatives echoed this assessment. Kabashima and Sato 1986, 310; U.S. House of Representatives 1983a, 254; *Congressional Quarterly* 6/25/83.

146. U.S. House of Representatives 1982, 242–43.

147. U.S. House of Representatives 1982, 240, 244.

148. Gayle 1993, 182.

149. Dunn 1987, 239; Rubenstein 1991, 124. The congressional pressure that led Japan to make this decision resulted from the concerns of policy makers about the overall U.S.-Japanese trade deficit rather than lobbying from the U.S. automobile industry. Aggarwal et al. 1987, 365.

150. Florida and Kenney 1991, 94.

151. *Ward's Automotive Yearbook 1986*, 9. A 1987 U.S.-Japan automotive industry conference in Michigan was titled, "Is There Enough Business to Go Around?" The consensus of the conference participants was no. Arneson 1988. "In North America, over 2 million units of overcapacity will be in place in 1990 as a result of the transplants," the keynote speaker at another conference predicted. Michael de Portu cited in *Automotive News* 5/20/89.

152. Hart 1992, 252.

153. *Automotive News* 4/7/86.

154. *Automotive News* 8/18/86.

155. Domestic and foreign-produced fleets were averaged separately when determining whether auto companies met the CAFE targets (75% domestic content was the cutoff point). This requirement was designed to discourage firms from offsetting domestic production of large vehicles by simply importing smaller cars rather than producing energy-efficient vehicles locally. *Automotive News* 6/11/90.

156. U.S. General Accounting Office 1988, 31.

157. For the EPA, however, the car still counted as an import because the agency averaged the Accords built in Japan with those built in the United States, thus arriving at a lower domestic content level. *Automotive News* 4/2/90, 8/20/90, 3/4/91.

158. Quotes from U.S. House of Representatives 1989a, 164; also see *Automotive News* 2/3/86, 1/26/87.

159. *Automotive News* 5/13/91, 6/10/91.

160. *Automotive News* 11/13/89.

161. *Automotive News* 3/2/87.

162. *Automotive News* 12/3/90.

163. U.S. House of Representatives 1987b, 10, 14.

164. The first quote is from *Automotive News* 2/3/86, and the second is from U.S. House of Representatives 1990b, 169. Also see Morris 1988, 87.

165. Morris 1988, 87.

166. U.S. Senate 1987e, 62; U.S. House of Representatives 1987b, 10.

167. The Treasury Department recognized the negative effects of incentive bidding wars but acknowledged, "Under our federalist system of government, the states are within their rights to reject our advice on incentives." U.S. House of Representatives 1987b, 122.

168. Florida and Kenney 1991.

169. *Automotive News* 1/21/91.

170. McDonald cited in *Ward's Automotive Yearbook* 1987, 15. Ford CEO cited in *New York Times* 2/8/87. Also see *Automotive News* 1/22/90. In 1989, Iacocca declared: "The transplants are murdering all of us—all of the Big 3." *Automotive News* 11/27/89. He later remarked, "It's amazing to me that, in the last few years, seven Big Three assembly plants have closed, and seven Japanese transplants have opened. You don't have to be a rocket scientist to figure out there's a correlation between the two." Cited in Ingrassia and White 1994, 25.

171. U.S. House of Representatives 1989d, 140–41.

172. McCulloch 1991, 172.

173. U.S. vehicle makers agreed. Interviews with industry executives, October 1994. *Automotive News* 6/30/86, 8/4/86.

174. *Automotive News* 3/10/86.

175. *Automotive News* 2/29/88.

176. U.S. House of Representatives 1989c, 28; U.S. House of Representatives 1989d, 111.

177. *International Trade Review* 10/1/86.

178. Cited in *Automotive News* 6/19/89; also see U.S. House of Representatives 1989c, 159, 191.

179. APAA concurred that these reforms would be optimal but itself called only for a freeze on new subzones. U.S. House of Representatives 1989d, 36, 110; *Automotive News* 6/12/89.

180. U.S. House of Representatives 1989d, 16, 157; *Automotive News* 7/3/89.

181. *International Trade Review* 9/2/87.

182. U.S. House of Representatives 1989d, 36, 104–7; *Metalworking News* 11/6/89. Even GM's "import-buster" Saturn plant had requested subzone status. *Automotive News* 10/30/89.

183. In a letter to the Ways and Means Committee, the company also asked that the government carry out public interest evaluations before subzones were granted in the future. U.S. House of Representatives 1989d, 287.

184. *Automotive News* 3/9/92.

185. *Automotive News* 9/7/87.

186. The group had remained silent at the earlier hearings over Toyota's application in August 1987. *Automotive News* 8/17/87, 10/14/91.

187. *Automotive News* 11/30/92; *New York Times* 6/14/93.

188. The MVMA and the APAA asked the FTZ Board to delay any final decision or even temporary permission to expand until the new administration had time to appoint a new board. *JIJI Press Service* 12/8/92.

189. *Detroit News* 3/24/93; interviews with industry executives, October 1994.

190. *Automotive News* 7/26/93.

191. *Automotive News* 3/29/93; *New York Times* 6/14/93.

192. *International Trade Review* 8/10/92.

193. Interview with industry executive, October 1994; also see *New York Times* 2/6/92; *Automotive News* 7/20/92.

194. *International Trade Review* 8/19/92.

195. U.S. House of Representatives 1993, 154.

196. *Automotive News* 2/24/86, 8/25/86.

197. *Automotive News* 10/12/87.

198. MEMA and APAA, calling the minimum percentage "inadequate," proposed raising it to at least 60%. *Automotive News* 3/788, 5/23/88.

199. Molot 1993, 9.

200. Eden and Molot 1993b, 182.

201. *Automotive News* 2/17/92.

202. *Nikkei Weekly* 3/14/92; *Automotive News* 6/24/91.

203. *Toronto Star* 3/25/92.

204. The rules did not count capital equipment and were written to give larger producers with more models or more plants more room to average out their regional content levels. As one analyst commented, "Asian producers tend to have fewer plants and fewer models and more parts imports. Who then is the rule aimed at?" Waverman 1993, 51.

205. Gestrin and Rugman 1994; Johnson 1993, 126–27; Krueger 1993; Angel Olea 1993.

206. Cited in Eden and Molot 1993b, 186. Nissan, since it already had Mexican operations, split from the other Japanese automakers and did not oppose Detroit on this issue. Eden and Molot 1993b, 186–88; *Ward's Automotive Yearbook 1992*; *Japan Economic Newswire* 10/18/92.

207. Molot 1993, 11–12. Peter Morici (1993, 248–49) adds that the final rules were less draconian than some observers had expected, given the beleaguered state of the industry and the politicized tone of the negotiations.

208. Reich 1993, 84. The Big Three defended their position by arguing that allowing newcomers to enjoy the benefits of NAFTA immediately hurt those firms that already had operations in Mexico since they had invested under vastly different Mexican government policies and so were now saddled with fixed investments and inefficient supplier contracts that would take time to restructure. New plants without these entanglements would make for an uneven playing field. Interviews with industry executives, October 1994.

209. Murray Smith and Ronald Wonnacott (1993, 285–301) argue that U.S. government officials were also concerned that agreeing to looser rules of origin, which would lead to the diversion of Asian IFDI from the United States to Mexico, would set a bad precedent for the possible expansion of NAFTA to other low-wage Latin American countries.

210. Eden and Molot 1993a, 221.

211. Interviews with industry executives, October 1994.

212. *Automotive News* 4/9/90.

213. Monica 1991, 639–41.

214. Unlike Ford and GM, Chrysler exported vehicles to Europe instead of manufacturing them there. *Automotive News* 4/9/90.

215. U.S. House of Representatives 1992a, 382.

216. Interviews with industry executives, October 1994.

217. *Automotive News* 5/20/91.

218. *Automotive News* 12/2/91. The minimum percentage of domestic parts was later raised to 60%, and Rep. Dan Rostenkowski revised the bill that spring, calling for imports and transplant production to be capped at 1992 levels and, from 1993 to 1999, to rise only as the sales of Big Three vehicles in Japan rose. *Automotive News* 12/23/91.

219. *Automotive News* 5/11/92. Super 301 was an expanded and strengthened version of Section 301, legislation aimed at foreign trade policies or practices that negatively affect U.S. commerce.

220. U.S. Senate 1992, 230–32.

221. Interview with industry executive, October 1994.

222. Japanese transplants pledged to increase their purchase of U.S-made parts by $19 billion a year, but skeptics pointed out that most of this money had already been promised individually by Japanese firms. *Ward's Automotive Yearbook 1992*. Moreover, the commitments were to suppliers located in the United States, not U.S.-owned companies. *Automotive News* 2/24/92.

223. *Automotive News* 5/18/92.

224. Gephardt had introduced parallel legislation defining any plant owned 25 percent or more by foreign interests as a transplant, thus including the output of the Flat Rock plant, the Geo Prizm from NUMMI, the Geo Metro and Tracker from CAMI, and the Eagle Summit, Eagle Talon, and Plymouth Laser at Diamond-Star. *Automotive News* 5/25/92. *Automotive News* (6/1/92) editorialized that "Ford and Chrysler play with fire when they endorse [the bill]."

225. *Ward's Automotive Yearbook 1992*.

226. Rep. Matsui, cited in *Automotive News* 6/22/92; see also *Congressional Quarterly* 5/16/92.

227. *Automotive News* 5/30/88.

228. According to one executive, "We want to equal, or even better, the domestic content levels of the Big 3 by 1996 in order to put that whole issue to rest." Cited in *Automotive News* 10/4/93.

229. *New York Times* 11/26/92; *Washington Times* 11/26/92.

230. *Automotive News* 11/30/92. A year later the Clinton administration announced that this body would participate in a government-sponsored project to develop a "super car" with vastly superior fuel efficiency. However, the project was confined to the Big Three, leading the Association of International Automobile Manufacturers to call the project a violation of national treatment. *New York Times* 1/9/94.

231. *Automotive News* 12/7/93.

232. *New York Times* 11/26/92.

233. *Sacramento Bee* 11/27/92; *USA Today* 11/27/92.

234. U.S. House of Representatives 1992b, 171.

235. Interviews with industry executives, October 1994.

236. Honda spokesperson cited in *Automotive News* 5/23/94. Mazda spokesperson cited in *Automotive News* 7/4/94.

237. Smith and Venables 1990, 150.

238. When the APAA's president was asked in 1992 congressional hearings whether he opposed IFDI by the Japanese assembly transplants, he responded, "I would prefer they didn't exist given their sourcing behavior, yes." U.S. House of Representatives 1992a, 249.

239. According to GM CEO Jack Smith, "You get realistic when you lose the kind of money we lost." Cited in *The Economist* 1/16/93.

240. Interview with industry executive, October 1994.

241. Interviews with industry executives, October 1994. Speaking of these simultaneous strategies, Chrysler president Harold K. Sperlich admitted in 1985: "It's contradictory as hell, but we have no choice. . . . We can't afford to bet the company on any one scenario, on whether Washington will wake up or won't wake up. We've got to have a strategy that will work no matter what happens." *Wall Street Journal* 10/28/85.

242. For example, a Ford executive stated, "We want liberalization, not protection." U.S. Senate 1992, 50.

243. U.S. House of Representatives 1992a, 331; *The Economist* 11/4/95.

244. Ingrassia and White 1994, chaps. 6–12.

245. *Wall Street Journal* 10/10/94; *International Trade Reporter* 3/17/93.

246. Pressure from Peugeot, Renault, Fiat, and VW prompted the European Community to negotiate an "understanding" with the Japanese in the summer of 1991. Although the terms of the deal were (purposely) left somewhat ambiguous, limits were placed on Japanese imports *and* transplant output. This agreement, according to Mark Mason (1994, 433), represents "the first major example among [advanced industrialized] countries in which restrictions are based on the nationality of the producer rather than the location of production." Also see *The Economist* 6/12/93.

247. Krueger 1993, 15.

248. Interviews with industry executives, October 1994; *New York Times* 2/7/94.

249. As Iaccoca said in a television interview (*Frontline* 12/1/92): "They go into a cornfield. They don't go in there in the ghettos. They don't want any of the problems." Industry officials claimed that these subsidiaries received unfair subsidies from state and local governments. Furthermore, they could hire younger workers—thus reducing health and pension costs—and sometimes these workers were non-union as well. U.S. Senate 1992, 38, 123.

250. Interviews with industry executives, October 1994.

251. Interviews with industry executives, September 1994.

252. *Automotive News* 11/20/89.

5. A LIBERAL RESPONSE: MACHINE TOOLS AND ANTIFRICTION BEARINGS

1. Alexander 1990, 11; Dertouzos et al. 1989, 232; Finegold et al. 1994, 36.

2. Quoted in *Production* 5/91; also see Cohen and Zysman 1987; Dertouzos et al. 1989. Machine tools are defined as power-driven devices, not handheld, that cut, form, or shape metal. Metal-cutting tools such as those used in drilling, bor-

ing, and gear cutting account for approximately three-fourths of the world industry's output; the remainder come from metal-forming tools, used in forging, bending, shearing, pressing, and punching. See Graham 1993, 140–42; Corcoran 1990, 227; and Finegold et al. 1994, appendix F, on the classification of machine tools. As a political unit the industry encompasses a wide range of subsectors. Reflecting this diversity, the National Machine Tool Builders Association (NMTBA) changed its name in 1988 to the Association for Manufacturing Technology (AMT) and voted to expand its membership to producers of other capital equipment. *American Machinist* 5/88.

3. A few statistics provide a sense of the magnitude of this collapse. In the mid-1960s the United States produced more than 28% of world output. By 1981 the share fell below 20%, and over the course of the 1980s, U.S. output fell to just over 7%. In the domestic market the decline was even more dramatic. By 1978 the United States first began to import more machine tools than it exported, running a trade deficit that rose sharply after 1982 and reached $1.7 billion by 1986. Foreign producers increased their market share from 10% in 1968 to 49% by 1986. Employment fell steadily in the 1980s; by 1992 the U.S. industry employed 40,500 workers, down from around 100,000 in 1980. Finegold et al. 1994, 11; Corcoran 1990, 235; Graham 1993, 140, 153; Holland 1989, 2; Alexander 1990, 6; *Ward's Auto World* 5/92.

4. Among the reasons: the increase of nonmetallic inputs by manufacturing industries, the rise of other metal-forming technologies, the decrease in the production of those products that use machined parts, the increased productivity of the machine tools themselves (thus reducing the amount of equipment customers have to buy), and the increased overseas production by other U.S. manufacturers. Over the 1980s U.S. consumption of machine tools declined by 37% in real terms. Alexander 1990, 3–4; Finegold et al. 1994, 18.

5. Alexander 1990, 1, 6; Dertouzos et al. 1989, 238.

6. Corcoran 1990, 238–39. Among the technological innovations in the industry, the most important was the computer-numerically controlled (CNC) tool, which gave manufacturers greater flexibility, diminishing changeover and set-up costs. CNC production was dominated by Fanuc, a Japanese firm that had taken technology licensed from the United States and (with Tokyo's help) developed a flexible, low-priced controller that quickly became the de facto world standard, giving Japanese machine tool manufacturers a significant first-mover advantage. The early adoption of CNC technology and modularization among Japanese firms allowed them to combine the benefits of scale economies with specialized customization. Boultinghouse 1994, 5–6.

7. Alexander 1990, 6; Hooley, 1987, 4. Another important center of machine tool production was West Germany. The German industry, primarily small and medium-sized firms, had long focused on high-precision specialized and customized machines. During the 1980s the Germans did not pose the same kind of competitive threat to U.S. producers as the Japanese and therefore were not subject to the same kind of political scrutiny. Indeed, like the U.S. industry, the German industry was thrown off balance by the Japanese surge in the early 1980s, though it was better able to recover through a strategy of upgrading quality and concentrating on the European market. Finegold et al. 1994, 12, 25.

8. Graham 1993, 147; Sarathy 1989, 136–37.

9. In 1991 the Americans had a little over 1% of the Japanese market and less than 2% of the German and Italian markets (which import almost a third of their machine tools and are the two largest European markets). Finegold et al. 1994, 67.

10. Julie Graham (1993, 161) writes: "Only the very large [U.S.-owned] firms have made sustained efforts to enter foreign markets, either through FDI or the export of machines and service. In general, the export market has been used as a buffer against bad times at home, rather than a target of a well-developed marketing effort." Also see Milner 1988, 114–15; O'Brien 1987, 31; Young 1990, 27.

11. U.S. House of Representatives 1991b, 1007.

12. Milner and Yoffie 1989, 268–69.

13. In 1989, for instance, the United States imported 55% of its machine tools, and European countries imported 35% to 65%, but the figure for Japan was around 7%. Thus Japan was an important market from which to be excluded. Its consumption was estimated around 16% of total world production, compared with 12% for the United States. Finegold et al. 1994, 75; *American Machinist* 10/90.

14. *Metalworking News* 5/21/90, 6/4/90; *American Machinist* 12/91.

15. Prestowitz 1988, 380.

16. Holland 1989, 185; Prestowitz 1988, 389–90.

17. According to one poll, 15% of the NMTBA's four hundred members did not support the petition. Lynn and McKeown 1988, 70, 122. Many of these dissenters were actually foreign-owned firms; NMTBA bylaws required only greater than 50% U.S. content for a firm to qualify for membership. Incidentally, Houdaille itself decided that the new petition probably would not succeed and that even if it did, relief would be too late. It therefore decided to seek a joint venture with a Japanese company called Okuma Machinery Works and after 1984 exited the machine tool business. Holland 1989, 233–38.

18. Alexander 1990, 22.

19. Saxonhouse 1986, 234.

20. Ellis Kraus and Simon Reich (1992, 882) argue that the national security argument was less persuasive to President Reagan than the claim that temporary protection would allow the industry to revitalize itself. Other evidence (for example, in Hooley 1987) suggests that the national security argument was crucial to building widespread support for the industry's position. Ultimately, the two claims are not mutually exclusive. The prospect of recovery was a prerequisite for the industry's effort to obtain government assistance; but without the national security argument, machine tool producers would have been just one more industry—and not a particularly powerful one—begging for trade protection.

21. U.S. Department of Commerce 1983, 2. An NMTBA spokesman said, "Our major concern is a major portion of our manufacturing tools are being built overseas. And anyone who thinks that in the middle of a war we're going to be able to ship machine tools across the Pacific from Japan or across the Atlantic from Germany hasn't looked at a map." Cited in *Ward's Auto World* 4/86.

22. Graham 1993, 161–63; O'Brien 1989, 31.

23. *Metalworking News* 8/27/90.

24. Mazak was the first to invest. A subsidiary of the Japanese company Yamazaki Corporation and one of the world's leading machine tool firms, it has had

a manufacturing presence at its Florence, Kentucky, plant since 1974 and expanded several times before doubling in size in 1988. A further $60 million expansion in 1990 increased production of lathes and machining centers by 50%. Toyoda's plant was in Arlington Heights, Illinois, and the company (an affiliate of Toyota) also purchased a production facility in Howell, Michigan. Okuma Machinery, Inc., spent $30 million to double capacity at its Charlotte, North Carolina, plant. Company officials attributed the stepped-up U.S. production to the VRAs. Other Japanese companies that relocated production included Mori Seiki, OSG Manufacturing, Sonoike Manufacturing, and Hitachi-Seiki (which opened a plant in Alabama at the end of 1989). Of the foreign acquisitions that occurred during this period, the most prominent was Makino's buyout of LeBlond, an old U.S. manufacturer (Makino also opened a new plant in Mason, Ohio). *Metalworking News* 7/20/87, 3/4/88, 5/15/89; *Cincinnati Inquirer* 9/5/91; *Financial Times* 9/20/88.

25. *Financial Times* 7/3/87.

26. Cited in *Metalworking News* 8/25/86.

27. Graham and Krugman 1995, 100.

28. *Metalworking News* 9/12/88.

29. Interview with industry executive, Washington, D.C., March 1995.

30. *Industrial Automation and Mechanical Engineering* 1/31/90.

31. Until then the only control makers that could claim domestic status were Allen-Bradley and DynaPath, a subsidiary of Hurco. *Metalworking News* 7/20/87, 4/25/88, 9/12/88.

32. *Japan Economic Journal* 9/8/90.

33. For instance, in October 1987 Customs officials seized a shipment of Taiwanese machine tools, claiming that the boring tool (a category of machine tool not covered by the VRA), once imported into the United States and combined with a tool changer, would become a machining center (which was covered). This action was followed by four similar seizures. In the summer of 1988 Commerce reportedly launched an investigation into content labeling at Hitachi Seike's plant in Congers, New York, though no formal action was taken. These problems were partly the result of what one Commerce official called "semantic problems about what to precisely call a given type of machine tool or whether to call disassembled parts machine tool 'kits.'" Cited in *Metalworking News* 10/26/87; also see 2/8/88, 8/1/88, 3/5/90.

34. *Metalworking News* 10/26/87.

35. *Metalworking News* 9/5/88.

36. Interview with industry executive, March 1995.

37. *Metalworking News* 1/23/89, 5/15/89; Alexander 1990, 28.

38. *International Trade Review* 2/15/90; *Metalworking News* 3/5/90, 5/14/90.

39. U.S. House of Representatives 1992c, 95.

40. *Metalworking News* 6/19/89.

41. Mitsubishi Heavy Industry announced plans in 1990 to build a new plant in Kentucky, which would produce machining centers and lathes, and Hitachi Seiki put up a new plant in Alabama. Okuma's North Carolina subsidiary increased production and expanded its product line. Kitamura began producing machining centers at its Chicago subsidiary in 1990. Miyano expanded its U.S. pro-

duction of milling machines, Mazak increased capacity at its Kentucky plant by 50%, and Amada expanded CNC punch presses in Los Angeles also by half. *Japan Economic Journal* 5/26/90.

42. On this wave of investments, see *Industrial Automation and Mechanical Engineering* 2/1/90, 4/11/90, 4/20/90, 4/24/90, 5/29/90, 7/11/90, 7/12/90, 8/16/90.

43. *Tooling and Production* 3/89.

44. Graham 1993, 158; Milner and Yoffie 1989, 268–69.

45. *Ward's Auto World* 5/92; Holland 1989, 271; Finegold et al. 1994, 12.

46. *Los Angeles Times* 10/20/91.

47. In the treaty's first year (1987), although imports declined by 8.3%, the U.S. industry's orders were no better than in 1986 (and 25% below 1984's level). *Metalworking News* 7/27/87; *Japan Economic Institute Report* 7/15/88.

48. *Financial Times* 9/7/90; *Machining and Tooling* 3/89; *Chicago Tribune* 9/3/90; Finegold et al. 1994, 11. A Commerce official concurred: "Holding the Japanese to a specified market share provided a certain security for U.S. firms. But there has been a direct line between the restraints and direct investment by the Japanese." Quoted in *Reuters Newswire* 2/22/90.

49. U.S. House of Representatives 1991b, 15; *New York Times* 4/16/92.

50. See Finegold et al. 1994, 121; *Machining and Tooling* 11/91.

51. *National Journal* 10/19/91.

52. *Chicago Tribune* 10/5/91.

53. *Tooling and Production* 11/91; *Legal Times* 9/2/91.

54. Alexander 1990, 25; *Washington Times* 12/21/91. For statements to this effect by executives from Toyoda, Makino, Okuma, and Mazak, see *Metalworking News* 1/15/90, 8/27/90; *Daily Yomiuri* 10/1/91; *Nikkei Weekly* 11/9/91.

55. "If there is not a clear national security consensus, then this VRA is gone," one administration official told the *National Journal* (10/19/91).

56. *Japan Economic Newswire* 12/3/91; testimony of NMTBA-AMT in U.S. House of Representatives 1991c, 974.

57. *Gannet News Service* 11/13/91. As an example, they pointed to Maho Group, a German machine toolmaker with a transplant in Connecticut, which had introduced an advanced laser-mill machine but limited pilot installation to users around its German plant. *National Journal* 10/19/91.

58. *Financial Times* 1/3/90.

59. Hurco's president, Brian McLauglin, argued, "Preserving yesterday's technology in a 'museum' of companies that can no longer compete on a world basis in no way serves our national defense." He also added that if national security were the real issue, the limits would have been focused on CNCs and software. "Most significantly," the Hurco position paper argued, "almost all the companies supporting VRA extension on national security grounds are buying computer numerical controls from Fanuc of Japan." Hurco executives pointed out to administration officials and congressional aides that most of the sophisticated weapons used in the Gulf War (such as the Patriot missile) depended on computer controls made by Fanuc, whose technology was developed in Tokyo. McLaughlin cited in *Los Angeles Times* 10/20/91; Hurco position paper cited in *Legal Times* 9/30/91; also see *Los Angeles Times* 10/30/91; *Financial Times* 11/1/91. After one meeting with congressional staff, according to the *Los Angeles Times* (10/30/91), "none of the aides would speak for attribution, but apparently the Hurco executives' argu-

ments have swayed some minds." *New York Times* 10/7/91; *American Machinist* 11/91, 12/91.

60. Bush administration cited in *International Trade Reporter* 1/1/92; AMT cited in *American Machinist* 2/92.

61. *Japan Economic Newswire* 7/10/92; *JIJI Press Service* 7/13/89; *Industrial Automation & Mechanical Engineering* 3/2/93.

62. *Ward's Auto World* 5/92.

63. U.S. House of Representatives 1994a.

64. Cited in *Metalworking News* 10/30/89; also see *Automotive News* 11/6/89.

65. Also see the testimony of Stanley Huffman on behalf of the National Tooling and Machining Association (NTMA). Most of the firms who lost bids, he claimed, felt that the bidding invitations they had received were not made seriously but rather were "merely a way for the Japanese to obtain information on American companies. The few members who have been successful at getting through the transplants' doors have been awarded only crumbs from a large pie." U.S. Senate 1990a, 75–78. Jim Mack, from the AMT, reiterated these complaints before the House hearings on the Trade Enhancement Act of 1992. Because that bill (discussed in the previous chapter) dealing with the automobile industry emerged at the same time the toolmakers were fighting for the VRA renewal, Mack claimed that the AMT had not had the opportunity to fully consider whether or not to support the legislation, though he expressed sympathy and agreement with the bill's aims. The group did not join in the campaign, however.

66. *Ward's Auto World* 4/86.

67. *American Machinist* 10/90; *Air Force Magazine* 5/10/91; Tolchin and Tolchin 1992, 62.

68. *Los Angeles Times* 1/29/91.

69. *Mergers & Acquisitions* 3/92; *New York Times* 1/18/91; *International Trade Reporter* 1/1/92; *Financial Times* 2/21/91; *Washington Post* 2/20/91.

70. One lawyer who dealt with foreign acquisitions told his clients whose bids could spark controversy to wait until things settled down. "Unless you need to do it now, this is a terrible time. It's open season on the Hill for every Japan-basher." Cited in *New York Law Journal* 1991. Also see *New York Times* 1/7/91; *Los Angeles Times* 2/20/91.

71. Ten members of Congress, led by Rep. Mel Levine (D-Calif.), the chairman of the House Energy Committee, wrote President Bush: "Allowing Moore to fall into foreign hands would pose an unacceptable national security risk to U.S. nuclear weapon production capability, as well as worsening the already disturbing trend of growing dependence on foreign machine tool vendors. We strongly urge you to recognize the value of a U.S. owned and controlled industrial base, particularly in machine tools and other national security areas, and to take all steps at your disposal to block this sale to a foreign company." Cited in *Financial Times* 2/21/91; also see *JIJI Press Service* 1/29/91.

72. *Washington Post* 1/13/91.

73. *New York Times* 2/20/91.

74. Interview with industry executive, March 1995.

75. Finegold et al. 1994, 227.

76. The Buy American Act, originally enacted in 1933, stipulated that the

federal government could spend its funds only on domestic products. There were a number of exceptions—for example, if the product was not made in the United States in sufficient quantity or quality or with a reasonable cost, if the purchase would be inconsistent with national interests, or if it was for use outside the United States.

77. *American Machinist* 9/87.

78. *International Trade Reporter* 10/22/86; *American Metal Market* 10/13/86; U.S. House of Representatives 1987a.

79. U.S. House of Representatives 1987a, 573.

80. For instance, Congress passed the Buy American Act of 1988 to monitor foreign procurement practices and impose sanctions on countries that discriminated against U.S. suppliers. The next year, it barred the Navy from buying certain kinds of foreign machine tools used in its ships for three years and all DOD facilities from buying foreign tools through 1989. Goehle 1989, 12; *Tooling and Production* 3/89; U.S. House of Representatives 1989b, 35–43; Vaughan 1989.

81. Goehle 1989, 11.

82. U.S. General Accounting Office 1994.

83. U.S. House of Representatives 1987a, 573–76.

84. U.S. House of Representatives 1987a, 573.

85. Interview with industry executive, March 1995.

86. Moran 1990, 82; U.S. General Accounting Office 1994.

87. U.S. Senate 1991, 48.

88. In fact, some argued the machine tool program was too obsessed with the short-term needs of the Pentagon. See the report from the National Research Council cited in *American Machinist* 9/87. A Rand study found that "ManTech-funded programs specifically focused on military applications often without broad commercial utility, and had no well-developed mechanisms of technology transfer to firms beyond the defense contractors that were the main program participants." Finegold et al. 1994, 41. Pentagon officials admitted as much but defended this approach. As the DOD's director of defense research and engineering testified, ManTech "has been, and will continue to be, driven by defense needs for technologies and systems that provide a superiority edge. The nature of our business dictates we be on the leading edge of creating technologies and products, that in the early development state, have no commercial market and are beyond the normal risk acceptable to industry." U.S. Senate 1994, 113.

89. *Business Week* 12/20/93.

90. U.S. Senate 1987a, 43–44; Mowery and Rosenberg 1989, 287–88.

91. Canadian firms were allowed in order to maintain the spirit of the Canada-U.S. Free Trade Agreement. *Metalworking News* 5/16/88; *Industry Week* 10/16/89; U.S. Senate 1987a.

92. *Wall Street Journal* 12/1/87.

93. *Metalworking News* 9/5/88.

94. Collis 1992, 252. One Defense Department official remarked that the antifriction bearing industry (whose outputs are found in almost every product with moving parts) ranked second only to semiconductors in terms of importance to national security. *Christian Science Monitor* 8/9/88.

95. Between 1980 and 1987, imports of bearings increased 16.7% (while exports declined 28.5%), and in 1987 U.S. producers of bearings saw their share of the world market fall to just 7.7%. European firms, like American ones, had long

held a substantial market share but suffered similar setbacks at the hands of the Japanese. Peterson et al. 1991.

96. Collis 1992, 265, 278, 296; *Japan Economic International Review* 8/14/87.

97. Collis 1992, 264, 277.

98. Ingersoll conducted a third of its business overseas, but according to Clyde H. Folley, the vice-chairman of the board, "Nobody has taken any retaliatory or punitive action against us." Cited in *New York Times* 11/24/88; also see 10/26/88. Torrington also had a 50–50 joint venture with a Japanese firm, NSK, which produced bearings in Japan.

99. Gordon and Lees 1986, 211; *New York Times* 7/16/84.

100. *American Metal Market* 3/4/85. NHBB was an important supplier of the precision-made spheres for missile guidance systems and computer components. But although the company relied on defense business for nearly half its sales, NHBB accounted for only around 5% of the total bearings bought annually by the Pentagon. *New York Times* 7/16/84; *American Metal Market* 11/19/84.

101. U.S. Senate 1984a, 16; *American Metal Market* 11/19/84.

102. U.S. Senate 1984a.

103. U.S. Senate 1988, 61.

104. *Federal Register*, cited in *Metalworking News* 4/11/88, 8/8/88; *Wall Street Journal* 8/5/88.

105. *Metalworking News* 4/6/87.

106. U.S. Senate 1987a, 33.

107. *States News Service* 7/17/87. The AFBMA was not unanimous in its support for the petition, but according to the group's chairman, that was only because of opposition from foreign-owned member companies. U.S. Senate 1987a, 36.

108. The Connecticut company alleged that nine countries (Japan, West Germany, Italy, France, the United Kingdom, Sweden, Singapore, Thailand, and Romania) dumped around $500 million worth of bearings (including needle, cylindrical, ball, tapered roller, and spherical roller) in 1987.

109. See the statement by commerce secretary C. William Verity, Jr., in *International Trade Reporter* 8/17/88. *National Journal* 12/3/88; *New York Times* 11/24/88; *Japan Economic Journal* 11/29/88.

110. *Wall Street Journal* 10/31/88; *International Trade Reporter* 5/3/89; *Purchasing* 5/4/89; *Metalworking News* 5/8/89.

111. *Metalworking News* 8/14/89; *Purchasing* 8/17/89; *Business Wire* 3/30/89. According to James Bovard (1991), a fierce critic of antidumping regulations, Torrington, and in fact all American companies, were renowned for poor service and unreliable bearings. A bearings buyer for Stowe Manufacturing Company testified to the ITC that the company had to build Torrington's "notorious unreliability into our production schedules." Needless to say, bearing makers strongly denied these charges.

112. *Japan Economic Journal* 5/13/89.

113. *Forbes* 5/28/90.

114. *Financial Times* 4/4/89.

115. Fifty percent of its U.S. sales were to be produced locally, and executives spoke of raising that figure to 85% by the next year. *Japan Economic Journal* 5/28/89.

116. Cited in *Metalworking News* 11/7/88; also see *Metalworking News* 8/14/89.

117. *New York Times* 11/24/88.

118. U.S. Senate 1988, 124; *Business Wire* 3/30/89. An industry executive testified: "Foreign-owned U.S. bearing transplant operations in the aggregate are not solvent. Evidence suggests they are lowering prices below costs to take market share from U.S.-owned producers. Foreign-owned companies have used the financial borrowing power of their parent organizations to build an asset base that allows them to secure market share regardless of uneconomical consequences. There appears to be substantial likelihood of foreign-owned companies engaging in faulty transfer pricing that may raise concerns under U.S. tax and trade laws." U.S. House of Representatives 1994a.

119. U.S. House of Representatives 1991a, 308.

120. Cited in U.S. Senate 1988, A-6-2.

121. U.S. Senate 1988, A-15-16.

122. The Moore takeover was an exception. In that case Moore's participation in the Department of Energy's nuclear weapon programs, the timing of the bid in the midst of widespread U.S.-Japanese tensions, and the actions of a small core of committed congressional policy entrepreneurs heightened visibility to the point where Fanuc decided to withdraw.

6. A STRATEGIC RESPONSE: AIRLINES AND TELECOMMUNICATION SERVICES

1. Hoekman and Primo Braga 1997, 1–2. Though information technology increasingly allows for the geographical separation of the producer and the consumer, Peter Dicken (1998, 392) notes that "even in those cases, there is generally a need for the supplying firm to have an actual presence in the foreign market to deliver the service more efficiently and effectively."

2. Peter Cowhey and Jonathan Aronson (1993, 7) define ICAs as "ongoing relationships between companies from two or more countries that involve significant markets, products, R&D, and other important process technologies that shape the strategy of global market leaders." These alliances may or may not involve direct equity holdings.

3. Reich 1991; Cowhey and Aronson 1993, 224–25, 233; *The Economist* 9/19/92.

4. The one exception was the objection on antitrust grounds by GM's competitors to its NUMMI venture with Toyota in 1984. However, at this early stage the Big Three still believed FDI in the United States would blunt the competitive advantage of Japanese assemblers; once they discovered this was not the case, they changed their view on the desirability of alliances.

5. See Beltz 1998 and Olbeter 1994 for contrasting arguments on the desirability of adopting this kind of a conditionality strategy in telecommunications.

6. Nayer 1995; Ott and Neidl 1995.

7. Specifically, a 1926 law limits foreign ownership to 25% of voting stock and requires two-thirds of the board and key management officials to be U.S. citizens. In the early 1990s the Department of Transportation began interpreting the statute to allow foreign carriers to hold up to 49% of a U.S. airline's nonvoting equity as long as the investment did not give a foreign company effective control. *Air Finance Journal* 2/94; *New York Times* 1/9/93. On Virgin Atlantic's unsuccessful attempt to challenge these restrictions, see *New York Times* 6/17/98.

8. See Kass 1994 on the debate concerning the continued relevance of these

security issues. The restrictions also result from the international regime governing aviation, specifically the Chicago convention, which essentially ties airlines to their home governments for the purpose of negotiating routes. Staniland 1999.

9. U.S. Senate 1997.

10. "Code-sharing" means that an international flight involving both partners is listed on a travel agent's computerized reservation system as involving a single airline; the agent is more likely to book this flight, and customers prefer (at least the illusion) of traveling on a single airline.

11. *Air Finance Journal* 2/94.

12. *National Journal* 1/12/91.

13. *New York Times* 9/20/89.

14. *Newsday* 1/13/91.

15. U.S. Senate 1991; *Air Transport World* 1/91.

16. Specifically, KLM could serve any U.S. city by subcontracting with Northwest to provide the planes and using Northwest's ground support and airport gates. In return, Northwest received some of the revenue from these passengers as well as access to KLM's international route system. *Air Transport World* 3/93.

17. Delta Airlines press release on *Business Wire* 2/3/93; *Minneapolis–St. Paul City Business* 9/18/92; *New York Times* 9/10/92; Ott and Neidl 1995, 124–25.

18. *Aviation Week & Space Technology* 7/27/92.

19. Although BA would have only 21% of the voting stock, 44% of USAir equity, and four seats on the board of directors (which would be expanded from thirteen to sixteen members), key decisions on issues such as the approval of fleet purchases, the use of capital, and personnel changes would require a supermajority (80%), thus giving the British veto power. BA saw this authority as essential for protecting its investment, but the structure of the deal raised the issue of whether the investment gave BA "control" of an American company and so required a DOT ruling.

20. Cited in Newhouse 1993, 46; also see *Aviation Week & Space Technology* 7/27/92.

21. *Wall Street Journal* 7/24/92.

22. *New York Times* 10/3/92.

23. Secretary of Transportation Card admitted as much. *Aviation Week & Space Technology* 1/4/93, 12/14/92.

24. USAir had already laid off seventy-six hundred employees during the previous two years to cut costs. *Air Transport World* 9/92; *New York Times* 10/3/92.

25. *Aviation Week & Space Technology* 12/14/92; *Washington Post* 12/18/92.

26. Newhouse 1993, 48; *The Economist* 9/5/92.

27. Tarry 1996, 6; *The Economist* 11/21/92. Crandall also went further than other airlines in demanding that the deal's approval be linked to "beyond rights" (the ability to land in London and continue to, say, Asia) as well as increased access to Heathrow. BA claimed it had little control over either of these issues since the first required negotiations with the third country's government and the second was a function of Heathrow's physical capacity. The rest of the industry backed away from AA's more strident demands but still supported using approval as a bargaining tool. The smaller airlines (Continental, Northwest, TWA) stayed on the

sidelines since they also hoped to attract foreign partners to bolster their own competitive position. Newhouse 1993, 48; *Aviation Week & Space Technology* 7/27/92; *Boston Globe* 12/23/92.

28. Newhouse 1993, 49.

29. *New York Times* 1/22/93. In "wet leasing," one airline uses the crew and plane of another for its flights.

30. *Aviation Weekly & Space Technology* 2/1/93, 2/8/93; *Wall Street Journal* 2/2/93.

31. U.S. House of Representatives 1994c, 29. In a filing with the DOT, AA questioned the motives of the more wary firms, arguing that Northwest opposed renunciation because it had "virtually merged" with KLM and did not want U.S. competitors flying from points beyond London Heathrow and that United did not want to jeopardize a recently signed agreement with Germany that made possible an alliance with Lufthansa. Moreover, AA continued, Northwest and United benefited from a "duopolistic franchise" in the U.S.-Japan market and so did not want to set a precedent of renouncing protectionist agreements. *Aviation Daily* 3/14/94.

32. *National Journal* 2/20/93.

33. The remark is cited in *Washington Post* 3/12/92.

34. President Clinton reportedly became personally involved in the review process and strongly supported the final decision. *National Journal* 6/19/93; *New York Times* 3/16/93, 3/17/93. Eventually, the issue became moot when BA decided on its own not to expand its investment because of USAir's inability to control costs or return to profitability; BA later decided to sell its stake in USAir after announcing a new partnership with American Airlines. *Air Transport World* 4/94.

35. Delta also took actions that seemed to conflict with its earlier positions. In April it entered into a marketing alliance with Virgin Atlantic in order to allow it to send its passengers into Heathrow on Virgin jets. Delta CEO Ronald Allen urged President Clinton not to delay or derail the partnership by "holding it hostage to the conclusion of a new bilateral" (which is exactly what Delta had done with the BA-USAir pact). *Aviation Week & Space Technology* 7/4/94.

36. *Aviation Week & Space Technology* 10/14/96. See also testimony in U.S. Senate 1997, 23.

37. *Aviation Week & Space Technology* 6/17/96; also see an interview with Crandall in *Financial Times* 9/17/96.

38. U.S. Senate 1997.

39. *National Journal* 10/5/96; *Washington Post* 7/26/96. Also see statements by United, USAir, and Delta executives in U.S. Senate 1997, 109–10; *Aviation Week & Space Technology* 6/17/96, 7/1/96.

40. "Simply put, open skies are worthless if the ground is closed," one Continental executive asserted. U.S. Senate 1997, 15; also see 16–17, 50–51, *Aviation Week & Space Technology* 6/17/96.

41. U.S. Senate 1997, 25, 100.

42. Oh 1996; Crandall 1997.

43. Strange 1996, 102. One British Telecom executive remarked, "The resources required in terms of capital, people, and technology are so vast that no player could deliver to the market [what] the market needs in the time frame [the] market needs it or at an acceptable cost." *Industry Week* 7/17/95.

44. Breitfeld 1997; Cowhey 1990, 177.

45. A common carrier is a company that provides communication and transmission services to the public. Because the prohibition applied only to firms holding a radio license, there was a bit of "wiggle room" for foreign investors. For instance, British-owned Cable & Wireless used all wire-line facilities to establish an American network. Cowhey 1995, 186.

46. One analyst testified before Congress that "it makes no sense to maintain ownership rules dating to 1914, when a German-owned highpower radio transmitter on Long Island, N.Y. sent messages to German naval ships in the Atlantic in violation of American neutrality." Eli Noam before the U.S. Senate (1995, 83). Another economist argued, "Few informed persons today believe that concerns over national security continue to motivate the FCC's current enforcement of the foreign ownership restrictions." Sidak 1997, 5; also see Globerman 1995, 22–23.

47. Noam (1994, 367) concludes, "One has to partner one's way into a market rather than invest one's way in."

48. Strange 1996, 104; see Gaster et al. 1996, 41–42, for comparative productivity figures.

49. A 1993 Office of Technology Assessment Report estimated that 85% of the EU's market was closed to foreign competition. Cited in Gaster et al. 1996, 62.

50. The statute actually limited foreign ownership to 25%, but other various foreign owners already held 5% of MCI. The two companies created a $1 billion joint venture (dubbed Concert Global Communications), of which MCI would own 25%. MCI would market phone service from this venture to MNCs in the Americas while BT would market to Europe, Asia, and Africa.

51. *Financial Times* 3/8/93. AT&T argued that approval should be contingent on AT&T's receiving a license from Britain's Department of Trade and Industry to provide similar service in Britain. *The Economist* 6/5/93; *Telecommunications* 5/93.

52. One industry expert commented, "This is AT&T's worst nightmare." *Telecommunications* 8/93.

53. Beltz 1998, 353.

54. *Washington Post* 8/24/93; Gaster et al. 1996, 139.

55. The Justice Department also examined the deal and required some minor changes to prevent the alliance from using its market power in Britain to harm its rivals; despite pressure from AT&T, DOJ did not consider the larger reciprocity issue. *Washington Post* 6/16/94.

56. Gaster et al. 1996, 144; press release by AT&T on *PR Newswire*, 9/22/93.

57. *Market Entry and Regulation of Foreign-Affiliated Entities*, Report and Order, IB Dkt. No. 95-22, 11 FCC Rcd 3873, cited in Sidak 1997, 186.

58. Gaster et al. 1996, 146–52; *Telecommunication* 5/96. The final version of the rules was incorporated into the Telecommunications Act of 1996.

59. *Telephony* 3/6/95.

60. *Business Week* 6/14/93. AT&T itself had formed a much looser alliance, called World Partners, with Singapore Telecom and KDD of Japan and had joined Unisource, an alliance of smaller operators from Holland, Sweden, and Switzerland. However, these alliances were not adequate substitutes for a more intensive partnership with stronger foreign carriers. The *Economist* (8/1/98) characterized both Unisource and World Partners as "dismal failures." AT&T had difficulty

finding partners because its size and strength caused European firms to fear that if they joined AT&T, they would simply be swallowed up. *Financial Times* 10/3/95.

61. *Financial Times* 11/4/96; Gaster et al. 1996, 63.
62. Gaster et al. 1996, 268. Also see *Telephony* 8/8/94.
63. *Wall Street Journal* 11/5/96.
64. *New York Times* 11/4/96; *Financial Times* 11/4/96.
65. *Washington Post* 1/5/96.
66. *Washington Post* 11/10/96.
67. Sidak 1997, 177–78.
68. *Journal of Commerce* 11/7/96.
69. For instance, AT&T asked for access to BT cable installations and networks at cost and the chance to place its own switching facilities into them as well as the removal of the three-digit code that customers had to dial to have their calls routed on a non-BT network. *The Independent* (London) 11/10/96.
70. *Associated Press* 7/8/97. In the end, following disappointing financial news from MCI, BT reduced the terms of its offer, and another company, World-Com, stepped in to acquire MCI. Later WorldCom attempted to merge with Sprint, but the deal foundered as a result of antitrust concerns in the United States and Europe.
71. *Communications Daily* 11/25/94.
72. *Communications Daily* 8/30/95.
73. *Industry Week* 7/17/95; *Reuter Business Report* 9/1/95; *Financial Times* 9/4/95; Sidak 1997, 187; Beltz 1998, 350.
74. *EuroWatch* 10/11/95.
75. MCI and BT also argued that the test should be applied as well to co-marketing arrangements and non-equity alliances like those of AT&T. Beltz 1998, 353.
76. *Communications Daily* 4/7/95; *Network World* 4/24/95.
77. *Communications Daily* 12/5/95.
78. Sidak 1997, 188–91; Gaster et al. 1996, 154–55.
79. Sidak 1997, 192–93; *Communications Daily* 12/18/95.
80. *Business Week* 7/24/00.
81. *Wall Street Journal* 7/25/00.
82. *New York Times* 7/25/00.
83. *Wireless Review* 10/15/00.
84. *Business Week* 8/28/00; *Wireless Review* 10/15/00.
85. *New York Times* 10/24/00.
86. Gaster et al. 1996, 155–56.
87. Milner and Yoffie (1989, 271) base their pessimistic prediction about the growth of contingent protection on the assumption that "foreign government intervention in these [strategic] sectors in Japan, Europe, and the newly industrializing countries has also been rising." At least in the service industries the opposite is the case; most countries have liberalized and deregulated these sectors.

7. POLITICAL VARIABLES AND POLICY PREFERENCES
1. DeSouza 1994, 170.
2. Kudrle and Bobrow 1982, 360–62.
3. Spero 1990, 126.

4. By this logic, it should also not matter whether profits are reduced by domestic or by foreign competition, and firms should demand policies to harm their domestically owned competitors as well. In fact, they do just that. Eugene Salorio's study of administered protection in the agribusiness industry convincingly demonstrates that producers formulate their demands on trade policy with an eye toward improving their relative position within the domestic industry. He concludes, "Firms may oppose protection for their own domestic industry if the threat to them of imports is less than the competitive benefits domestic rivals would derive from protection." Salorio 1991, 16–17.

5. E.g., Corden 1993.

6. An example of lobbying strategy priorities can be seen in the battle over the Trade Enhancement Act of 1992, when the auto industry agreed to drop the controversial portions of the bill dealing with transplant production in order to improve the chance that the import-related sections would become law.

7. Graham and Krugman 1995, 59. Marc Levinson (1987, 47) makes a similar argument about import competition.

8. The exception was the steel industry, in which, as discussed in chapter 3, IFDI came in the form of joint ventures.

9. See Gilpin 1975, 144; Lipson 1985, 200–57.

10. See Mason 1994 for a fuller comparison of the U.S. and European cases.

11. Only two non-Japanese manufacturing investments attracted significant opposition. The first involved the Huels AG acquisition bid for Monsanto's semiconductor material division (although the fact that the Japanese controlled the rest of this market was a major reason for the concern). Industry officials said they would have opposed the deal even more vigorously had the bidder been Japanese rather than German (interview with semiconductor industry executive, Washington, D.C., October 1994). The second was South Korean Pohang Steel Company's joint venture with U.S. Steel, which aroused some controversy because of its reliance on imported slab steel.

12. Ishihara 1989, chap. 2; Ohmae 1990, 202.

13. In the airline and telecommunication service industries in which European companies posed a competitive threat and market access in Europe was a problem, demands for contingently discriminatory policies did arise. But these industries do not lend themselves to comparing reactions toward trade with reactions toward IFDI.

14. There was some emphasis on reciprocity in the issue of foreign participation in federally funded R&D consortia such as Sematech, though U.S. firms made little effort to participate in similar Japanese consortia.

15. See Suarez 2000 on the ability of business to learn from experience in politics.

16. It was also true for some of the more domestically oriented upstream producers, which tended to be more hostile to IFDI across the board. These sectors (which were not examined in depth) included manufacturers of auto parts, picture tubes, and semiconductor materials and equipment.

17. Although the auto parts producers put forth strategic investment demands, the U.S. government lacked the domestic tools for restricting greenfield IFDI. The demands of the parts makers, then, were more indirect, focusing on is-

sues such as state incentives, free trade zones, rules of origin, and so forth rather than directly seeking to limit IFDI.

18. North 1981, 32, 205; Goldstein 1993, 17.
19. Pierson 1993.
20. Verdier 1994 is one exception.
21. E.g., see Alt and Gilligan 1994; Verdier 1994; McNamara 1998.

References

Aggarwal, Vinod K., Robert O. Keohane, and David B. Yoffie. 1987. "The Dynamics of Negotiated Protectionism." *American Political Science Review* 81:345–66.

Alexander, Arthur J. 1990. *Adaptation to Change in the U.S. Machine Tool Industry and the Effects of Government Policy.* Santa Monica: Rand Corporation.

Alic, John A. 1991. "Firm Weakness or Strength: U.S. Firms and U.S. Policies in a Global Economy." In *Strategic Partnerships: States, Firms, and International Competition,* edited by Lynn Krieger Mytelka, 149–66. Cranbury, N.J.: Fairleigh Dickinson University Press.

Alt, James E., Jeffry Frieden, Michael J. Gilligan, Dani Rodrik, and Ronald Rogowski. 1996. "The Political Economy of International Trade: Enduring Puzzles and an Agenda for Inquiry." *Comparative Political Studies* 29:689–717.

Alt, James E., and Michael Gilligan. 1994. "The Political Economy of Trading States: Factor Specificity, Collective Action Problems, and Domestic Political Institutions." *Journal of Political Philosophy* 2:165–92.

Altshuler, Alan, Martin Anderson, Daniel Jones, Daniel Roos, and James Womack. 1984. *The Future of the Automobile: The Report of MIT's International Automobile Program.* Cambridge: MIT Press.

Anderson, Kym, and Robert E. Baldwin. 1987. "The Political Market for Protection in Industrial Countries." In *Protection, Cooperation, Integration, and Development: Essays in Honour of Hiroshi Kitamura,* edited by Ali M. El-Agraa, 20–36. New York: Macmillan.

Angel, David P. 1994. *Restructuring for Innovation: The Remaking of the U.S. Semiconductor Industry.* New York: Guilford Press.

Angel Olea, Miguel. 1993. "The Mexican Automotive Industry in the NAFTA Negotiations." In *Driving Continentally: National Policies and the North American Auto Industry,* edited by Maureen Appel Molot, 353–70. Ottawa: Carleton University Press.

Arnson, Peter J., ed. 1988. *Is There Enough Business to Go Around? Overcapacity in the Auto Industry.* Ann Arbor: Center for Japanese Studies.

Baldwin, Robert. 1986. *The Political Economy of U.S. Import Policy.* Cambridge: MIT Press.

Baranson, Jack. 1981. *The Japanese Challenge to U.S. Industry.* Lexington, Mass.: Lexington Books.

Baumgartner, Frank R., and Beth L. Leach. 1998. *Basic Interests: The Importance of Groups in Politics and Political Science.* Princeton: Princeton University Press.

Beltz, Cynthia. 1998. "Foreign Ownership Restrictions, National Treatment, and Telecommunications." In *Foreign Ownership and the Consequences of Direct Investment in the United States: Beyond Us and Them*, edited by Douglas Woodward and Douglas Nigh, 327–59. Westport, Conn.: Quorum Books.

——, ed. 1995. *The Foreign Investment Debate: Opening Markets Abroad or Closing Markets at Home?* Washington, D.C.: American Enterprise Institute.

Bergsten, C. Fred, Thomas Horst, and Theodore H. Moran. 1978. *American Multinationals and American Interests*. Washington, D.C.: Brookings Institution.

Bergsten, C. Fred, and Marcus Noland. 1993. *Reconcilable Differences? United States–Japan Economic Conflict*. Washington, D.C.: Institute for International Economics.

Bhagwati, Jagdish, Elias Dinopoulos, and Kar-Yui Wong. 1992. "Quid Pro Quo Foreign Investment." *American Economic Review* 82:186–92.

Blonigen, Bruce A., and Robert C. Feenstra. 1997. "Protectionist Threats and Foreign Direct Investment." In *The Effects of U.S. Trade Protection and Promotion Policies*, edited by Robert C. Feenstra, 55–80. Chicago: University of Chicago Press.

Booz, Allen & Hamilton, Inc. 1985. *The Effect of Foreign Targeting on the U.S. Automotive Industry: A Report Prepared for the U.S. Department of Labor and the Office of the United States Trade Representative*. Washington, D.C.: Government Printing Office.

Borrus, Michael. 1983. "The Politics of Competitive Erosion in the U.S. Steel Industry." In *American Industry in International Competition: Government Policies and Corporate Strategies*, edited by John Zysman and Laura Tyson, 60–105. Ithaca: Cornell University Press.

——. 1988. *Competing for Control: America's Stake in Microelectronics*. New York: Ballinger.

Borrus, Michael, James E. Millstein, and John Zysman. 1983. "Trade and Development in the Semiconductor Industry: Japanese Challenge and American Response." In *American Industry in International Competition: Government Policies and Corporate Strategies*, edited by John Zysman and Laura Tyson, 142–248. Ithaca: Cornell University Press.

Borrus, Michael, and John Zysman. 1992. "Industrial Competitiveness and American National Security." In *The Highest Stakes: The Economic Foundations of the Next Security System*, edited by Wayne Sandholtz, Michael Borrus, John Zysman, Ken Conca, Jay Stowsky, Steve Vogel, and Steve Weber, 7–52. New York: Oxford University Press.

Boultinghouse, Brent. 1994. "The Japanese Machine Tool Industry." In *The Decline of the U.S. Machine Tool Industry and Prospects for Its Sustainable Recovery, Volume 2*, edited by David Finegold, Keith W. Brendley, Robert Lempert, Donald Henry, Peter Cannon, Brent Boultinghouse, and Max Nelson, 1–22. Santa Monica: Rand Corporation.

Bovard, James. 1991. "Toxic Dumping: Protectionism by Other Means." *New Republic* 205:18–19.

Brander, James A. 1986. "Rationales for Strategic Trade and Industrial Policy." In

Strategic Trade Policy and the New International Economics, edited by Paul R. Krugman, 23–46. Cambridge: MIT Press.

Breitfeld, Julie S. 1997. "The U.S. Export of Market-Based Industrial Policies for Telecommunications." *Journal of Public and International Affairs* 8:178–94.

Brouthers, Lance Eliot, and Steve Werner. 1990. "Are the Japanese Good Global Competitors?" *Journal of World Business* 25:5–11.

Burton, F. N., and F. H. Saelens. 1987. "Trade Barriers and Japanese Foreign Direct Investment in the Colour Television Industry." *Managerial and Decision Economics* 8:285–94.

Caves, Richard. 1996. *Multinational Enterprise and Economic Analysis*. 2d edition. New York: Cambridge University Press.

Chang, C. S. 1981. *The Japanese Auto Industry and the U.S. Market*. New York: Praeger.

Choate, Pat. 1990. *Agents of Influence: How Japan Manipulates America's Political and Economic System*. New York: Simon & Schuster.

Christelow, Dorothy B. 1995. *When Giants Converge: The Role of U.S.-Japan Direct Investment*. Armonk, N.Y.: M. E. Sharpe.

Clark, William Roberts. 1998. "Agents and Structures: Two Views of Preferences, Two Views of Institutions." *International Studies Quarterly* 42:245–70.

Cohen, Stephen S., and John Zysman. 1987. *Manufacturing Matters: The Myth of the Post-Industrial Economy*. New York: Basic Books.

Cole, Robert E., and Tazio Yakushiji. 1984. *The American and Japanese Auto Industries in Transition: Report of the Joint U.S.-Japan Automotive Study*. Ann Arbor: Center for Japanese Studies.

Coleman, John J., and David B. Yoffie. 1987. *The Semiconductor Industry Association and the Trade Dispute with Japan (A)*. Case Study no. 387-205. Boston: Harvard Business School Press.

Collis, David J. 1992. "Bearings: The Visible Hand of Global Firms." In *Beyond Free Trade: Firms, Governments, and Global Competition*, edited by David Yoffie, 251–310. Boston: Harvard Business School Press.

Corcoran, William J. 1990. "The Machine Tool Industry under Fire." In *The Promise of American Industry: An Alternative Assessment of Problems and Prospects*, edited by Donald L. Losman and Shu-Jan Liang, 227–48. Westport, Conn.: Quorum Books.

Corden, W. Max. 1993. "The Revival of Protectionism in Developed Countries." In *Protectionism and World Welfare*, edited by Dominick Salvatore, 54–79. New York: Cambridge University Press.

Cowhey, Peter. 1990. "The International Telecommunications Regime: The Political Roots of Regimes for High Technology." *International Organization* 44:169–99.

——. 1995. "Building the Global Information Highway: Toll Booths, Construction Contracts, and Rules of the Road." In *The New Information Infrastructure: Strategies for U.S. Policy*, edited by William J. Drake, 175–204. Washington, D.C.: Institute for International Economics.

Cowhey, Peter, and Jonathan Aronson. 1993. *Managing the World Economy: The Consequences of Corporate Alliances*. New York: Council on Foreign Relations.

Crandall, Robert W. 1981. *The U.S. Steel Industry in Recurrent Crisis: Policy Options in a Competitive World*. Washington, D.C.: Brookings Institution.

——. 1986. "Investment and Productivity Growth in the Steel Industry: Some Implications for Industrial Policy." In *Ailing Steel: The Transoceanic Quarrel*, edited by Walter H. Goldberg, 191–204. New York: St. Martin's Press.

——. 1997. "Telecom Mergers and Joint Ventures in an Era of Liberalization." In *Unfinished Business: Telecommunications after the Uruguay Round*, edited by Gary Clyde Hufbauer and Erika Wada, 107–24. Washington, D.C.: Institute for International Studies.

Curtis, Philip. 1994. *The Fall of the U.S. Consumer Electronics Industry: An American Trade Tragedy*. Westport, Conn.: Quorum Books.

Dallmeyer, Dorinda G. 1987. "National Security and the Semiconductor Industry." *Technology Review* 90:46–54.

Denzau, Arthur. 1989. "Trade Protection Comes to Silicon Valley." *Society* 26:38–42.

Dertouzos, Michael, Robert M. Solow, and Richard K. Lester. 1989. *Made in America: Regaining the Productive Edge*. Cambridge: MIT Press.

DeSouza, Patrick Jude. 1994. "The Regulation of Foreign Investment in the United States, 1973–1993, and the Making of American Foreign Economic Policy." Ph.D. dissertation, Stanford University.

Destler, I. M. 1992. *American Trade Politics*. 2d edition. Washington, D.C.: Institute for International Economics.

Destler, I. M., and John Odell. 1987. *Anti-Protection: Changing Forces in United States Trade Politics*. Washington, D.C.: Institute for International Economics.

Dicken, Peter. 1991. "The Changing Geography of Japanese Foreign Direct Investment in Manufacturing Industry: A Global Perspective." In *Japan and the Global Economy: Issues and Trends in the 1990s*, edited by Jonathan Morris, 14–44. New York: Routledge.

——. 1998. *Global Shift: Transforming the World Economy*. 3d edition. New York: Guilford Press.

Dunn, James A., Jr. 1987. "Automobiles in International Trade: Regime Change or Persistence?" *International Organization* 41:225–52.

Dyer, Davis, Malcolm S. Salter, and Alan M. Webber. 1987. *Changing Alliances: The Harvard Business School Project on the Auto Industry and the American Economy*. Boston: Harvard Business School Press.

Eads, George C. 1990. "Geography Is Not Destiny: The Changing Character of Competitive Advantage in Automobiles." In *Technological Competition and Interdependence: The Search for Policy in the United States, West Germany, and Japan*, edited by Gunter Heiduk and Kozo Yamamura, 212–32. Seattle: University of Washington Press.

Eden, Lorraine, and Maureen Appel Molot. 1993a. "Fortress or Free Market? NAFTA and Its Implications for the Pacific Rim." In *Pacific Economic Relations in the 1990s: Cooperation or Conflict?* edited by Richard A. Higgot, Richard Reaver, and John Ravenhill, 201–22. Boulder: Lynne Rienner.

——. 1993b. "Insiders and Outsiders: Auto Industry Policy Choices in the NAFTA Debate." In *The Challenge of NAFTA: North America, Australia, New*

Zealand, and the World Trade Regime, edited by Robert G. Cushing, John Higley, and Michael Sutton, 175–90. Austin: Lyndon B. Johnson School for Public Affairs.

——. 1993c. "Insiders and Outsiders: Defining 'Who Is Us' in the North American Automobile Industry." *Transnational Corporations* 2:31–64.

Encarnation, Dennis J. 1992. *Rivals beyond Trade: America versus Japan in Global Competition*. Ithaca: Cornell University Press.

Finegold, David, Keith W. Brendley, Robert Lempert, Donald Henry, Peter Cannon, Brent Boultinghouse, and Max Nelson. 1994. *The Decline of the U.S. Machine Tool Industry and Prospects for Its Sustainable Recovery, Volume 1*. Santa Monica: Rand Corporation.

Flaherty, M. Therese, and Ruth S. Raubitschek. 1990. "Local Presence and International Manufacturing Configurations in Technology-Intensive Industries." *Japan and the World Economy* 2:301–26.

Flamm, Kenneth. 1990. "Semiconductors." In *Europe 1992: An American Perspective*, edited by Gary Clyde Hufbauer, 225–92. Washington, D.C.: Brookings Institution.

——. 1996. *Mismanaged Trade? Strategic Policy and the Semiconductor Industry*. Washington, D.C.: Brookings Institution.

Florida, Richard, and Martin Kenney. 1991. "Japanese Foreign Direct Investment in the United States: The Case of the Automotive Transplants." In *Japan and the Global Economy: Issues and Trends in the 1990s*, edited by Jonathan Morris, 91–114. New York: Routledge.

——. 1992a. *Beyond Mass Production: The Japanese System and Its Transfer to the U.S.* New York: Oxford University Press.

——. 1992b. "Restructuring in Place: Japanese Investment, Production Organization, and the Geography of Steel." *Economic Geography* 68:146–73.

Frantz, Douglas, and Catherine Collins. 1989. *Selling Out: How We Are Letting Japan Buy Our Land, Our Industries, Our Financial Institutions, and Our Future*. Chicago: Contemporary Books.

Frieden, Jeffry A. 1991. "Invested Interests: The Politics of National Economic Policies in a World of Global Finance." *International Organization* 45:425–51.

——. 1999. "Actors and Preferences in International Relations." In *Strategic Choice in International Relations*, edited by David Lake and Robert Powell, 39–76. Princeton: Princeton University Press.

Frieden, Jeffry A., and Ronald Rogowski. 1996. "The Impact of the International Economy on National Policies: An Analytic Overview." In *Internationalization and Domestic Politics*, edited by Robert O. Keohane and Helen V. Milner, 25–47. New York: Cambridge University Press.

Garrett, Geoffrey, and Peter Lange. 1996. "Internationalization, Institutions, and Political Change." In *Internationalization and Domestic Politics*, edited by Robert O. Keohane and Helen V. Milner, 48–75. New York: Cambridge University Press.

Gaster, Robin. 1992. "Protectionism with Purpose: Guiding Foreign Investment." *Foreign Policy* 88:91–107.

Gaster, Robin, Erik R. Olbeter, Amy Bolster, and Clyde V. Presowitz Jr. 1996. *Bit by Bit: Building a Transatlantic Partnership for the Information Age.* Armonk, N.Y.: M. E. Sharpe.

Gayle, Dennis J. 1993. "Regulating the Automobile Industry: Sources and Consequences of U.S. Automobile Air Pollution Standards." In *Driving Continentally: National Policies and the North American Auto Industry*, edited by Maureen Appel Molot, 181–207. Ottawa: Carleton University Press.

Gestrin, Michael, and Alan M. Rugman. 1994. "The North American Free Trade Agreement and Foreign Direct Investment." *Transnational Corporations* 2:77–95.

Gilligan, Michael J. 1997. *Empowering Exporters: Reciprocity, Delegation, and Collective Action in American Trade Policy.* Ann Arbor: University of Michigan Press.

Gilpin, Robert. 1975. *U.S. Power and the Multinational Corporation: The Political Economy of Foreign Direct Investment.* New York: Basic Books.

Glickman, Norman J., and Douglas P. Woodward. 1989. *The New Competitors: How Foreign Investors Are Changing the U.S. Economy.* New York: Basic Books.

Globerman, Steven. 1995. "Foreign Ownership in Telecommunications: A Policy Perspective." *Telecommunications Policy* 19:21–28.

Goehle, Donna G. 1989. "The Buy American Act: Is It Irrelevant in a World of Multinational Corporations?" *Columbia Journal of World Business* 24:10–15.

Goldberg, Walter H. 1986. *Ailing Steel: The Transoceanic Quarrel.* New York: St. Martin's Press.

Goldstein, Judith. 1993. *Ideas, Interests, and American Trade Policy.* Ithaca: Cornell University Press.

Goldstein, Judith, and Robert O. Keohane. 1993. "Ideas and Foreign Policy: An Analytical Introduction." In *Ideas and Foreign Policy: Beliefs, Institutions, and Political Change*, edited by Judith Goldstein and Robert O. Keohane, 3–30. Ithaca: Cornell University Press.

Goodman, David, Debra Spar, and David Yoffie. 1996. "Foreign Direct Investment and the Demand for Protection in the United States." *International Organization* 50:565–91.

Gordon, Sara L., and Francis A. Lees. 1986. *Foreign Multinational Investment in the United States: Struggle for Industrial Supremacy.* New York: Quorum Books.

Gourevitch, Peter A. 1986. *Politics in Hard Times: Comparative Responses to International Economic Crises.* Ithaca: Cornell University Press.

Gowa, Joanne. 1987. "Public Goods and Political Institutions: Trade and Monetary Policy Processes in the United States." In *The State and American Foreign Economic Policy*, edited by G. John Ikenberry, David A. Lake, and Michael Mastanduno, 15–32. Ithaca: Cornell University Press.

Graham, Edward M. 1978. "Transatlantic Investment by Multinational Firms: A Rivalistic Phenomenon?" *Journal of Post Keynesian Economics* 1:82–99.

——. 1992. "Government Policies towards Inward Foreign Direct Investment: Effects on Producers and Consumers." In *Multinational Enterprises in the World Economy: Essays in Honor of John Dunning*, edited by Peter J. Buckley and Mark Casson, 176–93. Brookfield, Vt.: E. Elgar.

Graham, Edward M., and Paul R. Krugman. 1995. *Foreign Direct Investment in the United States.* 3d edition. Washington, D.C.: Institute for International Investment.

Graham, Julie. 1993. "Firm and State Strategy in a Multipolar World: The Changing Geography of Machine Tool Production and Trade." In *Trading Industries, Trading Regions: International Trade, American Industry, and Regional Economic Development*, edited by Helzi Noponen, Julie Graham, and Ann P. Markuson, 140–74. New York: Guilford Press.

Green, Eric Marshall. 1996. *Economic Security and High Technology Competition in an Age of Transition: The Case of the Semiconductor Industry.* Westport, Conn.: Praeger.

Greenwald, Gerald. 1984. "A Compact for Automotive Revitalization." In *The American Automobile Industry: Rebirth or Requiem?* edited by Robert E. Cole, 53–57. Ann Arbor: Center for Japanese Studies.

Grier, Kevin B., Michael C. Munger, Brian E. Roberts. 1994. "The Determinants of Industry Political Activity, 1978–1986." *American Political Science Review* 88:911–26.

Grossman, Gene. 1986. "Strategic Export Promotion: A Critique." In *Strategic Trade Policy and the New International Economics*, edited by Paul R. Krugman, 47–68. Cambridge: MIT Press.

Hall, Peter A. 1989. "Conclusion: The Politics of Keynesian Ideas." In *The Political Power of Economic Ideas: Keynesianism across Nations*, edited by Peter A. Hall, 361–91. Princeton: Princeton University Press.

Hansen, Wendy L. 1990. "The International Trade Commission and the Politics of Protectionism." *American Political Science Review* 84:21–46.

Hart, Jeffrey. 1992. *Rival Capitalists: International Competitiveness in the United States, Japan, and Western Europe.* Ithaca: Cornell University Press.

Helleiner, G. K. 1977. "Transnational Enterprises and the New Political Economy of U.S. Trade Policy." *Oxford Economic Papers* 29:102–16.

Hirschorn, Joel S. 1986. "Restructuring of the United States Steel Industry Requires New Policies." In *Ailing Steel: The Transoceanic Quarrel*, edited by Walter H. Goldberg, 205–46. New York: St. Martin's Press.

Hodges, Michael. 1988. "The Japanese Industrial Presence in the USA: Trading One Source of Friction for Another?" *Multinational Business* 1:1–14.

Hoekman, Bernard, and Carlos A. Primo Braga. 1997. *Protection and Trade in Services.* World Bank Policy Research Working Paper 1747. Washington, D.C.: World Bank.

Hogan, William T. 1991. *Global Steel in the 1990s: Growth or Decline?* Lexington, Mass.: Lexington Books.

——. 1994. *Steel in the 21st Century: Competition Forges a New World Order.* New York: Lexington Books.

Holland, Max. 1989. *When the Machine Stopped: A Cautionary Tale from Industrial America.* Boston: Harvard Business School Press.

Hooley, Richard. 1987. *Protection for the Machine Tool Industry: Domestic and International Negotiations for Voluntary Restraint Agreements.* Pew Case Studies in International Affairs, Case 120. Pittsburgh: Pew Charitable Trusts.

Howell, Thomas R., Brent L. Bartlett, and Warren Davis. 1992. *Creating Advantage: Semiconductors and Government Industrial Policy in the 1990s.* Washington, D.C.: Semiconductor Industry Association/Dewey Ballantine.

Howell, Thomas R., William A. Noellert, Jesse G. Kreier, and Alan Wm. Wolff. 1988. *Steel and the State: Government Intervention and Steel's Structural Crisis.* Boulder: Westview Press.

Ikenberry, G. John. 1988. "Conclusion." In *The State and American Foreign Economic Policy,* edited by G. John Ikenberry, David A. Lake, and Michael Mastanduno, 219–43. Ithaca: Cornell University Press.

Ingrassia, Paul, and Joseph B. White. 1994. *Comeback: The Fall and Rise of the American Automobile Industry.* New York: Simon & Schuster.

Irwin, Douglas. 1994. *Trade Politics and the Semiconductor Industry.* NBER Working Paper 4745. Cambridge: National Bureau of Economic Research.

Ishihara, Shintarō 1989. *The Japan That Can Say No: Why Japan Will Be First among Equals.* New York: Simon & Schuster.

Jenkins, Barbara. 1986. "Reexamining the 'Obsolescing Bargain': A Study of Canada's National Energy Program." *International Organization* 40:139–65.

——. 1992. *The Paradox of Continental Production: National Investment Policies in North America.* Ithaca: Cornell University Press.

Johnson, John R. 1993. "NAFTA and the Trade in Automotive Goods." In *Assessing NAFTA: A Trinational Analysis,* edited by Stephen Globerman and Michael Walker, 87–129. Vancouver: Fraser Institute.

Jones, Kent Albert. 1986. *Politics vs Economics in World Steel Trade.* Boston: Allen & Unwin.

——. 1994. *Export Restraint and the New Protectionism: The Political Economy of Discriminatory Trade Restrictions.* Ann Arbor: University of Michigan Press.

Kabashima, Ikuo, and Hideo Sato. 1986. "Local Content and Congressional Politics: Interest-Group Theory and Foreign-Policy Implications." *International Studies Quarterly* 30:295–314.

Kang, C. S. Eliot. 1997. "U.S. Politics and Greater Regulation of Inward Foreign Direct Investment." *International Organization* 51:301–33.

Kass, Howard E. 1994. "Cabotage and Control: Bringing the 1938 U.S. Aviation Policy into the Jet Age." *Case Western Reserve Journal of International Law* 26:143–81.

Katzenstein, Peter J., ed. 1978. *Between Power and Plenty: Foreign Economic Policies of Advanced Industrial States.* Madison: University of Wisconsin Press.

——. 1996. *The Culture of National Security: Norms and Identity in World Politics.* New York: Columbia University Press.

Kearns, Robert L. 1992. *Zaibatsu America: How Japanese Firms Are Colonizing Vital U.S. Industries.* New York: Free Press.

Kimura, Masato, and David A. Welch. 1998. "Specifying 'Interests': Japan's Claim to the Northern Territories and Its Implications for International Relations Theory." *International Studies Quarterly* 42:213–43.

Kowert, Paul, and Jeffrey Legro. 1996. "Norms, Identity, and Their Limits: A Theoretical Reprise." In *The Culture of National Security: Norms and Identity in*

World Politics, edited by Peter Katzenstein, 451–97. New York: Columbia University Press.

Kraus, Ellis S., and Simon Reich. 1992. "Ideology, Interests, and the American Executive: Toward a Theory of Foreign Competition and Manufacturing Trade Policy." *International Organization* 46:857–97.

Krueger, Anne O. 1993. *Free Trade Agreements as Protectionist Devices: Rules of Origin*. NBER Working Paper 4352. Cambridge: National Bureau of Economic Research.

Krugman, Paul R. 1987. "Strategic Sectors and International Competition." In *U.S. Trade Policies in a Changing World Economy*, edited by R. M. Stern, 207–43. Cambridge: MIT Press.

Kudrle, Robert. 1991. "Good for the Gander? Foreign Direct Investment in the United States." *International Organization* 45:397–424.

Kudrle, Robert, and Davis B. Bobrow. 1982. "U.S. Policy toward Foreign Direct Investment." *World Politics* 34:353–79.

Langlois, Richard N., Thomas A. Pugel, Carmela S. Haklisch, Richard R. Nelson, and William G. Egelhoff. 1988. *Microelectronics: An Industry in Transition*. Boston: Unwin Hyman.

Lavergne, Réal. 1983. *The Political Economy of U.S. Tariffs*. New York: Academic Press.

Lawrence, Robert Z. 1993. "Japan's Low Levels of Inward Investment: The Role of Inhibitions on Acquisitions." In *Foreign Direct Investment*, edited by Kenneth A. Froot, 85–111. Chicago: University of Chicago Press.

Levinson, Marc. 1987. "Asking for Protection Is Asking for Trouble." *Harvard Business Review* 67:42–47.

Lima, Jose Guilherme de Heraclito. 1991. *Restructuring the U.S. Steel Industry: Semi-Finished Steel Imports, International Integration, and U.S. Adaptation*. Boulder: Westview Press.

Lipson, Charles. 1985. *Standing Guard: Protecting Foreign Capital in the Nineteenth and Twentieth Centuries*. Berkeley: University of California Press.

Lynn, Leonard H., and Timothy J. McKeown. 1988. *Organizing Business: Trade Associations in America and Japan*. Washington, D.C.: American Enterprise Institute.

MacKenzie de Sola Pool, Adam. 1988. "A New American Policy on Foreign Investment? An Assessment of the Public Policy Process in the Fujitsu-Fairchild Takeover Battle." M.A. thesis. Cambridge, Mass.: Sloan School of Management.

Malerba, Franco. 1985. *The Semiconductor Business: The Economics of Rapid Growth and Decline*. London: Francis Pinter.

Marks, Stephen V., and John McArthur. 1990. "Empirical Analyses of the Determinants of Protection: A Survey and Some New Results." In *International Trade Policies—The Gains from Exchange between Economists and Political Scientists*, edited by John S. Odell and Thomas D. Willett, 105–39. Ann Arbor: University of Michigan Press.

Martin, Cathy Jo. 1995. "Nature or Nurture? Sources of Firm Preferences for National Health Reform." *American Political Science Review* 89:898–913.

Mason, Mark. 1994. "The Political Economy of Japanese Automobile Investment in Europe." In *Does Ownership Matter? Japanese Multinationals in Europe*, edited by Dennis Encarnation and Mark Mason, 411–38. New York: Oxford University Press.

Maxfield, Sylvia, and James Nolt. 1990. "Protectionism and the Internationalization of Capital: U.S. Sponsorship of Import Substitution Industrialization in the Philippines, Turkey, and Argentina." *International Studies Quarterly* 34:49–81.

McCulloch, Rachel. 1985. "U.S. Direct Foreign Investment and Trade: Themes, Trends, and Public Policy Issues." In *Multinationals as Mutual Invaders: Intra-Industry Direct Foreign Investment*, edited by Asim Erdilek, 129–59. New York: St. Martin's Press.

——. 1991. "Why Foreign Corporations Are Buying into U.S. Business." *Annals of American Political and Social Science* 516:169–82.

——. 1993. "New Perspectives on Foreign Direct Investment." In *Foreign Direct Investment*, edited by Kenneth Froot, 37–79. Chicago: University of Chicago Press.

McKeown, Timothy J. 1984. "Firms and Tariff Regime Change: Explaining the Demand for Protection." *World Politics* 36:215–33.

McNamara, Kathleen. 1998. *The Currency of Ideas: Monetary Politics in the European Union*. Ithaca: Cornell University Press.

Meltzer, Ronald I. 1987. "Color-TV Sets and U.S.-Japanese Relations: Problems of Trade Adjustment Policymaking." *Orbis: A Journal of World Affairs* 34:428–46.

Millstein, James E. 1983. "Decline in an Expanding Industry: Japanese Competition in Color Televisions in American Industry." In *International Competition: Government Policies and Corporate Strategies*, edited by Laura Tyson and John Zysman, 106–41. Ithaca: Cornell University Press.

Milner, Helen V. 1988. *Resisting Protectionism: Global Industries and the Politics of International Trade*. Princeton: Princeton University Press.

Milner, Helen V., and David B. Yoffie. 1989. "Between Free Trade and Protectionism: Strategic Trade Policy and a Theory of Corporate Trade Demands." *International Organization* 43:239–72.

Molot, Maureen Appel, ed. 1993. *Driving Continentally: National Policies and the North American Auto Industry*. Ottawa: Carleton University Press.

Monica, John R., Jr. 1991. "United States Exports with a Japanese Label: Potential Effects of EC 92 on Automobiles Manufactured by Japanese Companies on U.S. Soil." *George Washington Journal of International Law and Economics* 24:623–45.

Moran, Theodore H. 1990. "The Globalization of America's Defense Industries: Managing the Threat of Foreign Dependence." *International Security* 15:57–100.

Moravcsik, Andrew. 1998. *The Choice for Europe: Social Purpose and State Power from Messina to Maastricht*. Ithaca: Cornell University Press.

Morici, Peter. 1993. "NAFTA Rules of Origin and Automotive Content Requirements." In *Assessing NAFTA: A Trinational Analysis*, edited by Stephen Globerman and Michael Walker, 226–50. Vancouver: Fraser Institute.

Morris, Julian C. 1988. "The US-Japan MOSS Talks and the Future of the Auto Parts Industry." In *Is There Enough Business to Go Around? Overcapacity in the Auto Industry*, edited by Peter J. Arnson, 86–98. Ann Arbor: Center for Japanese Studies.

Morrow, James D. 1994. *Game Theory for Political Scientists*. Princeton: Princeton University Press.

Moses, Frederick A., and Thomas A. Pugel. 1986. "Foreign Direct Investment in the United States: The Electronics Industry." In *Uncle Sam as Host: A Research Annual*, edited by H. Peter Gray, 111–61. Greenwich: JAI Press.

Mowery, David C., and Nathan Rosenberg. 1989. *Technology and the Pursuit of Economic Growth*. New York: Cambridge University Press.

Mundell, Robert A. 1957. "International Trade and Factor Mobility." *American Economic Review* 47:321–35.

National Advisory Commission on Semiconductors. 1989. *A Strategic Industry at Risk: A Report to the President and Congress*. Washington, D.C.: Government Printing Office.

——. 1991. *Toward a National Semiconductor Strategy: Second Annual Report*. Washington, D.C.: Government Printing Office.

National Research Council. Commission on Engineering and Technical Systems. Manufacturing Studies Board. Committee on the Machine Tool Industry. 1983. *The U.S. Machine Tool Industry and the Defense Industrial Base*. Washington, D.C.: National Academy Press.

——. Office of International Affairs. Committee on Japan. 1992. *U.S.-Japan Strategic Alliances in the Semiconductor Industry: Technology Transfer, Competition, and Public Policy*. Washington, D.C.: National Academy Press.

Nayer, Baldev Raj. 1995. "Regimes, Power, and International Aviation." *International Organization* 49:139–70.

Nelson, Douglas. 1988. "Endogenous Tariff Theory: A Critical Survey." *American Journal of Political Science* 32:796–837.

——. 1994. *The Political Economy of U.S. Automobile Protection*. NBER Working Paper 4746. Cambridge: National Bureau of Economic Research.

Nevin, John J. 1978. "Can U.S. Business Survive Our Japanese Trade Policy?" *Harvard Business Review* 56:165–78.

Newhouse, John. 1993. "The Battle of the Bailout." *New Yorker*, January 18, 42–51.

Nicolaides, Phaedon, and Stephen Thomas. 1991. "Can Protectionism Explain Direct Investment?" *Journal of Common Market Studies* 24:635–64.

Noam, Eli. 1994. "Direct Foreign Investment in Telecommunications: Comments." In *The Race to European Eminence: Who Are the Coming Tele-Service Multinationals?*, edited by Erik Bohlin and Ove Granstrand, 365–67. New York: North-Holland.

North, Douglass. 1981. *Structure and Change in Economic History*. New York: W. W. Norton.

O'Brien, Peter. 1987. "Machine Tools: Growing Internationalisation in a Small Firm Industry." *Multinational Business* 9:23–34.

Odell, John S., and Thomas D. Willett. 1990. "United States Trade Policy: Underlying Forces for Stability." In *International Trade Policies: Gains from Exchange between Economics and Political Science*, edited by John S. Odell and Thomas D. Wilett, 30–42. Ann Arbor: University of Michigan Press.

Oh, Jong-Geun. 1996. "Global Strategic Alliances in the Telecommunications Industry." *Telecommunications Policy* 20:713–20.

Ohmae, Kenichi. 1990. *The Borderless World: Power and Strategy in the Interlinked Economy.* New York: HarperCollins.

Olbeter, Erik R. 1994. "Opening the Global Market for Telecommunications." *Issues in Science and Technology* 11:57–58.

Ott, James, and Raymond E. Neidl. 1995. *Airline Odyssey: The Airline Industry's Turbulent Flight into the Future.* New York: McGraw Hill.

Perkins, Robert A. 1983. "Internationalization of the Japanese Auto Industry: Real Progress or a Snail's Pace?" In *Automobiles and the Future: Competition, Cooperation, and Change,* edited by Robert E. Cole, 11–18. Ann Arbor: Center for Japanese Studies.

Peterson, Donna J. S., Gerald T. Kelley, and Myron G. Myers. 1991. *An Assessment of the Economic Status of the Antifriction Bearing Industry.* Bethesda: Logistics Management Institute.

Pierson, Paul. 1993. "When Effect Becomes Cause: Policy Feedback and Political Change." *World Politics* 45:595–628.

Powell, Robert. 1994. "Anarchy in International Relations Theory: The Neorealist-Neoliberal Debate." *International Organization* 48:313–44.

Prestowitz, Clyde V., Jr. 1988. *Trading Places: How We Are Giving Our Future to Japan and How to Reclaim It.* New York: Basic Books.

Pugel, Thomas A. 1987. "Limits of Trade Policy toward High Technology Industries: The Case of Semiconductors." In *Trade Friction and Economic Policy: Problems and Prospects for Japan and the United States,* edited by Ryuzo Sato and Paul Wachtel, 185–223. New York: Cambridge University Press.

———. 1989. "Japanese and American Response to Trade Friction: The Semiconductor Industry." In *Trade Policy and Corporate Business Decisions,* edited by Tamir Agmon and Christine Hekman, 173–97. New York: Oxford University Press.

Pugel, Thomas A., and Ingo Walter. 1985. "U.S. Corporate Interests and the Political Economy of Trade Policy." *Review of Economics and Statistics* 67:465–73.

Ray, Edward John. 1991. "Foreign Takeovers and New Investments in the United States." *Contemporary Policy Issues* 9:59–71.

Reich, Robert. 1991. *The Work of Nations: Preparing Ourselves for 21st Century Capitalism.* New York: Knopf.

Reich, Simon. 1993. "NAFTA, Foreign Direct Investment, and the Auto Industry." In *Driving Continentally: National Policies and the North American Auto Industry,* edited by Maureen Appel Molot, 63–99. Ottawa: Carleton University Press.

———. 1989. "Roads to Follow: Regulating Foreign Direct Investment." *International Organization* 43:543–84.

Rodrik, Dani, and Chang-Ho Yoon. 1989. *Strategic Trade Policy When Domestic Firms Compete against Vertically Integrated Rivals.* NBER Working Paper 2916. Cambridge: National Bureau of Economic Research.

Rogowski, Ronald. 1989. *Commerce and Coalitions: How Trade Affects Domestic Political Alignments.* Princeton: Princeton University Press.

———. 1999. "Institutions as Constraints on Strategic Choice." In *Strategic Choice in International Relations*, edited by David Lake and Robert Powell, 115–36. Princeton: Princeton University Press.

Rubenstein, James M. 1991. "The Impact of Japanese Investment in the U.S." In *Restructuring the Global Automobile Industry: National and Regional Impacts*, edited by Christopher Law, 114–42. New York: Routledge.

Safarian, A. E. *Multinational Enterprises and Public Policy: A Study of the Industrial Countries.* Brookfield, Vt.: E. Elgar.

Salorio, Eugene M. 1991. "Trade Barriers and Corporate Strategies: Why Some Firms Oppose Import Protection for Their Own Industry." DBA dissertation. Boston: Harvard Business School.

Salvatore, Dominick. 1991. "Trade Protection and Foreign Direct Investment in the U.S." *Annals of American Political and Social Science* 516:91–105.

Sarathy, Ravi. 1989. "The Interplay of Industrial Policy and International Strategy: Japan's Machine Tool Industry." *California Management Review* 31:132–61.

Saxonhouse, Gary R. 1986. "The National Security Clause of the Trade Expansion Act of 1962: Import Competition and the Machine Tool Industry." In *Law and Trade Issues of the Japanese Economy: American and Japanese Perspectives*, edited by Gary R. Saxonhouse and Kozo Yamaura, 218–37. Seattle: University of Washington Press.

Saxonhouse, Gary R., and Robert M. Stern. 1989. "An Analytical Survey of Formal and Informal Barriers to International Trade and Investment in the United States, Canada, and Japan." In *Trade and Investment Relations among the United States, Canada, and Japan*, edited by Robert M. Stern, 293–353. Chicago: University of Chicago Press.

Sazanami, Yoko. 1989. "Trade and Investment Patterns and Barriers in the United States, Canada, and Japan." In *Trade and Investment Relations among the United States, Canada, and Japan*, edited by Robert Stern, 90–126. Chicago: University of Chicago Press.

Scheuerman, William. 1986. *The Steel Crisis: The Economics and Politics of a Declining Industry.* New York: Praeger.

Scheve, Kenneth F., and Matthew J. Slaughter. 2001. *Globalization and the Perception of American Workers.* Washington, D.C.: Institute for International Economics.

Schoenberger, Erica. 1985. "Foreign Manufacturing Investment in the United States: Competitive Strategies and International Location." *Economic Geography* 61:241–59.

Schwartzman, David. 1993. *The Japanese Television Cartel: A Study Based on Matsushita v. Zenith.* Ann Arbor: University of Michigan Press.

Semiconductor Industry Association. 1990. *Four Years of Experience under the U.S.-Japan Semiconductor Agreement: "A Deal Is a Deal."* San Jose, Calif.: Semiconductor Industry Association/Dewey Ballantine.

Sen, Amartya. 1986. "Behaviour and the Concept of Preference." In *Rational Choice*, edited by Jon Elster, 60–81. New York: New York University Press.

Sidak, J. Gregory. 1997. *Foreign Investment in American Telecommunications*. Chicago: University of Chicago Press.

Sikkink, Kathryn. 1991. *Ideas and Institutions: Developmentalism in Brazil and Argentina*. Ithaca: Cornell University Press.

Smith, Alasdair, and Anthony J. Venables. 1990. "Automobiles." In *Europe 1992: An American Perspective*, edited by Gary Clyde Hufbauer, 119–58. Washington, D.C.: Brookings Institution.

Smith, John F. 1983. "Prospects and Consequences of American-Japanese Company Cooperation." In *Automobiles and the Future: Competition, Cooperation, and Change*, edited by Robert E. Cole, 19–26. Ann Arbor: Center for Japanese Studies.

Smith, Murray G., and Ronald J. Wonnacott. 1993. "Alternative Approaches to North American Trade and the Auto Industry." In *Driving Continentally: National Policies and the North American Auto Industry*, edited by Maureen Appel Molot, 285–301. Ottawa: Carleton University Press.

Snidal, Duncan. 1986. "The Game *Theory* of International Politics." In *Cooperation under Anarchy*, edited by Kenneth A. Oye, 25–87. Princeton: Princeton University Press.

Spencer, Linda M. 1988. *American Assets: An Examination of Foreign Investment in the United States*. Arlington, Va.: Congressional Economic Leadership Institute.

Spero, Joan Edleman. 1990. *The Politics of International Economic Relations*. 4th edition. New York: St. Martin's Press.

Staniland, Martin. 1999. "Transatlantic Air Transport: Routes to Globalization." Paper presented at the conference "Creating a Transatlantic Marketplace: Government Policies and Business Strategies," Washington, D.C., November 4–5.

Stegemann, Klaus. 1989. "Policy Rivalry among Industrial States: What Can We Learn from Models of Strategic Trade Policy?" *International Organization* 43:73–100.

Steinmueller, Edward W. 1988a. "Industry Structure and Government Policies in the U.S. and Japanese Integrated Circuit Industries." In *Government Policy toward Industry in the United States and Japan*, edited by John B. Shoven, 31–54. New York: Cambridge University Press.

——. 1988b. "International Joint Ventures in the Integrated Circuit Industry." In *International Collaborative Ventures in U.S. Manufacturing*, edited by David C. Mowery, 319–54. Cambridge, Mass.: Ballinger.

Stevens, Candice. 1990. "Technoglobalism and Technonationalism: The Corporate Dilemma." *Columbia Journal of World Business* 25:42–49.

Stockman, David. 1991. "Remarks on Trade and Investment Friction between the Japan and the U.S." *Japan and the World Economy* 3:103–11.

Stowsky, Jay S. 1989. "Weak Links, Strong Bonds: U.S.-Japanese Competition in Semiconductor Production Equipment." In *Politics and Productivity: How Japan's Development Strategy Works*, edited by Chalmers Johnson, Laura D'Andrea Tyson, and John Zysman, 241–74. New York: Ballinger.

Strange, Susan. 1996. *The Retreat of the State: The Diffusion of Power in the World Economy*. New York: Cambridge University Press.

Suàrez, Sandra L. 2000. *Does Business Learn? Tax Breaks, Uncertainty, and Political Strategies*. Ann Arbor: University of Michigan Press.

Takacs, Wendy E. 1981. "Pressures for Protectionism: An Empirical Analysis." *Economic Inquiry* 19:687–93.

Tarry, Scott E. 1996. *Bailing Out USAir: The Politics of Balancing Domestic and Foreign Economic Interests*. Pew Case Studies in International Affairs 216. Washington, D.C.: Institute for the Study of Diplomacy.

Thelen, Kathleen, and Sven Steinmo. 1992. "Historical Institutionalism in Comparative Politics." In *Structuring Politics: Historical Institutionalism in Comparative Analysis*, edited by Sven Steinmo, Kathleen Thelen, and Frank Longstreth, 1–32. New York: Cambridge University Press.

Tolchin, Martin, and Susan Tolchin. 1988. *Buying into America: How Foreign Money Is Changing the Face of Our Nation*. New York: Random House.

———. 1992. *Selling Our Security: The Erosion of American Assets*. New York: Knopf.

Tyson, Laura D'Andrea. 1992. *Who's Bashing Whom? Trade Conflict in High-Technology Industries*. Washington, D.C.: Institute for International Economics.

Tyson, Laura D'Andrea, and David B. Yoffie. 1993. "Semiconductors: From Manipulated to Managed Trade." In *Beyond Free Trade: Firms, Governments, and Global Competition*, edited by David B. Yoffie, 29–78. Boston: Harvard Business School Press.

United States Congress. Joint Economic Committee. Subcommittee on Trade, Productivity, and Economic Growth. 1986. *Trade in Semiconductors*. 99th Congress, 1st session. Washington, D.C.: Government Printing Office.

United States Congress. Office of Technology Assessment. 1983. *International Competitiveness in Electronics*. OTA-ISC-200. Washington, D.C.: Government Printing Office.

United States Department of Commerce. 1983. *Petition for Machine Tool Import Quotas*. Filed by the National Machine Tool Builders Association under Section 232 of the Trade Expansion Act of 1962. March 10. Washington, D.C.: Government Printing Office.

———. International Trade Commission. 1985. *A Competitive Assessment of the U.S. Semiconductor Manufacturing Equipment Industry*. Washington, D.C.: Government Printing Office.

———. 1986. *Prehearing Briefs of Texas Instruments, Intel, and Motorola. Investigation nos. A-588-505 (256K DRAMs and Above from Japan), 731–TA-270 (64K DRAMs from Japan), and 731-TA-288 (EPROMs from Japan)*. April 15 and 25, May 12, November 12. Washington, D.C.: Government Printing Office.

United States Department of Defense. Defense Science Board. 1987. *Defense Semiconductor Dependency*. Washington, D.C.: Government Printing Office.

United States General Accounting Office. 1988. *Foreign Investment: Growing Japanese Presence in the U.S. Auto Industry*. Washington, D.C.: Government Printing Office.

——. 1990. *Sematech's Efforts to Strengthen the U.S. Semiconductor Industry*. Washington, D.C.: Government Printing Office.

——. 1994. *Industrial Base—Assessing the Risk of DOD's Foreign Dependence*. Washington, D.C.: Government Printing Office.

United States House of Representatives. 1982. Committee on Ways and Means. Subcommittee on Trade. *Fair Practices in Automotive Products Act*. 97th Congress, 2d session. September 21. Washington, D.C.: Government Printing Office.

——. 1983a. Committee on Energy and Commerce. Subcommittee on Commerce, Transportation, and Tourism. *U.S. Auto Trade Problems*. 98th Congress, 1st session. April 12 and 28, May 6. Washington, D.C.: Government Printing Office.

——. 1983b. Committee on the Judiciary. Subcommittee on Monopolies and Commercial Law. *Acquisitions and Joint Ventures among Large Corporations*. 98th Congress, 1st and 2d sessions. July 28. Washington, D.C.: Government Printing Office.

——. 1984a. Committee on the Judiciary. Subcommittee on Monopolies and Commercial Law. *Acquisitions and Joint Ventures among Large Corporations*. 98th Congress, 2d session. March 23. Washington, D.C.: Government Printing Office.

——. 1984b. Committee on Energy and Commerce. Subcommittee on Commerce, Transportation, and Tourism. *Future of the Automobile Industry*. 98th Congress, 2d session. February 8. Washington, D.C.: Government Printing Office.

——. 1986a. Committee on Government Operations. *Adequacy of Federal Enforcement of Steel Import Program*. 99th Congress, 2d session. April 4. Washington, D.C.: Government Printing Office.

——. 1986b. Committee on Government Operations. *Plight of American Steelworkers Whose Jobs Have Been Adversely Impacted by Imported Steel*. 99th Congress, 2d session. April 25. Washington, D.C.: Government Printing Office.

——. 1986c. Committee on Ways and Means. Subcommittee on Trade. *Certain Tariff and Trade Bills*. 99th Congress, 2d session. February 6 and 7. Washington, D.C.: Government Printing Office.

——. 1987a. Committee on Banking, Finance, and Urban Affairs. Subcommittee on Economic Stabilization. *New Industrial Base Initiative*. 100th Congress, 1st session. July 8 and 28, September 15. Washington, D.C.: Government Printing Office.

——. 1987b. Committee on Small Business. *Global Competition in the Auto Parts Industry*. 100th Congress, 1st session. July 21. Washington, D.C.: Government Printing Office.

——. 1989a. Committee on Government Operations. Subcommittee on Commerce, Consumer, and Monetary Affairs. *Foreign Trade Zones*. 101st Congress, 1st session. March 7. Washington, D.C.: Government Printing Office.

——. 1989b. Committee on Government Operations. Subcommittee on Legislation and National Security. *Implementation of the International Government Procurement Agreement and the Buy American Act of 1988*. 101st Congress, 1st session. September 27. Washington, D.C.: Government Printing Office.

——. 1989c. Committee on the Judiciary. *International Competition in the Steel*

Industry. 101st Congress, 1st session. September 30. Washington, D.C.: Government Printing Office.

———. 1989d. Committee on Ways and Means. Subcommittee on Trade. *Operation of the Foreign Trade Zones Program of the United States and Its Implications for the U.S. Economy and U.S. International Trade.* 101st Congress, 1st session. October 24. Washington, D.C.: Government Printing Office.

———. 1989e. Committee on Ways and Means. Subcommittee on Trade. *Steel Import Stabilization Extension Act and Other Proposals Related to the Steel Voluntary Restraint Agreement Program.* 101st Congress, 1st session. June 15. Washington, D.C.: Government Printing Office.

———. 1990a. Committee on Energy and Commerce. Subcommittee on Commerce, Consumer Protection, and Competitiveness. *Foreign Investment in the United States.* 101st Congress, 2d session. June 13. Washington, D.C.: Government Printing Office.

———. 1990b. Committee on Ways and Means. Subcommittee on Trade. *U.S. Trade Relationships with the Soviet Union and Eastern Europe, Implications of Europe 1992 on American Direct Investment and Foreign Investment in the United States.* 101st Congress, 2d session. January 25. Washington, D.C.: Government Printing Office.

———. 1991a. Committee on Armed Services. *Future Uses of Defense Manufacturing and Technology.* 102d Congress, 1st session. September 24. Washington, D.C.: Government Printing Office.

———. 1991b. Committee on Science, Space, and Technology. *Critical Technologies: Machine Tools, Robotics, and Manufacturing.* 102d Congress, 1st session. Washington, D.C.: Government Printing Office.

———. 1991c. Committee on Ways and Means. *Factors Affecting U.S. International Competitiveness.* 102d Congress, 1st session. July 16, 17, and 18, September 12. Washington, D.C.: Government Printing Office.

———. 1992a. Committee on Energy and Commerce. Subcommittee on Commerce, Consumer Protection, and Competitiveness. *Trade Enhancement.* 102d Congress, 2d session. March 5 and 25, April 8. Washington, D.C.: Government Printing Office.

———. 1992b. Committee on Energy and Commerce. Subcommittee on Commerce, Consumer Protection, and Competitiveness. 1992b. *Anti–Car Theft and Content Labeling.* 102d Congress, 2d session. September 10. Washington, D.C.: Government Printing Office.

———. 1992c. Committee on Foreign Affairs. *Jobs and U.S. Machine Tool Exports.* 102d Congress, 2d session. July 22. Washington, D.C.: Government Printing Office.

———. 1993. Committee on Government Operations. Subcommittee on Commerce, Consumer, and Monetary Affairs. *The North American Free Trade Agreement and Its Impact on the Textile & Apparel/Fiber and Auto & Auto Parts Industries.* 103d Congress, 1st session. May 4. Washington, D.C.: Government Printing Office.

———. 1994a. Committee on Government Operations. Subcommittee on Commerce, Consumer, and Monetary Affairs. *United States–Japan Trade Talks.*

103d Congress, 2d session. February 24. Washington, D.C.: Government Printing Office.

——. 1994b. Committee on Ways and Means. *Trade Agreements Resulting from the Uruguay Round of Multilateral Trade Negotiations.* 103d Congress, 2d session. February 1. Washington, D.C.: Government Printing Office.

——. 1994c. Committee on Public Works and Transportation. Subcommittee on Aviation. *U.S. International Aviation Policy.* 103d Congress, 2d session. Washington, D.C.: Government Printing Office.

United States Office of Federal Procurement Policy. 1990. *Buy American Act: A Study of Alternatives to the Rule of Origin.* Washington, D.C.: Government Printing Office.

United States Senate. 1984a. Committee on Armed Forces. Subcommittee on Preparedness. *Mineaba Acquisition of New Hampshire Ball Bearings.* 98th Congress, 2d session. September 26. Washington, D.C.: Government Printing Office.

——. 1984b. Committee on Finance. Subcommittee on International Trade. *U.S. Steel Industry.* 98th Congress, 2d session. June 8. Washington, D.C.: Government Printing Office.

—— 1984c. Committee on Commerce, Science, and Transportation. *Fair Practices in Automotive Products Act.* 98th Congress, 2d session. May 16. Washington, D.C.: Government Printing Office.

——. 1987a. Committee on Armed Services. Subcommittee on Defense Industry and Technology. 1987a. *Manufacturing Capabilities of Key Second-Tier Defense Industries.* 100th Congress, 1st session. July 23. Washington, D.C.: Government Printing Office.

——. 1987b. Committee on Commerce, Science, and Transportation. 1987b. *Acquisitions by Foreign Companies.* 100th Congress, 1st session. June 10. Washington, D.C.: Government Printing Office.

——. 1987c. Committee on Energy and Commerce. Subcommittee on Commerce, Consumer Protection, and Competitiveness. *Trade and Competitiveness.* 100th Congress, 1st session. March 10. Washington, D.C.: Government Printing Office.

——. 1987d. Committee on Finance. *Impact of Imports and Foreign Investment on National Security.* 100th Congress, 1st session. March 25. Washington, D.C.: Government Printing Office.

——. 1987e. Committee on Labor and Human Resources. Subcommittee on Employment and Productivity. *MOSS Talks/US Auto Parts Industry.* 100th Congress, 1st session. March 30. Washington, D.C.: Government Printing Office.

——. 1988. Committee on Small Business. *Problems Confronting the Domestic Ball and Roller-Bearings Industry.* 100th Congress, 2d session. September 8. Washington, D.C.: Government Printing Office.

——. 1989. Committee on Armed Services. Subcommittee on Defense Industry and Technology. *The Future of the U.S. Semiconductor Industry and the Impact on Defense.* 101st Congress, 1st session. November 29. Washington, D.C.: Government Printing Office.

——. 1990a. Committee on Commerce, Science, and Transportation. Subcommittee on the Consumer. *FTC and International Antitrust Laws.* 101st Congress, 2d session. July 19. Washington, D.C.: Government Printing Office.

———. 1990b. Committee on Commerce, Science, and Transportation. Subcommittee on Science, Technology, and Space. *Foreign Acquisition of Semi-Gas Systems.* 101st Congress, 2d Session. October 1. Washington, D.C.: Government Printing Office.

———. 1991. Committee on Armed Services. Subcommittee on Defense Industry and Technology. *Manufacturing Technology Programs Being Undertaken by the Department of Defense and the Department of Commerce.* 102d Congress, 1st session. April 9. Washington, D.C.: Government Printing Office.

———. 1992. Committee on Finance. *Opening Market Proposals, Auto Trade, and Customs Modernization.* 102d Congress, 2d session. July 22 and 29. Washington, D.C.: Government Printing Office.

———. 1994. Committee on Armed Services. Subcommittee on Defense Technology. *Acquisitions and Industrial Base.* 103d Congress, 2d session. March 18. Washington, D.C.: Government Printing Office.

———. 1995. Committee on Commerce, Science, and Transportation. *Hearing on Telecommunications Policy Reform.* 104th Congress, 1st session. March 21. Washington, D.C.: Government Printing Office.

———. 1997. Committee on the Judiciary. Subcommittee on Antitrust, Business Rights, and Competition. *The British Airways–American Airline Alliance: Antitrust Implications.* 105th Congress, 1st session. April 22. Washington, D.C.: Government Printing Office.

Uriu, Robert M. 1996. *Troubled Industries: Adjusting to Economic Change in Japan.* Ithaca: Cornell University Press.

Vaughan, David A. 1989. "The Buy American Act of 1988: Legislation in Conflict with U.S. International Obligations." *Law and Policy in International Business* 20:603–19.

Verdier, Daniel. 1994. *Democracy and International Trade: Britain, France, and the United States, 1860–1990.* Princeton: Princeton University Press.

Vogel, Steven K. 1999. "When Interests Are Not Preferences: The Cautionary Tale of Japanese Consumers." *Comparative Politics* 31:187–207.

Walters, Ingo, and Kent A. Jones. 1981. "The Battle over Protectionism: How Industry Adjusts to Competitive Shocks." *Journal of Business Strategy* 2:37–46

Walters, Robert S. 1983. "Industrial Crises and U.S. Public Policy: Patterns in the Steel, Automobile, and Semiconductor Experiences." In *An International Political Economy*, edited by Ladd Hollist and F. Lamond Tullis, 153–74. Boulder: Westview Press.

Warshofsky, Fred. 1989. *The Chip War: The Battle for the World of Tomorrow.* New York: Charles Scribner's Sons.

Wassman, Ulrike, and Kozo Yamamura. 1989. "Do Japanese Firms Behave Differently? The Effects of *Keiretsu* in the United States." In *Japanese Investment in the United States: Should We Be Concerned?* edited by Kozo Yamamura, 119–44. Seattle: Society for Japanese Studies.

Waverman, Leonard. 1993. "The NAFTA Agreement: A Canadian Perspective." In *Assessing NAFTA: A Trinational Analysis*, edited by Stephen Globerman and Michael Walker, 32–59. Vancouver: Fraser Institute.

Weir, Margaret. 1992. "Ideas and the Politics of Bounded Innovation." In *Struc-*

turing Politics: Historical Institutionalism in Comparative Analysis, edited by Sven Steinmo, Kathleen Thelen, and Frank Longstreth, 188–216. New York: Cambridge University Press.

Wilkins, Mira. 1989. *The History of Foreign Investment in the United States to 1914*. Cambridge: Harvard University Press.

Wilson, Robert W., Peter K. Ashton, and Thomas P. Egan. 1980. *Innovation, Competition, and Government Policy in the Semiconductor Industry*. Lexington, Mass.: Lexington Books.

Winham, Gilbert, and Ikuo Kabashima. 1982. "The Politics of U.S.-Japanese Auto Trade." In *Coping with U.S.-Japanese Economic Conflict*, edited by I. M. Destler and Hideo Sato, 73–119. New York: Free Press.

Womack, James P., Daniel T. Jones, and Daniel Roos. 1990. *The Machine that Changed the World: The Story of Lean Production*. New York: Rawson Associates.

Woodward, Douglas, and Douglas Nigh, eds. 1998. *Foreign Ownership and the Consequences of Direct Investment in the United States: Beyond Us and Them*. Westport, Conn.: Quorum.

Yamamura, Kozo, ed. 1989. *Japanese Investment in the United States: Should We Be Concerned?* Seattle: Society for Japanese Studies.

Yamamura, Kozo, and Jan Vandenberg. 1986. "Japan's Rapid-Growth Policy on Trial: The Television Case." In *Law and Trade Issues of the Japanese Economy: American and Japanese Perspectives*, edited by Gary R. Saxonhouse and Kozo Yamamura, 238–83. Seattle: University of Washington Press.

Yanarella, Ernest J., and William C. Green, eds. 1990. *The Politics of Industrial Recruitment: Japanese Automobile Investment and Economic Development in the American States*. New York: Greenwood Press.

Yoffie, David. 1983. *Power and Protectionism: Strategies of the Newly Industrializing Countries*. New York: Columbia University Press.

———. 1988. "How an Industry Builds Political Advantage." *Harvard Business Review* (May–June):82–89.

———. 1993a. "Introduction: From Comparative Advantage to Regulated Competition." "Conclusions and Implications." In *Beyond Free Trade: Firms, Governments, and Global Competition*, edited by David Yoffie, 1–25, 429–450. Boston: Harvard Business School Press.

———. 1993b. "Foreign Direct Investment in Semiconductors." In *Foreign Direct Investment*, edited by Kenneth Froot, 197–222. Chicago: University of Chicago Press.

Young, Stephen. 1990. "Japanese Move the Machine Tool Industry Up a Gear." *Multinational Business* 12:25–36.

Ziegler, Nicholas J. 1991. "Semiconductors." *Daedalus* 120:155–82.

Zürn, Michael. 1997. "Assessing State Preferences and Explaining Institutional Choice: The Case of Intra-German Trade." *International Studies Quarterly* 41:295–320.

Zysman, John. 1989. "Contribution or Crisis? Japanese Foreign Direct Investment in the United States." In *Japanese Investment in the United States: Should We Be Concerned?* edited by Kozo Yamamura, 97–110. Seattle: Society for Japanese Studies.

Index

Note: *t* with page number indicates tables.